MAITREYA'S TEACHINGS

The Laws of Life

Edited and introduced

by

Benjamin Creme

*The cover picture is reproduced from a painting by Benjamin Creme entitled **Approach** (1965).*

TABLE OF CONTENTS

CHAPTER 4. CAUSE AND EFFECT — UNDERSTANDING ENERGIES 81

MARKET FORCES 102

CRIME AND VIOLENCE 111

RELIGIONS AND RELIGIOUS LEADERS 142

Islamic fundamentalism 149; Working together, sharing together 149; Do not teach with attachment 149; Religious leaders 149; The duty of spiritual leaders 150; Joining the club 150

CHAPTER 7. THE SCIENCE OF LIGHT   230

CHAPTER 8. THE EMERGENCE OF MAITREYA   241

INTRODUCTION

Since early 1975, I have been presenting information about the return to the everyday world, as World Teacher, of Maitreya, Head and Leader of our Spiritual Hierarchy of Masters of Wisdom. He does not come alone, but with many other Masters, Who, in the esoteric tradition, are the custodians of the Plan of Evolution on Planet Earth.

Lord Maitreya descended from His retreat in the high Himalaya on 8 July 1977, stayed some days in the plains of Pakistan to acclimatize Himself, and on 19 July entered London, England, His 'point of focus' in the modern world. Since then He has lived in London's large Asian community, awaiting the moment to emerge openly as the World Teacher for all groups, religious and non-religious alike.

From September 1977 until May 1982, Maitreya gave through me 140 communications (later published by *Share International* as *Messages from Maitreya the Christ*). In this way, He revealed fragments of His teachings, demonstrating His concerns and His hopes for a better life for all through sharing of resources, and the establishment, thereby, of justice and peace in the world.

A later phase of Maitreya's teaching began in 1988 and continued to 1993. Profound, yet simple, this spiritual teaching concerns everyone, not only those from religious traditions, and will characterize His approach to humanity in the centuries ahead. The teachings were given to a close associate of Maitreya in the Asian community, and from him to two independent journalists, Patricia Pitchon and Brian James, who passed them regularly to me for publication in the monthly magazine *Share International*, of which I am chief editor. Those predictions relating to future world events were distributed to the world's media in a series of news releases. In this way Maitreya released to the world an extraordinary body of teachings and analyses of world problems — political, economic, social and environmental. In the political field, He made many predictions of uncanny accuracy including: the end

1

of the 'Cold War'; the break-up of the Soviet Union; the release of Nelson Mandela and the end of apartheid in South Africa; the fall from power of Mikhail Gorbachev and Margaret Thatcher.

Maitreya understands the Laws of Cause and Effect perhaps more than anyone else on this planet, thus enabling Him to foresee the effects of the causes we ourselves have set in motion. Through those forecasts, He shows us how these laws work by linking the violence of events such as those in the first Gulf War to subsequent natural disasters which can and do affect people not directly involved, but who nevertheless have to endure the consequences of a disturbed planet.

Maitreya's unique stature, His ages-long experience on the evolutionary path, enable Him to present His profound spiritual teachings in the simplest terms, free of all doctrinal 'clutter' and theological dogma. There is no imposition; everyone is left, and encouraged to be, freely themselves.

Above all Maitreya teaches the art of Self-realization. Three practices, simple, yet needing discipline to achieve, are at the core of His teaching on Self-realization: honesty of mind; sincerity of spirit; and detachment.

Practise these three, Maitreya says, and come to Self-realization which is God-realization.

"It has nothing to do with religion, politics or any form of ideology." "Anyone, at any stage, can learn the art of Self-realization and find he will enjoy life. Life is to be enjoyed, with detachment."

"Salvation is not in religion, not in politics, not in philosophies or ideologies. It exists in practising the art of living with a strong sense of detachment."

"Even when you see Me, do not run after Me. I have not come to create followers. If you parade Me, you do not know who I am. What you experience yourself is your wealth."

These few quotations from Maitreya's teachings, I hope, will give readers a taste of the simple directness of His thought and prepare them for the feast of Truth which, I believe, this book presents.

Special note to readers:

Communicated as they were to two journalists by a close associate of Maitreya, these teachings are written in a different style from the messages given by Maitreya through myself. Maitreya gave His teachings to a group of swamis around Him and this specific associate was also present. The associate relayed Maitreya's teachings while recalling visions given to him by Maitreya, and described his experiences with comments. Therefore, the writing style mixes Maitreya's direct expression with explanatory comments by the associate. In the associate's own words: "I am only an ordinary man. I make mistakes. But Maitreya enables me to see 'with the third eye' events which happen in the world. Through the visions, I can understand. Otherwise it would be difficult to understand some things. If you have a vision you cannot forget it."

In spite of the different writing styles, the teachings presented in this book all originated from Maitreya. Therefore, for the sake of readability, we have simplified the format and eliminated the quotation marks indicating who said what except when they were direct quotations of Maitreya's words. Unless otherwise indicated, the double quotation marks indicate Maitreya's direct words regardless of whether this is stated or not.

The sentences in brackets are my comments or editor's notes.

The dates when the teachings were given are noted when that information would be helpful in understanding the teachings themselves. Otherwise, the dates have been eliminated.

Benjamin Creme, London, February 2005

CHAPTER ONE

THE LORD IS WITH YOU;
BE WHAT YOU ARE

Who is Maitreya? — In Maitreya's view, titles like "the Messiah" can lead to illusion. Although some may find the qualities of Jesus in Him, "Those who look for Me as a Teacher are nearer the mark, for that is what I am. I seek to express that which I am through you; for this I come".*

The true quality of the teacher will be seen in the teaching. "The Master is within you. If you follow the disciplines of life the Teacher teaches you, the Master reveals Himself within you. Do not be attached to the human form." The living truth is a matter of experience. Maitreya adds: "I cannot be monopolized. I belong to everyone."

[*These words appear also in *Messages from Maitreya the Christ*, No. 10, received through Benjamin Creme on 8 November 1977.

Note: Throughout this book, Maitreya's direct words are in double quotations regardless of whether this is stated or not.]

The Master within — "First you are the disciple. When you realize, as Jesus did, that 'The Father and I are One', you become the Master. The Master is within you. The Almighty is within you."

Light itself is a Master.

Experience Me within you — "I do not want you to believe in Me. First experience Me within you. When you experience Me then you become aware of My presence within you. It is not a matter of belief first."

"When I am with you, you have nothing to fear. When you are aware, you know I am with you and you are with Me.

"Thought cannot enter the Kingdom of God. You must enter the Kingdom of God."

Awareness is nothing but the reflection of your real Self. When you merge with your real Self you can transmigrate, transmute, transform.

"Everyone is important in the eyes of the Lord."

Self-respect — Maitreya is working now in every part of the world irrespective of creed, nationality, race, etc, at all levels of existence.

The Lord Maitreya inspires everyone through mind, spirit and body to generate, in the first place, self-respect, out of which the blessings of salvation will emerge which will make life meaningful for one and all.

No matter what the degree of your crime, you can train yourself in self-respect by practising sincerity of spirit and honesty of mind, and by feeding your body with natural food. It is your natural heritage. Use it.

The most important temples in life are the spirit, which must be fed with sincerity, the mind, which must be fed with honesty, and the body, which must be fed with right food. This will create harmony in mind, spirit and body.

Self-respect is the seed of awareness.

The present political system is fast undergoing changes inspired by Maitreya. In short, each and every country will generate self-respect and let each and every nation enjoy the fruits of life. Whatever you see in the world of suffering, crime and violence will begin to disappear in a short space of time.

Detachment — Each and every soul is one with Me. You do not disappear in this oneness; you create harmony.

Start from the beginning: practise detachment. What is the Ego? It is an Energy-Governing Organ. Your mind, spirit and body can become wrapped in that energy. If you are freed from that energy, you can come and go at will. You can use it.

If you want to know Me you have to give up everything. Whatever you experience in life, always have detachment and you will remain with Me, because you are not attached to anything.

A real disciple is one who will respect the traditions.

Respect your own religions, your own ideologies, in brief, your own thoughtform, and you will experience the Master.

Complacency — No understanding of the spiritual crisis in the world is possible without clear consideration of causes. Complacency is the root of all evil in the world. What can be summed up as the 'I'm all right Jack' mentality leads both individuals and institutions to become estranged from the realities of life, and therefore to ineffective solutions. Complacency is a form of corruption which is not 'outside' but inside. The mind itself is potentially constructive or destructive.

Be what you are — "Be what you are. Do not follow one another. If you practise honesty of mind, sincerity of spirit and detachment, you will know your Self, you will know Me, you will know the Lord."

To follow another means to copy, imitate or identify with another, forgetting your real Self. As an example, consider pop stars. Many fans try to dress and behave like them. This does not lead to happiness or fulfilment. "The same thing can happen to disciples." The task of the Master is to awaken the Self within. When you, in turn, know your Self, you can awaken others. To awaken another does not mean to cast your shadow over him. When the Self awakens, development follows naturally; the person fulfils his own destiny and enjoys the blessings of the Lord.

The pace of development of each person can thus be respected. This is why Maitreya says: "Let the pagan believe in the stone, because without the Lord there is no stone." Correct relationship between the Self and mind, spirit and body is what matters.

Look within — Do not copy one another. Be what you are and the struggle will come to an end. Look within. Will you then

7

copy one another, or compare? When you look within, you become sacred, immune to chaos and confusion.

Do not copy — Mahavir Swami* is described historically as a pious Jain who became a monk and 'discarded clothing', instructing 11 disciples before his death. Having followed their master, these disciples also discarded their clothes, becoming naked sannyasis.

"The moment Mahavir experienced the Lord in his totality, he gave away everything he had, even his clothes. This was due to a sense of awe. Why copy this? Mahavir's spiritual journey did not end there.

"When there is no genuine discovery or experience, merely copying becomes another type of bondage.

"When swamis, gurus, etc experience uneasiness they give up the world and go into retreat in caves and mountains. This is called 'peace' but it is not peace; it is often a state of shock such that they cannot face the vibrations of life."

[*Spiritual leader of Jainism (a probable contemporary of Gautama Buddha) who died around 476 BC at Pava in India.]

The Almighty — Everyone will accept that there is someone behind creation — the Almighty Who has no human form or name. Those who go to church or to the temple or the mosque, and those who have no religion at all, will respect this concept. Common sense will show this to be so.

Spiritual teachers and isms — In the past, when a spiritual teacher died, if he remained attached to his mission he could appear (in his astral body) to his disciples and could even, on rare occasions, materialize. But this did not solve the problems with which disciples were faced. Ultimately, in the past, 'isms' were created every time.

This time, Maitreya says: "I, Myself, have come. I cannot be caught in any isms." The time will come when people will understand this naturally, without fuss, because they will feel free within. This is why Maitreya says: "I have not come to create followers." What is important is your Self, free from compulsions, able to fulfil your duty without a sense of burden, not bothered by praise or criticism.

The moment you feel divinity within you, you realize everything is within you. The master key is within you.

Direct experience — If you have a direct experience of the Lord, will it matter, then, whether you become a millionaire, a king or a beggar?

This experience alone is sufficient to create equilibrium in mind, spirit and body. This experience can never change. It is eternal. Once you have it, it is always with you, even if you leave your mind, spirit and body. When you experience the Almighty, you do not create divisions.

I am with you — "You are experiencing Me at every moment. Every moment, I am with you. Only those whose mind, spirit and body are tranquil, in a state of equilibrium, become aware of God's presence.

"There are times when you become aware that someone is behind you, within you, over you, around you — something is present. That 'something' is the Almighty. It does not participate; it observes. No one need struggle for this step. Everyone qualifies at this stage. Then, as your awareness grows, if you practise the discipline of detachment, you will know Me in My totality. The moment you think of Me, I am with you."

You are unique and equal — "I have not come to puzzle or startle people. When people experience Me, they will not run after Me. For the first time people will know the purpose of life."

You will not feel you are leading a futile life, but one in which the Master is within you, guiding you. This sense of inwardness will give you another perspective in life.

You will feel you are enjoying life. Fulfilment will take place within. Everything is within you. When this happens you will not react in anger. With a sense of detachment you will experience the power of God. God is behind everything.

Knowing the Lord — When the spirit is dry, you go to church, temple or mosque. By going there, you are following one aspect of life. To know the Lord in His totality, practise honesty, sincerity and detachment. Then you will know the Lord is 'within' and 'without'. Maitreya says: "I have not come to command you. I have come to free you. With detachment, My powers can be used by you for the good of all."

Simplicity — The Archbishop of Canterbury and other religious leaders around the world will eventually leave their palaces to live in simpler surroundings, because simplicity is a significant factor in order "to remain with the Lord in the heart". If you surround yourself with the luxuries of life you have a situation where the senses become possessive and life becomes struggle, confusion, chaos.

The moment you experience the Lord within, you tend to become free of all these attachments in life. Simplicity is not a burden for mind, spirit and body. These are the temples of the Lord and they must be free of possessiveness. The necessities, however, will be there. These are automatic processes which express the natural course of inner evolution.

The trend towards greater simplicity will also be observable among many rich people around the world who will surrender the excess and share with the people.

"If you are serving me, I am everywhere."

The Lord's message is indivisible and applies to one and all.

Death — "I come at the eleventh hour to save My sparks of life. The sparks of life are each and every individual Self. If someone is in trouble and he is My disciple, I come to console and guide him."*

"Death is also the eleventh hour. Does it hurt you when you change your clothes? When you leave your body, it will not hurt you. You may panic. This is your eleventh hour. At this moment, everything stands still. I am with you, and with everyone, at their eleventh hour. I help the one who is slain and

10

the one who slays, I give experiences to both. When Jesus was on the cross, I was by the side of both crucified and crucifier at the eleventh hour. When Jesus saw this He said: 'Father, forgive them, for they know not what they do.'" Maitreya says: "In victory and in defeat, I am with you." When the moment of death comes, the person experiences a sort of loneliness, as if things are moving away from him. "At that moment, I am also helping the person to become detached."

[*"My disciple" is one who applies the teaching.]

The eleventh hour — "I come at the eleventh hour." Maitreya explains this through the symbolism of numbers: eleven (11) is understood as one plus one (1+1). Therefore, "At the eleventh hour there is none except you and Me". "When there is none except you and Me everything dissolves around you. There is tranquillity, peace, grace. All karmas (conditioned activities) cease."

At the twelfth hour Creation began. Twelve (12) is understood here in its symbolic meaning of one plus two (1+2). In effect this makes three, the Trinity. In the East the Trinity is known as Shiva-Vishnu-Brahma. In the West it is the Father, the Son and the Holy Ghost.

Shiva, Vishnu, Brahma — Vishnu is One who controls the powers of life. The merging of positive and negative currents creates light, energizes. Vishnu controls and nourishes Shiva and Brahma. When He turns the wheel, equilibrium is created between Brahma and Shiva.

Individuality is sacred — Individuality is the soul. People will come to realize this. Individuality is sacred. The child respects his own individuality. People will experience, for the first time, even in marriage, the sacredness of their individual entities. Marriage will become less disturbed.

Individuality — the soul — will be respected in temple, church and mosque. Nations will enact laws that will preserve individuality, and will promote conditions to enshrine this sacredness.

Rules and regulations will not be imposed as they are now. The individual will be important. He will act not out of compulsion, but out of a sense of duty and responsibility towards others, as if he were acting for his own Self.

Do not worship Me — Do not try to worship Me. If you worship Me, you are trying to lower yourself. I do not want this. I want you to be equal. You are a spark of the Supreme Being. Do not think you are below Me.

My army is everywhere — The last time Maitreya (Christ) came, He was nailed to a cross. This time He cannot yet be found, but that does not mean He is afraid to appear. His appearance will follow naturally.

"I cannot be destroyed," Maitreya has told the politicians. "My army is everywhere, in every nation and individual, for I am in the hearts of one and all."

Creation — Every country and nation is equally sacred in the eyes of Maitreya, just as is every individual. When creation goes to sleep, and there is danger, the Lord takes care of us all.

Keep the mirror clean — Recently in China there were soldiers who refused to shoot.* This is because an experience of awareness was given to them such that they perceived the persons who were being shot as resembling themselves. This is why Maitreya teaches His disciples: "Be a clean mirror." Thus others will see themselves in you. "When you see your Self in Me, will you run after Me?" (Jun 1989)

Be what you are.
I teach you.
I am with you.
Keep the mirror clear.

[*In June 1989 in Tiananmen Square, Beijing, Chinese students who were demonstrating for democracy were shot indiscriminately by soldiers sent by the government.]

Salman Rushdie — When the baby cries out for a lollipop and does not get it, he gets angry and confused. He ends up calling his mummy bad names.

So it was with Salman Rushdie.* He was looking for divine experiences through religion and when he failed he began describing his difficulties and disillusion. But his failure to experience anything does not negate divinity, because it does not exist in evolution. It exists only in the Supreme Being.

A writer or a poet fails because he or she is seeking the ultimate. But that cannot be found in life — in evolution. So when they fail to find the ultimate they embark on founding religions and philosophies. They begin to create doubts about the existence of God. These writers are neither right nor wrong in looking for new goals and new experiences. But when they create disturbances through their work those who read them begin to panic because they do not want to lose their certainties. Salman Rushdie and the devout Muslims are in the same boat because they are clinging to their beliefs and are frightened of losing them.

Maitreya has come to guide us to experience Him in our hearts. That experience cannot happen in the mind, spirit or body because they exist in evolution. Divinity is pure and eternal. The Self exists in the heart which is where you experience God. (Feb 1990)

[*Anglo-Indian novelist Salman Rushdie was condemned to death (fatwa) by the former Iranian spiritual leader Ayatollah Ruhollah Khomeini on 14 February 1989, after publishing *Satanic Verses.*]

Enjoy life — "Remain open-minded. Enjoy life. When you enjoy life, it is as if you are sitting on the beach looking at the vast ocean. At that moment you experience serenity, tranquillity, detachment within. You do not think of your bank account at that moment. Nobody lectures you at that moment. The gift of life flowers within you.

"Experience this and you will realize you are a unique person. You are unique in this creation."

Happiness — Human beings are looking for happiness such as is found in the lap of the mother. You will find happiness when you begin to realize that the Almighty is always with you, 24 hours of the day. Then you will experience freedom from within. There is no room then for unhappiness, greed or anger.

Make yourself happy — "Do not make Me happy. Make yourself happy and you have made Me happy. If you look after yourself, you look after Me."

In unity, diversity — "In unity there is diversity. The time has come to awaken. Be what you are. Do not follow one another. Gradually you will become evolved. No two persons are alike. No two persons can be carbon copies. The moment you take on another's personality you are creating a distance between Me and you. The moment you are what you are, you begin to enjoy bliss, serenity, tranquillity. Then there is no distance between us."

Immortality — "I am the nectar. I am the poison. The moment you realize you are not mind, spirit and body, not even the life force, that is immortality. At that stage you can take charge of your own destiny. You are a spark of the Almighty."

"I am with everyone, as much with a prostitute as with a so-called saint. I never give up anyone."

The basic chord of truth — The truth has many faces, but the main chord is within the individual. The moment you feel Oneness, when you speak, the basic chord of truth sings within. "Experience Me. Be what you are. The moment you try to be what you are, you experience who you are, why you are.

"People respond. But if you try to twist the truth or to make money out of it, it becomes so distorted that people begin to lose interest in it."

Oneness — "When all forms are dissolved, you know the Lord in all His Oneness. There is the Lord. The Lord and You."

CHAPTER TWO

THE SELF, AWARENESS AND DETACHMENT

Being and Becoming — Being and Becoming are two modalities. Being is unchanging, whereas becoming is a process in time and space. Man, in his Being, is the Self. In his becoming, he is the soul — the reflection of the Self. Mind, spirit and body are the temples of the Lord which man inhabits. Spirit is Shiv-shakti, which is energy. Mind is Brahma, which is thought-formation. Body is Prakriti, which is material substance and can also be thought of as material activity. These terms can be thought of as nouns, but they can also be thought of as movement or processes.

The destiny of the Self is to be free. Considered in its freedom, in its Being, it is called Atman. Within the limitations of time and space, in its becoming, it is the soul, or Jiva.

The Self is not energy (Shiv-shakti, spirit); the Self is not thought-formation (Brahma, or mind); the Self is not material activity (Prakriti, the body). The destiny of the Self is to enter and leave these temples of the Lord at will.

Detachment is the process whereby man ceases to identify with the body (material aspect), with the mind (thought aspect) and with spirit (energy or power aspect). Thus he comes to know and be his real Self.

Any action you perform should be done according to these three principles: honesty of mind, sincerity of spirit and detachment. Any action performed with dishonesty of mind, an insincere spirit and attachment is destructive.

If a person is overpowered by Shiv-shakti, he can perform miracles. Yet the person looks withdrawn, blank. If a person is overpowered by Brahma, he can be a philosopher, but he can be imprisoned in that thought-formation.

15

When we consider the trinity, as Shiva, Brahma and Vishnu (the sustaining aspect), it is also possible for a person to be overpowered by the Vishnu aspect. He can give, and give generously, perhaps become a saint, but that, too, can be a prison. During the sixties, hippies responded to the Vishnu aspect. They were disillusioned with power (Shiv-shakti) and mind (Brahma).

What changes? — When the mind is quiet, free from dogmatic views, it will absorb the truth. "If you want to test the truth of anything, speak with a child."

The mind, spirit and body are like the elements of nature. They do not change. "God created the entire universe, in which He placed mind, spirit and body for the Self to realize the Being and Becoming of the Lord."

The one who changes through experiences is the Self.

If you use this mirror to look at the religions of the world, you will see they are based on the personal experiences of the prophets, gurus, saints, etc. When people follow them they are bound to experience suffering, because they are not following their own Self. If you close your eyes and allow someone else to lead you, you are bound to stumble.

Everyone has free will. When that free will is not functioning or is being misled, "the Lord intervenes".

When you open up the secrets of your life through honesty, sincerity and detachment, the Self begins to move and can enter the mind, the spirit, and even the body (through the breath) and depart at will. Otherwise the mind, spirit and body endure starvation, and the Self becomes the prisoner of consciousness and sub-consciousness, which govern the mind and spirit with the forces of instinct.

Take a person walking in the street. Suddenly, he takes a knife and stabs another person. This happens through instinct.

"Self-realization is God-realization." Self-realization has nothing to do with religion, politics or any form of ideology.

'Second nature' — "I do not want you to accept or reject Me. It is your inner experience which counts." Every individual

16

will find he can make his contribution to society. Everything that has materialized is called "Prakriti". It is your 'second nature'. At present, your 'second nature' controls mind, spirit and body. As awareness grows, its strength diminishes. As long as you are controlled by your 'second nature' you cannot understand the art of existence.

Maitreya is inspiring one and all to fulfil their destiny, to be free of this 'second nature' through growing self-awareness.

The power of thought — Recently much attention in Great Britain has focused on child abuse. Here it is necessary to understand the power of thought. In many cases, a single, powerful thought has taken hold of the mind, to the exclusion of all else. This is destructive. In order to help the person to detach himself from that thought, it is necessary to lead him to an awareness of the Self, the 'observer', the 'watcher'. The Self is not the mind. This will create a space inside the person and this awareness will enable him to free himself. There are no short-cuts to this process, but it is itself part of a method which also includes beneficial breathing techniques. Maitreya is training certain people who are fitted for this type of work. Appropriate training will yield results.

The time is fast coming when young people will be very difficult to understand. Wrong training, excessive emphasis on material values, on competition, leads to hopelessness. Education at present does not create self-awareness. Yet it is self-awareness which leads to self-realization, the destiny of us all.

Sufficiency — Money multiplied by money contributes to the stress of modern life. Money is not the priority; sufficiency is the priority. When sufficiency becomes the priority, it orders society in a different way, creating stability. In this regard, sharing is both a moral value and a method of implementation. This will create a more peaceful atmosphere, in which people will not struggle to make millions. They will fulfil their duties, care for their families, and children will be able to evolve.

"You have been given mind, spirit and body to express My Being and Becoming in thought, speech and action. Therefore, be honest in mind (which is the natural food of mind), be sincere in your spirit (the natural food of spirit) and feed your physical body with the right food. Anyone who deprives you of these three things will fall into destruction."

Personification — Those who experienced the truth of Light in the past classified themselves as prophets, saints and gurus. They personified their experiences and lost the true meaning of the teaching of the Lord. "The moment you personify the spiritual force in you, a process of destruction begins. You will experience corruptive forces around you." This is not a prediction, rather a universal law. "The mind is not to be personified. The spirit is not to be personified."

If you set a goal, achieve it, but cannot then dissolve it, your development is arrested. What you are able to personify, you should be able to dissolve. As an example, if you practise meditation and personify what occurs, you are automatically surrounded by (spiritual) powers that imprison you. This happens to yogis and saints.

The Self becomes enveloped, imprisoned, in a powerful force. In light of this teaching, all religions are suffering from contradictions now, due to personification. Thus the evolution of the spiritual force is arrested. When the flow is blocked, it spills over and surrounds mind, spirit and body. People who do not want to know anything other than the thought to which they are stuck cannot make further progress.

The spiritual forces let loose in the Middle East led to destruction through this process. "In the name of spiritual forces the spiritual leaders inspired the masses and achieved destruction."

Life is not something whereby 'you set the goal and that's the end of it'. "Life is ever-flowering." Likewise politically, if you set the goals, achieve them and remain stuck there, the system will crack open.

Harmony created in the political spectrum depends on understanding each other, on an awareness that all shades of the political spectrum are equally important. To say that a particular political ideology is the only way of life is, in itself, destructive.

We have reached a critical point now. No one will be able to disagree with this, because the evidence is before our eyes. "The effects of ancient habits are gathering speed now."

In the Muslim world, people do not personify Allah, and this is their great contribution. Among the Hindus, people have personified the Lord through a multitude of gods and goddesses. Now they are beginning to realize everything comes from One Source. Before, the minority among Hindus knew this truth, kept control of it and created divisions. This has led to a loss of authority. But people now are beginning to revere the One Lord.

If you allow any thought to personify in you, it is not you any longer. That thought possesses you. The law of inertia becomes effective. This is why one experiences attachment, tension, depression. Thought should be like water, fluid and able to change shape. When it personifies, it solidifies. That creates strife. When a thought takes a natural course it never personifies. It fulfils its role, materializes naturally and disappears.

How can you say Jesus is the only begotten Son of God, if the Light which exists in Jesus exists in the entire creation? Equilibrium and harmony will automatically evolve out of this realization. Likewise, "if you personify Me, run after Me, you will create nothing but confusion, chaos, destruction". "Even My signs create only momentary happiness. The happiest moment is when you see Me within your heart."

Religion — All religions are at fault for the suffering in the world. "Instead of teaching salvation, religions are creating pockets of imprisonment. You are to teach the individual that to Self-realize is his destiny — the ultimate freedom and the ultimate salvation. The moment you personify teachings, you create demi-gods and dogmas which imprison." Further, "If you personify the teaching, embodying it, you are creating something different".

Jesus and the Buddha — The experiences the Lord gave Jesus are being given to certain disciples today. But in the case of Jesus, his mind initially became possessive of those experiences. The mind tried to use these spiritual powers to achieve certain goals. He began to preach. The priests challenged him: "Can you free yourself, if you are God?" Jesus could do nothing at that moment.

When Jesus was on the Cross and asked: "My Lord, My Lord, why hast Thou forsaken me?" he was given a vision. He understood then that the mind should not run after spiritual forces. He was taught at that moment that the entire creation is the Lord's.

The prayer* given out now by Maitreya was given to him. "Without the Lord's will, nothing takes place." Upon experiencing the vision, Jesus said: "Father, forgive them, for they know not what they do."

Jesus was concerned about disparities between rich and poor. "In the eyes of the Lord, no one is rich or poor." One should try to realize the Self. Thus one will use what one needs and pass on the excess. Jesus should have taught at that time: "Be not attached to riches or poverty"; "When you try to preach, you create nothing but limitation." The true teaching is: "I am with you if you are honest, sincere, detached."

If you preach out of a personal desire, to cling to power, to maintain your position, you create "positive fear" because no one has experienced the Almighty.

The moment you experience the Almighty, you are no longer what you were. You merge into Light straightaway. This is why the Lord gives a vision in the form the mind can understand and the spirit can absorb.

When you are free of attachments, as the Buddha was, you are given the vision of the Absolute (nirvana).

But Jesus was attached to that which he wanted to achieve (parity between rich and poor; justice). As his teaching was relative (because it was submerged in opposites), the Lord

20

gave him a vision of Light. Then Jesus knew that the relative and the absolute are the two sides of Light. Jesus realized, in mind, spirit and body, that it is the same Light. Then silence prevailed. He was satisfied.

"Even if you have reached a very high state of evolution, you cannot say: 'I am the Lord.' You can simply say: 'I am the messenger of the Lord.'"

[*The Prayer for the New Age]

Krishnamurti — When Krishnamurti* was asked to take up certain positions, he declined, saying he was not a guru of anything. He was a true disciple of Maitreya.

The teachings of Krishnamurti are the teachings of Maitreya. Madame Blavatsky and Alice Bailey had glimpses of the teaching, but they became involved in the processes of teaching. In Maitreya's view, everyone in the Theosophical Society except Krishnamurti failed in the sense that they got more involved in the mechanism of the forces of evolution and the search for their sources instead of realizing the teachings of the Lord. Krishnamurti wanted no one to interpret his teaching. Those who were interested could listen to his taped talks.

[*Krishnamurti (1895-1986), spiritual teacher]

Bio-genetic engineering — Scientists today are in a similar position. They are involved in the mechanism of the forces of evolution. They do not know where these forces lead, but they will definitely get a glimpse of the end of the trail.

"The universe comes forth from Light. Each and every soul is just a spark of that Light. When that spark of Light comes closer to the whole Light, it merges." The same thing happens with knowledge and wisdom. When these approach the point where the soul makes an exit (from mind, spirit and body), they dissolve. Knowledge and wisdom as we know it cannot follow the soul (ie the Self).

If scientists persist in experiments with bio-genetic engineering they will be able to create beings which are half-man, half-animal. But scientists will never be able to understand mutation, which is beyond knowledge and wisdom.

The same Light which is in the spine of a snake is in the spine of a man. If the Light leaves one form and enters another, it carries the previous characteristics (the evolutionary forces which were there in the snake at the time). To use this to 'play God' is dangerous. "Only God understands mutation."

Through mutation the soul takes different bodies. The scientists are interfering with the natural course of mutation.

"You are able to do certain things, but you should not do them. Why do you not spend money rightly so that people can be given the right food to eat, that they may die natural deaths?"

Playing with the forces of creation — The scientists experimenting with human genes are like babies playing with a live wire — they invite destruction. They are opening the doors to the dark forces of life. None of them have the proper disciplines of mind, spirit and body and yet they want to play with the forces of creation.

Modern science deals only with the physical world and refuses to accept the realities of the mental and spiritual. Yet even a surgeon after he has operated on a patient must wait for the consciousness to return before he can say that he is successful. Where did that consciousness go? Where does it come from? He has no idea. Yet that is the secret of life. When Jesus was alive he did not need laboratories to achieve miracles and cures. How did he do it? He did it through awareness of the Supreme Being around him and that awareness meant that he could use the powers of creation to heal the world's suffering.

"I am behind you. Become aware of My powers and use them to heal and for the enrichment and betterment of your lives."

Conditioning — In the biblical story of the Garden of Eden, Adam and Eve were told not to eat the fruit of the tree of knowledge of good and evil. This means "Do not follow

22

prakritis". This Sanskrit word refers to material activity or matter in broad terms, but prakritis (in the plural) also means human activities which are the result of conditioning. Thus Adam and Eve were tempted by the snake, the symbol of prakritis, that is, conditioning — the opposite of freedom.

Once you 'eat' knowledge (a possessive act) rather than facing knowledge with awareness, whereby you understand that you must not 'grab', you are no longer free.

When Krishnamurti became aware in this way, he declined the role of guru: the true Lord is in the heart. If you want to know Him, try to understand the voice of silence. In silence there is freedom from prakritis, from conditioning. Silence is that space which is free from conditioning. What is important is the Lord within you.

"Be sincere in your spirit, be honest in your mind, be detached." When you surrender the Self to mind, spirit and body (when you identify with thought, power and matter), everything becomes predestined. This means that you are subject to conditioning, your thoughts and acts are the result of conditioning, you lose your free will.

Thus attachment is loss of freedom. Detachment is freedom. "Even when you see Me, do not run after Me. I have not come to create followers. If you parade Me, you do not know who I am. What you experience yourself is your wealth."

Experience of the Almighty — Jesus as a person, as an individual entity, experienced the sustenance, the support, of the Almighty. People everywhere are beginning to experience this now. What will the signs be? People will be able to explain in simple sentences what Jesus experienced in Christ. When you experience the One who sustains you, who is the source of all creation, you know that without Him nothing takes place. At such a time, the Self is oblivious to everything that is happening around it. This is why Jesus said: "Father, forgive them, for they know not what they do." When you are honest, sincere, detached, you can reach this stage. The teaching of Maitreya inspires you to look within. This is not religion. This is not politics. This is not ideology. Karma itself is Dharma. Without karma there is no salvation. But do not remain attached. That is imprisonment. The day the Self within is free of the stresses and strains inherent in the processes of Being and Becoming, yet fulfils Its duty in a detached manner, the Kingdom of the Lord is experienced by the Self in the heart.

[Note: "Karma is Dharma" means that human activity is itself the path of duty.]

Sex — Maitreya discussed briefly the Martin Scorsese film, *The Last Temptation of Christ*, with a group of swamis. In Maitreya's view the issue of whether the film should be shown or not is not so important. He did say, however, that it is not the case that "To know the Lord you have got to give up sex." He added: "I do not make these regulations. If you condemn sex, you must ask yourself how you were born. Where did you come from? The Lord does not say, give up your wife and children. Does anyone make a fuss about birth and death? Who is not born of sexual intercourse?" He contrasted the attitudes of priests and film-makers. He said that because religious men are themselves running after Christ, they give up everything. The Lord gives them certain experiences to quiet the mind. These men then stipulate that you must give up what they have given up in order to reach the stage they have reached (ie to have those experiences).

"Do not preach that sex is dirty. It is natural and does not need to be taught. It develops with the evolutionary forces of life. The true Master is awareness, which teaches at the right moment. To educate about sex prematurely is also not advisable. Things should be allowed to take their natural course."

In discussing temptations, Maitreya said temptations of mind, spirit and body force the self to do something against the will of the real Self. He explained that Jesus passed through these stages. In passing through these stages Jesus was also tempted. "Does anyone know what he did?" Maitreya added: "The Lord says: 'Do not condemn sex. If you condemn sex you will never know who I am.' You will find that the sexual act, performed with sincerity of spirit, honesty of mind and detachment, becomes divine. If it is divine, it does not cling to mind, spirit and body. You are free even at that moment. You know the results of the sexual act performed with possessiveness and attachment. The hunger grows, the person can become oversexed and eventually can commit sexual crimes, which are carried out with dishonesty of mind, an insincere spirit and attachment. Any act performed thus becomes destruction."

However, even if Jesus had had sexual intercourse in his lifetime, one cannot say "Sex is against the Lord".

The film-makers, on the other hand, clothe this matter with 'inquisitive mind'. The mind wants to find things out, but inquisitiveness alone creates division. Detachment and sincerity of spirit would have produced a different film. On the other hand, many religious leaders are running away from the realities of life.

Do not run after Me — "I have not come to found a new religion. Each of you should continue to develop within your own religious tradition. I have not come to create followers. Even when you see Me, do not run after Me. If you run after Me, you will lose Me." "I have come to teach the art of Self-realization." This is neither an ideology nor a religion, and benefits people of all religions and none. "I belong to everyone."

The Self alone matters — "The Self alone matters." You are that Self, "an immortal being". Suffering is caused by identification with anything and everything which is not the Self. Ask yourself: "Who am I?" You will see that you are identified either with matter (the body), or with thought (the mind) or with power (spirit). But you are none of these. "Mind, spirit and body are the temples of the Lord." The Self experiences in these "the supreme Being and Becoming of the Lord." Being is eternal, Becoming is the unfolding in time and space. The Self experiences both.

You do not contact the Self via mediums. You contact the mind — the state of mind of the person concerned. But the Self can never be contacted. The 'spirit', the 'mind', are not yours. What you experience in mind and spirit you claim as yours. It is there for you as long as the Self is in contact with mind, spirit and body. Mind, spirit and body are universals the Self steps into. The medium develops the art of communication with mind and spirit. But the Self is beyond mind, spirit and body.

Attachment — If you do not know yourself as the Self, you can become attached to body, mind or spirit.

If you are attached to the body, you will find that there is no end to material desires and sensual gratifications. Greed grows, the search continues, and satisfaction always eludes you. If you are attached to the mind, you can become entangled in thought constructions, ideologies, isms to which there is no end. The more you search, the further afield you go. The more you find, there will always be unknown regions. In fact, you can get lost here. You do not feel fulfilled. If you are attached to spirit (power) you will dabble in regions which can never be fully understood, via a host of isms such as occultism, spiritualism, etc. To dabble means to misuse.

As an example, spiritualists believe they can contact the dead. So-called mediums are in fact "tuning in" to vibrations which are still within the realm of mind, spirit and body. "Where is the Self who has departed?" He is no longer in the body, which has been either cremated or buried. He is no longer in the mind, which the Self experienced, as a temple of the Lord, for a fixed period of time. Likewise, the Self is not the power (spirit) which is experienced by the Self as a temple of the Lord. "No spiritualist can recall the Self." Since you are the Self, who is the medium recalling? Only a Master can recall the Self, on rare occasions dictated by spiritual law.

This is why Maitreya advises: "Do not be attached to the physical form of a Master. Otherwise, when He is not there, you will grieve. When you know yourself as the Self within, such grief disappears."

Jesus warned against the misuse of powers. "Even if you come across them, even if they develop in you, do not become attached to them. Do not try to possess them. If you do, they will destroy you. They are not yours."

Gurus can fall — Many teachers and gurus have fallen through attachment to powers which manifested themselves through them either as a result of natural development or through the grace of the Lord. As soon as you try to claim anything for yourself, as soon as you identify with those powers instead of understanding that you are the immortal Self and the powers belong to the Lord, you are lost. This is a difficult test, and even today the lives of many followers who identified with their guru or teacher have been shattered when the teacher or guru, forgetting the Self within, attaches himself to material, mental or spiritual powers. Thus some begin to accumulate wealth, some misuse thought and imprison others mentally, creating divisions and intolerance instead of respecting the freedom of each individual, and others become attached to power and misuse it. That is why Maitreya says: "Do not become attached to My spiritual powers."

Detachment — When you are detached, the Self experiences these powers and allows the fulfilment of divine purpose. To possess is not only to misuse but to misdirect and to interfere. As an example, true spiritual healers allow the Lord to work through them but remain detached both from cause (the Lord's will) and effect (the healing of a particular individual). This is why it is important to remain detached both from success and failure. Some individuals are healed; some are not. If you do not claim anything for yourself, pride cannot flourish and all is directed according to spiritual law. You do not heal; the Lord heals. The Self knows this. Practise with detachment and leave the consequence to the Lord.

Experience the Self within — If you follow others instead of being yourself, you lose your sparkle; you cannot reflect the light of individuality. Without that light, there is no progress in life. Similarly, when you experience the Self within and come to know you are an immortal entity, completely separate from mind, spirit and body, you learn to use these temples of the Lord creatively, with awareness. Processes of healing follow automatically.

This is why Maitreya has said that even people with AIDS will be healed through prayer and through the practice of honesty of mind, sincerity of spirit and detachment.

Without detachment there is no salvation. The prayer given out previously by Maitreya can lead people to experience that Self within who is detached from mind, spirit and body. It is included here for those who do not know it:

> I am the creator of the universe.
> I am the father and mother of the universe.
> Everything came from me.
> Everything shall return to me.
> Mind, spirit and body are my temples,
> For the Self to realize in them
> My Supreme Being and Becoming.

Heart to heart — People have asked: "How do we begin: How do we practise sincerity?" Consider an expression which is often used, such as "having a heart-to-heart talk" with someone. What does this mean? It means you will express yourself as you really are, you will communicate from the centre — your centre — the Self. Practise this. It will transform you and those around you.

Honesty of mind — When you think one thing, say another, and do something which is different again, you are lost. Honesty of mind leads to honest speech and honest action. This harmony leads to peace and happiness. "Whether you are a thief or a saint, you can begin right now."

Education — Children need to be taught "the three Rs" (reading, writing and arithmetic). But this is not enough. They need to be taught who they really are. The children of today will understand the relationship between the Self and mind, spirit and body with greater ease than adults imagine. Even a child who is bullied and has no one to turn to, a child who has been abused, can be healed through this understanding. He will be able to know and experience that what has been abused, whether in mind, spirit or body, is not his true Self.

Innocence — Innocence is nothing but the fertile ground for mind, spirit and body to remain detached.

The most important thing in life is to learn true inwardness. If you fill a mind with ideology, it can last in this condition for about 20 years. Then it looks for drugs. Do not deprive children of their innocence. Innocence becomes a strong ground to resist the ideologies of the world. Innocence and detachment work together.

Gardens — The time is coming when every house will have a garden. The flowers growing there, of different colours, are the symbols of the children of the Earth.

Where you live, sleep and eat, your symbol of God is a garden. Spend at least 10 to 15 minutes a day looking after it, growing things in it, and come very close to Me. A mystery will evolve from that garden, cleansing mind and spirit.

The Glory of the Lord — The Glory of the Lord can never be comprehended by anyone, but it can be experienced. When Jesus experienced the Lord, the Lord immediately taught him one art: to remain detached from the Lord's glory by becoming the humblest of men. If you become humble, you do not claim anything for yourself.

Do not judge others — All are trying to understand the truth. For this, mind, spirit and body must be disciplined. Everything then falls into the right perspective. If you say: "My way is right; what others experience is not right," you create destruction. People experience the Lord in different ways. Do not judge others. Judge situations and become aware, but remain detached.

Divine radiation — Scientists believe radiation (of the sun) causes cancer. There are those who are able to come closer to (divine) radiation. Yet it is much more powerful than the sun's radiation.

Divinity and blessings — Divinity does not belong to anyone. It cannot be possessed. It must be revered, respected. If you touch it, it will disappear.

Blessings can only be experienced. If you try to impose them, they are curses.

Awareness and conditioning — When you surrender the Self to mind, spirit and body, everything is predestined. Anything you do through Self-awareness is not predestined, because it does not arise out of conditioning.

The truth of divinity — All religions are undergoing a process of purification, in that individuals experience for the first time the truth of divinity: it is not outside, but situated in the heart and, simultaneously, in the universe, in creation everywhere. In this process, the Self experiences its own identity as distinct from all external and internal happenings.

That individual Self experiences for the first time that the One who is behind him, who makes him aware, cannot be limited, but is universal. The One is the Guide of the individual Self in its Being and Becoming. His presence is felt everywhere.

Change — It is the individual alone who can set himself or herself free from this karmic cycle (the cycle of conditioned human activity). Nations and governments are simply guardians, protectors of the values of life, but they cannot change the individual. Change comes from the individual himself.

Equilibrium — If you look outside all the time you will lose sight of your inner self. Life then becomes too materialistic. If the reverse is the case, and you look inside yourself much of the time, you lose contact with external reality. Equilibrium between inner and outer leads to right relationship developing in mind, spirit and body. The point of equilibrium must be maintained.

Help yourself — Until you have helped yourself, you cannot help others.

Loneliness — To be honest, sincere and detached is to experience oneness with God. But so often this oneness is interpreted by people as loneliness and something to be feared. Yet the feeling of loneliness is the supreme blessing in disguise because it shows that a person is approaching oneness with the Lord.

People who cannot have children are brainwashed into believing that they should have children. Yet their loneliness is a blessing in disguise. It is their genetic evolution that makes them different from other married couples.

Everyone runs away from loneliness but you should not fear it.

When 13- and 14-year-old children run away from home to live in cardboard boxes, they are seen as problem children with problem family backgrounds. Instead, they should be seen as people who have evolved to the point where they need to experience that oneness with God. They feel imprisoned in their mind, spirit and body, so they will go to any lengths to be free. The Self cannot climb a mountain loaded down, tired and exhausted. Instead of blaming the family or the young person, the emphasis must be on creating an environment where they can feel free and at peace. Then everything will fall into perspective.

Environment — People are concerned about the environment. Observe how this is happening around the world. If you want to feel that you are part of the Almighty, the environment becomes the mirror for the Self to realize that it is part of the entire creation.

Awareness leads to looking into the environment. A clean, neat and tidy environment brings you closer to God. Even a few years ago, no politician took the environment seriously. Now the concern is there.

Respect environment — We must respect our environment, not destroy it. When you want to reach the roof of your house, you need a ladder. Once you get there, you should not throw it away and abandon it, for there are others who are following on who need it. So it is with the environment for the generations that follow us.

Teacher's task — To say "I am the Messiah" can create opposition. "Messiah" is a word coined by the human race. People want someone to free them from all their sufferings. It is detachment which frees you from suffering.

A Master cannot master the universe of energy (Shiva). If you use the word Master to mean teacher, then know that the teacher's task is to teach you to be free of attachment to mind, spirit and body. That is your destiny. That is salvation.

Preaching at people — Preaching at people will not work. If you approach a prostitute and you lecture her, she will reject your words as ideology. But if you say: "Whatever you are doing, be yourself, be honest, sincere and detached," this will create an experience in that individual which will dissolve the isms in mind, spirit and body. The same applies to a thief. It is the experience which will free mind, spirit and body from isms, from conditioning. When the person experiences himself as he is, he can feel the 'observer' within. The observer within is not a limited, finite person. It is infinite, and many call it "divinity". The observer is divine. This is the connection between the Self and the Divine.

To the Swamis: "Do not make speeches; do not lecture. If a thief comes to you, welcome him and advise him to follow the three principles (honesty of mind, sincerity of spirit and detachment). If the thief practises these, he will achieve salvation."

Awareness, more powerful than nuclear bombs — "Awareness alone is more powerful than nuclear bombs, more powerful than anything else in the universe. Awareness is even 'beyond light' and is growing fast now."

Mr Gorbachev — What made one person change all of Russia? Awareness in one person can spark awareness in millions of people. Awareness is growing in people everywhere today.

Growing interdependence — In awareness, you experience Oneness. Awareness of interdependence, of oneness, inspires people to help one another.

It is necessary to respect the forces of interdependence. As scientists deepen their understanding of the laws of life and mind, there will be a greater understanding of interdependence. It is the cement that sustains creation.

What is changing? — It is the individual who is changing, experiencing a greater and deeper awareness.

In awareness everything becomes purified.

In awareness everyone is forgiven.

In awareness the Self realizes he is not the doer, but the witness of creation. The Self witnesses the functions of mind, spirit and body but is free of them. Is there then any stress, confusion, chaos?

The problem of isms — Replacing communism with capitalism will not, of itself, solve the problem. Corruption, crime, homelessness, etc, also exist in the West.

When awareness is still dormant, isms control mind, spirit and body and create divisions. This is maya — ie illusion. When awareness controls and guides you, isms cannot come close to you. Awareness can even make a king give up his kingdom. Privileges divide, denying oneness to the entity within you. Isms are not thrown away all at once. They are steps on the way. Awareness controls the pace of evolution. When the Almighty bestows His grace on you, you keep your identity and throw away the ladder which enabled you to climb. However, the ladder is useful for those still on the ground.

Society — Society at present is like a den. You know that there are too many snakes in the jungle, so in your den you are the master and you do not allow others to come in. In society as we know it, the like-minded stick together and deny (themselves and others) a wider awareness.

To know Me — "To start with, I come to you 'like a thief in the night', so that you will not become too excited. Slowly, as you become aware, you can 'digest' what is 'eaten'. In awareness you will know Me. In isms you will fight against Me."

The actor and the Self — The most important thing to remember is that, in adhering to isms, it is not you who is acting; rather, the mysterious forces of creation are playing around and giving you the impression that you are the actor.

But the Self is never an actor. In awareness, the Self simply observes. In awareness, the Self is able to recognize who the actor is, because in that state there is understanding, knowledge, wisdom and intelligence free from isms.

Awareness centres — In a variety of towns and cities there are centres called 'Body Talk'. Soon there will be "awareness centres", which focus on communication between individuals rather than on the body alone. This idea is being considered by a number of individuals at present. Like scientists, people will experiment with a variety of approaches in working with people where genuine communication becomes paramount. People who come for help will suddenly experience "that" (ie awareness) within, and through this inner event they will experience relief.

[Note: Once this process is set in motion, people themselves will participate actively in finding solutions to their problems.]

In the Light, there are no arguments — "The Lord is not evil. You (the Self) are not evil. Because you cleave to form you are attached to traditions, creeds, ideologies. When you part from them you experience regrets, unhappiness. In Reality neither form nor belief divide. In the Light, in Oneness, there are no arguments; everyone can see. In darkness, even just two people will argue. Because you cannot communicate with Reality you experience contradictions and chaos."

Awareness and children — Awareness will be respected in the home and in the school as a sacred, God-given gift. Awareness is the mother of creation. Awareness can never be divided, nor imposed. Textbooks cannot describe it, because there is no beginning nor end to it. Awareness can only be experienced. To inspire a very young child to look for God is undivine, because in this way you create isms. Awareness is a seed in all creation and in every individual. If you allow the child to have his natural growth, you will allow his awareness to grow; the child will enjoy normal life and will not be dogmatic. In awareness you do not possess children, yet they come closer to you. Even now, children as young as nine or 10 are raising funds to feed the hungry. Imagine what they will be like when they are tomorrow's citizens. Children can do it. Politicians cannot do it.

Life after death — Life in the universe is absolute; in creation it is always relative. That is why people should not cry at death; it is not something horrible or ghastly. Their friends and loved ones have simply returned to their homeland. The books and writings received by writers through channelled sources are a sign that this message about life on the other side of death is beginning to get through to humanity.

The human race is now being inspired to experience a feeling of awareness. People will not be able to explain it. They just know that they feel different about life.

Awareness purifies — Awareness is something so sacred that it purifies the Self and frees it from creation. It brings about salvation and oneness with the Creator. Now that Maitreya Himself has come to teach us we no longer need gurus or saints. We are made aware through Him.

Attachment to forces — Forces are not 'satanic' in themselves. The same forces can be used to build and to destroy. If you become attached to evolutionary forces, you

35

can become psychic, clairvoyant, etc, because you are using these forces to fulfil your thought-formations.

Detachment is the most powerful 'drug' — The Self is endless. Awareness is endless. Mind, spirit and body have a beginning and an end. With detachment, the Self experiences phenomena in mind, spirit and body, but it does not get attached to the miraculous powers of which mind, spirit and body are capable.

The laws of creation are in the mind. The universal energy is in the spirit and the forum for the materialization of the creation is the physical body.

In effect, when the Self observes God's powers it is detachment which saves the Self from imprisonment in the bondages of life.

Detachment is the most powerful 'drug'. It becomes so effective that it immunizes the Self from the processes and proceedings of mind, spirit and body.

To learn detachment is an art. A scientist, with detachment, will learn the laws of physics and chemistry (the laws of creation) and will apply them, creating things which constitute God's work.

The artist, with detachment, will be able to describe God through his own experiences.

The destiny of one and all is to be, one day, free of mind, spirit and body. This in itself becomes salvation.

Why 'glorify'? — If you look into history (as man has conceived it), you will see that many events have been glorified (for example, battles, crusades, victories, etc). Anything you glorify leads ultimately to destruction.

If you glorify God in terms of any ism, you create 'crusades' in mind, spirit and body. Instead of creating harmony and equilibrium, you create issues of 'high' and 'low'. The moment you glorify, ask yourself who is glorifying and whom you are glorifying? "Do not glorify Me. If you try to glorify Me you create nothing but confusion and chaos in mind, spirit and body. Instead, know that I am within you. It is the Self which must experience the Lord in thought, speech and action."

Mysteries of life — When mind, spirit and body are in equilibrium and the Self thinks of anything in mind, that will materialize. The moment you desire an orange, it will be before you. The moment you desire to ride a horse, it will be before you.

When you experience this, it will no longer be a mystery. Until you reach this stage, it remains a supreme mystery of life. Anyone, at any stage, can learn the art of Self-realization and will find he can enjoy life. Life is to be enjoyed, with detachment.

Politicians — Politicians are groping in darkness, in isms. They look into science, agriculture, etc, to solve problems. When one problem is solved, another arises. Problems multiply like mosquitoes. No one is born to lead another. Everyone is born to experience the Lord in His creation. The moment you do so, you will enjoy life in the Lord's creation.

Thieves and saints — Saints, gurus, politicians, educators and doctors are all contradicting each other. When a thief comes to you, how can you solve his problem if you yourself have not thieved in your life? [Maitreya is addressing saints and gurus here.] How can you appreciate light if you do not know darkness? Darkness and light are both important. A thief is important. A saint is important.

If a thief comes to you, do not preach; it will not work. Teach him to be honest about what he is doing. The thief will gradually acquire detachment. Detachment enables the mysteries of life to become clearer. The thief, with detachment, eventually realizes the mind is reacting to a particular thought-formation.

"Even when you are thieving, know that without the divine hand of the Lord you would not be able to thieve." The Self only witnesses. Gradually the Self becomes aware of its mastership. Gradually, the Self controls mind, spirit and body.

Everyone has his own wealth, which no one can take away. This wealth is Self-realization.

Possessiveness — "The moment you experience Me with detachment, you will respect Me in My various forms. You will not cry for the form; you cry only when you are possessive."

One true experience alone is sufficient — This teaching is simple to understand, yet difficult to put into practice in your activities, because you need discipline. An experience of the Lord can help you. When the Self is taken away from mind, spirit and body (even momentarily), that experience alone is sufficient.

Why compare? — "I am not important. With whom shall I compare Myself? Similarly, when you are in your Self, you know Me and you are at-one with the entire creation. If someone comes to rob you, if someone comes to praise you, will it matter?"

Ignorance and knowledge — Whatever is done in ignorance is automatically forgiven. Whatever is done in knowledge of the consequences is sin, if by your actions you knowingly imprison yourself in the bondages of life.

Innocence attracts — If you have the mind and spirit of a baby, wherever you go you will attract people. The Self of a baby is detached. His innocence attracts.

A baby smiles at you, even if he has never seen you before. Why? It expresses his natural happiness. Why do adults behave differently? Because there is a crusade going on all the time in mind, spirit and body. The Self is experiencing nothing but conditioning in mind, spirit and body.

"This is not philosophy. I am teaching you live things, not 'past, present and future'. If you practise honesty of mind, sincerity of spirit and detachment while you are alive, you can embrace My totality in one single birth."

The Self — The Self is presence, awareness and light: presence in time, awareness in eternity, and light. "We are all sparks of the Almighty."

Environment and individuality — The environment has become the top priority today. Within a few years, the priority will be mind, spirit and body, in the life of an individual.

Renewal — In childhood you are detached. But as you grow, if you become attached, you lose the beauty of life. The Lord comes again, in your old age, to free you.

The 'bath' of mind, the 'bath' of spirit — Just as the body must be bathed, detachment is the 'bath' of mind, and awareness is the 'bath' of spirit. When you roam in mind, spirit and body remember that your resting place is in Self-awareness. When you sleep, if you sleep 'in mind' you wake up exhausted. If you sleep 'in spirit' you may experience extraordinary things. If you sleep in Self-awareness, it is a good sleep.

Life is balance — Creation has energy and if that energy is disturbed it can shake our world and even break it. But it can be rebuilt. "One has to be careful with energy. If you try to possess it, it will destroy you. You may be good at mathematics and become a first class mathematician. But what happens? You can become unbalanced if there is no equilibrium on the intellectual level.

"It is the same if you are caught up in spiritualism. You can become obsessive.

"Be detached and intelligently use that energy. Life is equilibrium and balance.

"It is the destiny and evolution of everyone to reach this state." Whatever you do in life practise detachment and you will achieve equilibrium and experience the forces of life passing through your mind, spirit and body and not be possessed by them.

"When you do this the 'third eye' is opened and you will be able to sense what is happening around you and foresee events."

The third eye — The 'third eye' will eventually develop. That is the destiny of one and all. It is our common heritage. When the third eye opens, you can see the four kingdoms. The pattern of events on Earth will be seen on the astral and mental planes. "There is no freedom or salvation there. Freedom and salvation lie in detachment."

[Note: 'Third eye' is not a physical eye but the name given to a centre (vortex) of energy in the head. It is the result of interaction between the crown centre and ajna centre.]

Perfection — Perfection is only in the Supreme Being. We are not in the Supreme Being. We simply experience the reflection of the Supreme Being in the process of creation. No one should make attempts to be perfect in creation, because this leads to a fight against the forces of life.

Causes of suffering — Neither scientists, intellectuals nor philosophers can understand why there is suffering in life, why we are inflicted by such terrible diseases as AIDS. They cannot understand because they have a materialistic approach to life. Man does not exist on the physical plane alone but on the mental and spiritual planes as well.

Man has worked very hard and created much material wealth and knowledge but has paid little attention to the mental and spiritual bodies.

Spiritual bankruptcy creates the suffering of disease in the world, while physical disasters such as earthquakes, explosions and murder come about because of ill-health on the mental plane.

World leaders, political and religious, have done nothing for the spiritual welfare of humanity. You do not have to look far to understand how the spiritual and mental worlds interact in human affairs — no further than an ordinary family.

No matter how far away a husband or wife may be from each other, they will often know or sense if something is wrong with the other, for they are spiritually and mentally related. It is the same with people and nations: if we wrong the Vietnamese refugees* then we shall suffer as well.

Life consists of the mind, spirit and body. If the body is starved it weakens and becomes sick; if the spiritual body is starved a person fades and dies; if the mental body is starved a person loses his direction in life.

The natural food for the mind, spirit and body is honesty, sincerity and detachment. If the natural evolution of these bodies is retarded or hampered by man-made laws there are always disastrous consequences.

[*The Vietnamese boat people, escaping the 1979 Chinese invasion and turned back by the West in the 1980s.]

Self and mind — Ask yourself who is trying to acquire knowledge and wisdom. Is it you, the Self? No. It is the mind. When the mind and spirit struggle, you (the Self) are caught in the crusade.

The role of the Self — What happens to the Self? The Self witnesses. The Self plays the 'mini-role' of the Almighty. The Self is the spark of the Almighty. The Self simply observes the processes of mind, spirit and body. In this sense also, the Almighty never interferes in the Becoming. The Self makes itself known through awareness. The Self makes mind, spirit and body aware of reality. Then mind, spirit and body respect the awareness of the Self and make decisions accordingly. "Let your awareness grow. Awareness, with intelligence, will guide mind, spirit and body. This will create harmony between mind, spirit and body and the Self." Then the Self can use the forces of Life to transform things, to effect 'miracles'. Mind, spirit and body are simply vehicles.

The road to awareness — Awareness is Vishnu, the aspect of Deity which sustains and nurtures mind, spirit and body. Awareness is universal. It does not 'belong' to any religion, nor to any guru, saint or politician. When you judge, saying 'I am right. You are wrong', you are caught in the web of attachment. The Self must always practise detachment. In this way, awareness will grow.

Friends and enemies — If you respect your Self, you respect the entire creation. Then there are no 'friends' or 'enemies'. Disputes between people do not take place in the Self, but in mind, spirit and body. What matters is the Self, the spark of the Almighty. "If you are a thief, I am with you. If you are a king, I am with you."

Who is your enemy? — "This time, I am speaking through people who carry My messages, and those who do will know that if you exclude one person you will not understand Me. If you do understand Me you will understand that there is no difference between you and your enemy."

"People who read these teachings are putting them into practice. The moment practice becomes habit it becomes your protection, the seal that guards you."

Conditioning — When Jesus went to various places preaching "Love thy neighbour as thyself", he also preached honesty and sincerity, because this creates love within you. The rabbis went to Mary to complain that her son was preaching things which were not in line with their teaching. Mary would ask Jesus why he was teaching in this way. At times there were arguments. Had tempers flared, Mary could have thought: "My son is mad." This is conditioning. Conditioning is like an egg. Once incubated, the life within bursts through the shell. When conditioning cracks, there is a sense of relief. Conditioning can crack with awareness or without awareness.

When conditioning cracks without awareness the result is a shock. It has such power it can even destroy part of the memory. Tremendous energy is tied up there, like a volcano when intense heat causes it to erupt. The destiny of conditioning is that it will burst. No one can remain conditioned for ever. "Be detached, then you will not be conditioned."

Conditioning and fear — When Rama came, all those around him, including his father, mother and siblings, were conditioned. There were intrigues to keep him out of the palace. He lived in the jungle for 14 years. When this conditioning 'cracked', Rama's family went to him and begged him to return.

The same applies to Krishna. He was also free from conditioning. Many prophecies surrounded the event of his birth. The king slaughtered as many babies as he could and the baby Krishna had to be hidden in a river. All those who were conditioned feared that one day Krishna would take over.

The same occurred at the birth of Moses; as a baby, he had to be hidden. Why? The conditioned fears the unconditioned. Whoever harbours conditioned teaching will feel fearful. The unconditioned is fearless.

Conditioning and karma — Cyclical patterns of cause and effect — karma — govern our lives. As long as we are conditioned, these cyclical patterns repeat themselves. Detachment releases us from repetitive cycles.

The energy tied up in conditioning is like the energy contained in a volcano. When the volcano erupts, all is drama. When the lava cools, when the energy cools down, it is possible to see how beautiful the patterns in the lava are.

We are all observers in this vast creation. If we observe with a strong sense of detachment, we will find beauty, equilibrium, harmony in it.

Evolution — Isms, ideologies and beliefs are essential stages in the life of every human being. They represent the 'second nature' of our lives. Evolution can only take place through them, and is in fact controlled by them. We should not tell people to abandon their beliefs and philosophies or trust and faith in them. Human beings are motivated by isms such as love, faith, trust and patriotism. It is important for survival in 'second nature' — in the world in which they live. The spark inside them has, one day, to be free from that nature and its illusions.

Even if, through meditation or spiritual awareness, you feel momentarily free of the world of the mind, spirit and body, you should not abandon it but continue to respect and honour it.

Every individual, every nation, is ruled by their 'second nature'. The laws of evolution governed by this nature surround the Self and it is up to the Self to learn to master them with awareness. Awareness builds up a movement in life which creates evolutionary progress. But awareness must not be confused with freedom, for that is the ultimate destiny of the journey through life.

While each person is locked into his journey through evolution, dependent on his 'second nature', he should be taught the art of self-discipline and through this he gradually becomes aware of how to use the laws of evolution.

We are evolving in cycles of time, experiencing birth and death. Salvation is in the Supreme Being where there is no movement, only continuous awareness. This is the spiritual journey of one and all: to learn the art of Self-awareness.

Creation is an automatic process. Every ism is automated. It is like throwing a stone into the water, automatically creating ripples. So every action creates effects automatically to remind the Self that it is not free. Once the Self looks for that freedom, then the journey towards salvation begins.

When Jesus reached the point of Supreme Being on the cross, he asked: "Father, why have you left me?" His Father told him: "Look around you; everything that is happening is not freedom or salvation. These you can only find with Me."

Jesus realized that all beings are created by God and that we are all reacting to the laws of nature.

Creation is a launching pad for freedom. Your mind, spirit and body are matter of creation evolving towards the Supreme Being — the freedom of complete awareness — so do not neglect them.

Look after your family. Remember it is the isms, beliefs and faiths that get us up in the morning and send us to work in order that we may pay the bills and care for our family. It is not a conscious thing. These isms are the 'second nature' which push us to perform our duties in life and thus be able to evolve. Awareness is the guiding force. The Self must respect the mind, spirit and body and learn to adopt honesty, sincerity and detachment.

Everyone is looking for a Messiah. It is our Self looking for guidance. Maitreya is a guiding force in creation, pointing towards our destiny of freedom. He is the helping hand needed by the majority of people. This pointing is nothing other than a realization of the forces of evolution around us. The moment you realize this, then this awareness becomes your guiding force.

But remember, Maitreya also obeys the laws of creation. He does not destroy them but points them out.

The new energy sweeping through the world is re-programming creation to make people aware of their mind, spirit and body. This awareness acts like water splashing away the mud of old beliefs and politics, bringing a new freshness to our lives.

New awareness — All the changes taking place in the world are creating awareness in people, who have decided that enough is enough; they have a right to be free and to enjoy life. They no longer want to be conditioned by politics, religion or commercialization.

Life has to be balanced, and we have to be aware of the Self in the heart.

It has taken Maitreya to release this awareness into the world. No politician came forward to say: "Let the voice of the people be the basis of democracy." They all hid behind their ideology. They did not talk about harmony.

The light, the bible, the prayer for one and all from now on, is the awareness that Maitreya is in you and you are in Him. His vibrant teachings are stirring the world now, and the politicians are silent.

The tongue — The most important part of the body is the tongue. The physical body needs it to talk and to taste. The

45

tongue of the mind is the memory. The tongue of the spirit is wisdom. The tongue of the Almighty is awareness.

In the physical body the tongue is needed to eat. Once the food is eaten, the taste for it is gone. You become detached and you do not want to eat the same thing every day or you would soon get tired of it. It is the same with the mind; if it is fed the same thing all the time it will lose interest. Be detached, though, with memory; use it but do not be obsessed with it.

When you see wisdom in the spiritual world do not become attached to it. It can appear like a snake or a man in white clothes. Experience the taste of it, but do not become addicted to it.

The process of awareness — Maitreya is trying to develop a sense of equilibrium between the Self and the Almighty. Recently He addressed a group of Swamis as follows: "You have given up certain things in life to concentrate on the Lord but you are not 'coming closer'. Rather, it is a process of awareness — the awareness that the Lord is behind you.

"Your destiny is freedom. No one is 'born in sin'. Rather, the Self is subject to conditioning during the process of evolution. The process of evolution is the Becoming.

"If you follow the three principles of honesty of mind, sincerity of spirit and detachment, evolution proceeds naturally. Your 'second nature' is conditioned nature, but practice of the three principles will free you from conditioning. No one is 'condemned' to conditioning.

"Please do not presume things. This amounts to 'a soft landing' which satisfies the mind. Isms are like small pills that give the mind little breaks in life. Mind, spirit and body feel a bit 'high', a bit happy. But the realities of life can never be comprehended via isms. They can only be experienced. Experience and vision go together.

"Do not struggle to attain special powers, such as the capacity to see with the 'third eye'. It is true that when you see with your third eye there are no isms, no imaginings. But to accelerate the processes of life unnaturally will destroy you. There is a natural pace of development.

"When you become desireless all the burdens of life are removed."

The nature of experience — "If you practise the three principles of honesty, sincerity and detachment you will develop your own sacred knowledge and wisdom."

However, difficulties can arise when you start to describe your experiences. The moment you open up, less evolved souls will feel drawn and will cling to the gems of knowledge and wisdom, just as bees are drawn to honey. If you become attached to this attention you will get trapped and fall into a cycle of karma (cause and effect) which amounts to another form of conditioning.

Your experience is your personal blessing. What you have experienced, you know. Others can only understand once they have experienced.

Effects follow the telling of certain experiences. If you become attached to these effects there is no salvation.

Experiences which follow from honesty of mind, sincerity of spirit and detachment are genuine, pure, spontaneous, un-conditioned. "Do not cheat yourself. Respect yourself."

Other dimensions — Many people, including those in positions of power, have no idea whatsoever about dimensions other than the physical. They think the world is governed by physical laws. "What about the laws that control physicality?"

Practice — "If you practise the three principles (honesty, sincerity and detachment), My universal consciousness will be revealed to you. Do not be attached to it. Use it for the betterment of yourself and others. Do not say: 'I am only a human being, I cannot do it.' You can do it. Whatever you are doing, I am with you."

AIDS — The newspapers have become very quiet about the AIDS epidemic and we are seeing fewer headlines. No one seems to be aware of the true story that is emerging: many patients are healing themselves.

Many AIDS sufferers have been joining Buddhist and other centres and learning Self-awareness through meditation. In this way they have learned how to discipline the mind, spirit and body and to tap into the powers of the Self to heal themselves.

Eventually this kind of self-discipline will help the unemployed, and those who have fallen into crime and drug abuse. Chaos, corruption and crime will recede in society as people gain happiness and peace through learning to control their lives through Self-awareness. (May 1990)

Prayer and meditation — Prayer is one of the easiest, sweetest and most elegant ways to remember the Lord. In prayer there is always detachment. In prayer you have no weight, no cares — this is a state of absoluteness. You experience the presence of the Almighty. "In prayer you will never be lost."

Meditation means a conscious process of detachment. There is a beginning of awareness of mind, spirit and body as vehicles for the Self. But in meditation you can be lost if you do not know the proper approach, that is, if there is an attachment to spiritual powers. The Self is able to move in and out of mind, spirit and body. But powers do exist around the Self. If the power of spirit is able to draw the Self to it, the Self gets engrossed and remains wrapped in that energy which can be either constructive or destructive. This leads nowhere. In power (spirit) *per se*, there is no salvation. In meditation, you can maintain equilibrium in mind, spirit and body through detachment. This is a long process.

Creation — What does Maitreya mean when He says: "It is your heritage to sit at the 'right side' of the Almighty"? We can see it this way: 70 per cent is creation and 30 per cent is the Supreme Being. In that so-called 30 per cent, the Self is resting, there is no relationship such as exists in creation. The 30 per cent is the kingdom of the Almighty. So, the Self is in the domain of 30 per cent, observing creation, the other 70 per cent.

In creation things evolve. There is 'high and low', 'good and bad'. Creation takes place in the 70 per cent. There is no creation in the 30 per cent. The Self, seated in that 30 per cent, remains free from the cyclic phenomena of creation.

When creation is approached from the Self you can view it from the standpoint of the Almighty, because within the domain of the 30 per cent you remain as the Almighty does: non-participant. In this domain there is grace, bliss, happiness.

All the isms are in the 70 per cent. In the 30 per cent you are free from isms.

Gurus, saints, scientists are penetrating the how/when/where of the 70 per cent domain. In this way, they are goaded into unknown problems of life, into attachments. For example, you decide you like a domain and do not want to move from it.

"When you try to be what you are, you begin to sit next to the Almighty. Here there is no creation as such, but a window to look into creation. The 'third eye' is a window between creation and the Supreme Being."

When you are fast asleep, mountains, rivers, people working, etc, appear. (Someone is observing this.) In time, your Self will be able to do this consciously. The Self will be able to observe through the 'third eye'.

In creation everything is moving. Do not step into creation. Observe it, watch it, with the clear understanding that everything belongs to the Almighty.

In creation, light — There are people who have experienced leaving their physical bodies. They speak of going through a tunnel, a dark hole. This is because what we call darkness is in the Supreme Being. When the Self returns to its 30 per cent domain, the sensation is of moving from light to darkness. This is because where the Self rests there is no movement.

Wherever there is light, there is creation. Without light there is no creation. Many scientists speak of a Big Bang. At this point, light emerged. Through colours, vibrations and sounds creation emerged.

Consciousness and awareness — In the domain of creation, we find consciousness. In the domain of the Supreme Being there is omnipresence, omnipotence, and, quite simply, awareness. Gurus, saints and rishis know that all elements in creation can be controlled, but the domain of the Supreme Being can never be controlled.

Why you should be detached — "Everything in creation is important for the Lord. Who are you to say that you are above and another is below? A master can become a servant, a servant can become a master. Things can change. So be detached."

Karma — What is hatred? In effect, the Self dislikes the burden of all the conditioning in the mental body. The mind then goads the Self into karmas (conditioned behaviour). The Self then loses direction, equilibrium, awareness and detachment. The Self 'ages' into that state of conditioning known as birth and death. At death the Self suddenly breaks out of the physical body, then the mental body, and rests in some form of the spiritual body. This cycle of birth and death goes on until the Lord Himself 'opens the door of heaven'.

"There is no heaven in mind, spirit and body. Heaven is beyond mind, spirit and body. It is in the Supreme Being."

In the context of this basic teaching, one can understand that in creation everything that is predestined is, in effect, preconditioned.

[Note: Maitreya is referring here to the great Law of Karma: effects invariably follow from causes which have been set in motion, and nothing in creation is outside this Law.]

Peace and war — What is peace? "In creation, peace means non-conditioning. What is war? War means conditioning."

We can understand that when people try to impose ideologies, they ultimately undergo processes of self-defeat, because the Self is at war. "The seeds of destruction lie in conditioning. The seeds of peace lie in non-conditioning."

"Be what you are, so that you are free from conditioning, so that you can approach whatever comes before you with an open mind, so that you do not fall into destructive processes."

Worshipping power — As the Self passes from one stage of life to another, experiences of creation are stored in the consciousness. That consciousness becomes the bank of awareness. The closer one comes to the Supreme Being, the more consciousness develops around the Self. So the Self experiences Godly powers, Godly presence and the presence of deities. "If you worship these deities you are in fact worshipping power. What happens if you worship these powers? You try to create awareness around the power, and sometimes you can use the power to transmute, etc, but will this bring salvation? No." "My powers are not to be followed, but to be respected with a strong sense of detachment." Once that process has been accomplished, even with Godly, spiritual powers, then the Almighty opens the door, and the Self "sits next to the Almighty" — that is, in the Supreme Being.

Life, light and creation — At the human level, it is very difficult to understand creation, because at the human level everything is conditioned. Only highly evolved souls, aware and detached, can guide humanity towards freedom and salvation. This is why Maitreya teaches honesty, sincerity and detachment, because these three, if practised, generate awareness and equilibrium in mind, spirit and body.

In light there is total creation. Light is the mother of creation. The 'beginning' and the 'end' are in light. But Life is beyond light. The source of Life is in the Supreme Being.

Nevertheless, creation around us is important to us. "Nothing is outside us. Everything is within mind, spirit and body. Those who learn the art of Self-realization in mind, spirit and body will experience that everything within and without is from one source which we call God. In effect, anything and everything belongs to the Almighty. Once that sense is developed in the mental body, then the spiritual body will follow the same pattern and the Self will be able to express equilibrium and detachment. The isms of desire such as 'mine' and 'yours' will fall into the right perspective.

The Self is not mind, spirit or body. The Self is immortal. Mind, spirit and body are the clothes given by the Almighty at birth and discarded at death. It is Life, which is experience, which becomes the source of energy. Experience is very important for the Self to be able to move in mind, spirit and body and establish mastery. When this is done, creation is mastered."

Detachment leads to fearlessness — Look at the mind, spirit and body of a little baby, which is honest, sincere and detached. The baby in his innocence likes to walk everywhere, without fear. Everyone has passed through this stage of fearlessness.

In adult life one becomes aware, with knowledge and wisdom, that if one becomes egoistic during the process of struggle between good and bad, right and wrong, then the shadow of fear is cast upon one. But if one is detached and humble, one becomes free of this shadow of fearfulness.

"Supreme Being is beyond mind, spirit and body. It is awareness which makes the Self experience the Supreme Being and the Becoming of the Lord.

"Awareness cannot be individualized. Awareness embraces the Supreme Being and the Becoming of the Supreme Being, and in awareness the Self experiences equilibrium. The practise of equilibrium is generated and sustained by detachment.

"What happens to one who ardently believes in particular ideologies when he dies? Can anyone answer this? On the deathbed, everything is left behind. Again, at that moment, the discipline of detachment works on mind, spirit and body. So detachment is a very significant factor in life."

"Invite politicians, philosophers, and scientists to answer the question: how significant is detachment in life? And if it is, why are you conditioning people with ideologies, thus creating nothing but confusion?"

Without detachment, no salvation — "What you have now may be taken away from you in time. This is why detachment is very important. One who practises attachment cannot achieve salvation."

Attachment to spiritual powers — Many yogis are attached to spiritual powers. Here a crisis arises: yogis in deep meditation open up windows of the mind and spirit. They can see creation in mind and spirit. But if the yogi cannot close these windows again, he becomes 'derailed'. No one can stand the cosmic dimension in mind and spirit. It is beyond human capacity to witness this.

This is why Maitreya says: "Never try to be what I am. Be what you are. I am with you. My relationship with you is like the relationship between a mother and her baby. The baby does not want to be the mother, but its destiny is to be a parent one day."

"One day you will be what I am."

Evolve at a natural pace — What will happen if, as in the case of some yogis and saints, you try to force the pace of evolution? You will not be able to endure the cosmic dimension of the Lord. The same thing happens to a baby. Evolution must be natural. The baby will be a parent one day without fuss and struggle if it evolves naturally.

Possessions — Nothing belongs to you. Everything belongs to the Lord. If you are honest with yourself, you are honest with the Lord. If you are sincere with yourself, you are sincere with the Lord.

The voice — The tone of voice can give an indication of the level of attachment or the degree of sincerity. A nasal timbre is different from a voice that speaks from the heart. A nasal tone indicates attachments. A deep resonance is not the same as sound mediated through throat and nose. The latter indicates strong emotions.

Do not 'possess' knowledge — When some people who were paralyzed came into the presence of Jesus, by a mere touch they were energized and relieved of suffering.

When Sai Baba is present, people who come close to Him are transformed.

In these situations there is no 'How, Why, What, When, Where?' You can become attached to these questions, which then become the seeds of confusion. These questions, if posed possessively, make people grab knowledge and wisdom under the illusion that it belongs to them. They create their own secret societies and begin to rule people around them. Those who have gained some special knowledge make it esoteric and create suspense. This, in turn, creates attachment. This is how such people exact respect, a position as leader, with followers.

"All gifts are of the Lord. Nothing is secret. If you are 'minus' one person, you are minus Me. Wholesomeness lies in honesty, sincerity and detachment.

"You have physical eyes. You can see what is good and what is bad, what is pleasant or harmful. When you practise honesty, sincerity and detachment, awareness grows. You can experience peace, grace, happiness, serenity. This is so even when everything around you is totally negative.

"Just as one rotten potato can rot others around it, one enlightened person can enlighten others around him. People around that person will be energized."

The path of awareness — The statement of Jesus: "I am the way and the truth and the life; no one comes to the Father but by Me," means that only through awareness can we reach the Almighty.

This truth is personified in Jesus in the Christian tradition. If you 'de-personify' this truth, it can be understood as the principle of awareness.

You cannot reach the Almighty through knowledge and wisdom alone. This path can lead you to deities, essentially creations of the mind. In this there is no salvation.

This is why the way to the Father is 'only through Jesus', or awareness, because in awareness there is no attachment, no desire. In awareness there is no time or space.

There should be no conscious attempt to seek God's 'whereabouts', because if you are honest, sincere and detached the door opens.

"Through awareness you evolve. Only the Lord can quicken the pace.

"Whatever is given to you is yours. Do not allow it to be disturbed. Consciousness is divine as long as it is not interfered with. But the moment it is played with it is undivine. You do not have to please Me. Make your Self happy and I am happy with you."

Imposition is undivine — What flowers naturally from within is divine, but imposition from without is undivine. "When you are honest, sincere and detached, who is your master? The Lord is in the heart. If you have found the Lord in the heart you do not go out looking for anyone. You fulfil your duties, you become what you are; you are the happiest person on Earth because you are not allowing anyone to play with your mind, spirit and body. In the manner of Jesus, Rama, Krishna, Sai Baba, you allow your intelligence and awareness to guide you in mind, spirit and body, and yet you remain humble."

A ship without a rudder — There are disciples who have followed a spiritual master and have not reached the ultimate goal of freedom and salvation despite the fact that they have been practising day and night. They return to society but not to normality. Their life is like a ship without a rudder. They create a class or group of their own.

Similarly, in the 1960s, expectations were not fulfilled in schools and universities. Young people began to live for the day, and to live together. They became 'hippies'. Many of these were unable to rejoin society in a satisfactory way.

This is why Maitreya says: "Detachment is the divine water which leads one to divine freedom and salvation." "Attachment is the root cause of destruction. If you get attached even to a spiritual principle, it will destroy you. Possessiveness, in this sense, leads to witchcraft."

The teachings of Jesus are about detachment. "Love thy neighbour as thyself" means that although your neighbour has made you angry, through love that anger will dissolve. You realize you are not that anger. In this way clouds come and go, but you remain the same. You are not conditioned, not imprisoned. This is divine freedom in creation. "You are in the Light, and the Light is in you."

Cause and effect — Human activities which are conditioned, known as 'karmas', are subject to the laws of cause and effect. "If you do not practise detachment in your life's activities, you experience hindrances, stagnation and imprisonment. Life becomes cyclic (ie repetitive). It remains chained to the laws of cause and effect. Then there is no peace, no grace, no happiness, no freedom, no salvation.

"This is why detachment is such an important discipline in life."

"Life without detachment is like a serpent without a head. In ancient times, the serpent became a powerful symbol: either you tamed the serpent or it would kill you."

A changing environment — If you aspire to certain goals and multiply your desires with attachment this will destroy you. If the environment changes and it is not what a person wants, it can lead to suicide. This was the fate, recently, of some Soviet politicians. (Aug 1991)

Be who you are — The simple foundation for the teachings of the New Age is this: Be who you are. If you are a Jew, be a Jew. If you are a Muslim, be a Muslim. If you are a Christian, a Hindu, a Buddhist, be who you are. If you can discover the secrets of mind, spirit and body, you will know who you are.

You can do this through honesty of mind, sincerity of spirit and detachment. You gain freedom in creation and salvation in the Supreme Being. It is detachment which takes you from creation into the Supreme Being. In this way you are not distracted by the powers of creation.

If you become attached, even to the divine power, you will be able to perform miraculous things, but this is not salvation.

Through detachment you begin to lead a life of wholesomeness; you experience oneness. If you are attached you experience something closing in upon you.

Temptation — People who have reached certain stages of evolution in life may experience psychic powers. "Do not fall into this trap. It is called temptation. You are free if you are detached. It all depends upon the clarity, the purity, of mind, spirit and body.

"If you are free of desires, the journey becomes easier for the soul to experience all these things in quick succession. But if there are too many isms the soul's journey becomes that much more difficult."

Self and ego — Whenever you think of 'me' or 'mine' you personify. The ego has the power to perform activities (karmas); it is still important. The Self is immune, in this sense: The Self does not have to perform any disciplines. The Self only witnesses.

Through honesty and sincerity the relationship between the Self and the ego grows. If detachment prevails, there is no personification. There is then no division. There is "Manyness in Oneness" and "Oneness in Manyness". This is divine love.

The ego comes and goes. The Self witnesses. "If you take one step towards Me, I will take two steps towards you. I will lend you My strength. I am always with you."

You and I are One — When you are detached in mind, spirit and body, then whatever happens around you and within you does not touch you. You are immune. This is salvation. As long as you are attached you will experience struggle, the ups and downs in life. Knowledge and wisdom create the strongest bonds of attachment. This is why Maitreya says: "Be what you are. You are not knowledge. You are not wisdom. You (the Self) and I (the Self) are One."

"Whoever, whatever, wherever you are, tread the divine water of cleanliness which is detachment. I have not come to teach you anything new. Be honest to yourself, sincere to yourself, and be detached.

"This method is so simple, so sweet, it is free from religions, ideologies, politics. It makes one experience who one is. Fulfil your role, yet be free."

Divinity and detachment — "If you become attached, even to divinity, it will destroy you. What is truly divine is detachment. In detachment you will see the divine powers of the Lord but you will be detached from them."

Love your neighbour — Recently a Swami asked Maitreya: "What is meant in the Bible by 'Loving your neighbour as yourself'?"

Maitreya says: "To love your neighbour as yourself has nothing to do with religion. When it comes to loving yourself, you love your neighbour because the Self in him is the Self in you."

Knowledge, wisdom and awareness — Knowledge becomes wisdom when it has been experienced. If you do not experience it, then it remains as a role model. The image that comes to mind is a library. Even what you experience can remain stacked up there. The moment you act with detachment awareness takes charge of you.

"You want to achieve salvation from the cycle of birth and death. This means you want to be free of the 'Big Bang's' influence. But knowledge and wisdom on their own will not help you. It is awareness which guides the true Self." This awareness is freedom and salvation. Awareness arises as a result of detachment.

The moment the 'fruit of the tree of knowledge' was eaten, Adam and Eve became conscious of the things around them. Knowledge, without detachment, entraps you. It becomes one of the bondages of life.

"The body needs bathing every day. You also need to bathe your mind and spirit. Your spirit is the source of energy. Your spirit can become exhausted. You need the water of detachment."

Going forward, not back — The entire creation came from the 'Big Bang'. Does this mean you have to go back to the Big Bang? No. You want to move on.

When you are detached and therefore aware, you are one with God. Your doubts disappear.

If you teach that Rama is God without understanding, this creates confusion in young minds. How many youngsters go to temples? Some are there, taken by their parents. But today knowledge and wisdom are necessary in order to face the problems of life, rather than the past.

Before Jesus was put on the cross he was crowned with thorns and was powerless to prevent it. At some point he appeared to have doubts. But the experience given to him on the cross made him say: "Father, forgive them, for they know not what they do." Jesus was freed from the bondages of knowledge and wisdom. He realized that in awareness he was one with God.

"You can control knowledge and wisdom. You can use it positively. But it should not take charge of your Self. It should not master you. The moment you are detached from it you master it."

The Art of Healing

Healing — Maitreya has given the art of healing to people in Hong Kong and the Middle East who cannot even sign their name on a piece of paper. (Healing in this way depends not on formal education but on awareness.) As the art of healing develops, there will be in the long run less employment in the medical field as we know it today. On the other hand, music, art and recreation will gain in prominence in the future. As more people work with the arts, crime rates will be reduced.

The problem of AIDS — A Swami who works closely with Maitreya in London recently asked him what he should do when people came to him suffering from AIDS.

Maitreya answered: "In your mind, spirit and body, practise detachment. Harmony between mind, spirit and body will be restored. You will find you are healed. AIDS will vanish."

The Swami then asked: "With this statement, why can't we go out and preach this?"

Maitreya replied: "First of all, if you go out and give this to someone when his hands are full, what will happen? It will slip from his grasp. But if there is a real hunger on the part of any individual (ie the individual must first experience a sincere yearning) and you give him this, you will heal him."

This is a form of what is called 'automatic healing', an ancient art.

"I am giving you one of the easiest ways to know Me: be honest in your mind, be sincere in your spirit, feed your body with right food.

"Then your awareness will grow. In anything you do with a sense of detachment, if it is a natural course of action, I am with you. But attachment, possessiveness, is undivine. There I cannot be with you."

The Swami then used this approach with a man who had AIDS, a West African intellectual who desperately wanted to overcome his situation. This man is now putting on weight, enjoying life, and has stopped using any medication for his symptoms.

Those close to Maitreya also work with people who have undergone a profound transformation as a result of a direct experience of Maitreya. It should not be thought that He presents Himself only to important people. On an individual level, many miracles have occurred. He has made Himself known to prostitutes and murderers as well as ordinary people in all walks of life and is continuing to do so.

One murderer experienced such a profound change that he approached the above-mentioned Swami and said: "Swami, I want to become a saint." The Swami answered: "The door is open."

An interesting psychological principle is operating here: when a violently energized person (ie a murderer) experiences a spiritual transformation, that same energy is transformed into ardent aspiration. The transformation of such a person, because of his very nature, cannot be lukewarm.

Another example would be Mary Magdalene.

AIDS — Many mothers and babies are now infected with AIDS. The genes have altered. This type of mutation in the body originates in the mind, which can cause genetic alterations. The physical body is not the sole sufferer. The body is controlled by the spirit or power aspect, which in turn is controlled by mind. The mind is controlled by 'Atma', the Self, also referred to as awareness.

Although the physical body may have no direct sexual contact, if the mind indulges in destructive ways it can affect the physical body and create symptoms of diseases. If there are genetic alterations these can affect the baby.

When the mental and spiritual 'bodies' (energy patterns) are sick, the physical body is affected. (Dec 1990)

Healing through prayer — Many people will be healed through the practice of prayer. This process has already begun, and although individual instances have not 'hit the news' as yet, people will begin to talk about their experiences in this regard. Cases of healing through prayer will become known publicly. (Jun 1988)

Vegetarianism — Vegetarianism is the human diet of the future. Eating heavy red meats creates self-destructive habits by accentuating the animal instincts. Eating a lighter diet of vegetables, which can also include eggs, cheese and fish, increases a person's self-awareness. Look at America, the biggest meat-eating country in the world. They have a huge crime problem and an obsession with guns.

Depression — When a person is depressed he goes to the doctor. Very often he is prescribed drugs so he does not experience a particular state of mind. When the effect of the drug wears off he goes back for more. "Everyone goes through processes of depression. Do not be afraid of them. Sit quietly and experience what you are going through. The Self will be able to identify that It is not depressed. It will be able to observe a state of consciousness, a state of mind which is undergoing change. It is the personification of this state which creates confusion and chaos. Personification is self-destructive. Whatever is personified is not the real Self."

"Observe. Be detached. When you experience depression you will be able to explain what it is. The Self can practise awareness through detachment and free the mind, spirit and body from imprisonment."

Schizophrenia and depression — Schizophrenia and depression are phases of de-conditioning of mind, spirit and body. These processes take place, not at birth, but due to certain circumstances of life. Split personalities and depression occur, not in the Self, but in our energy-governing organs. If the Self does not move freely in mind, spirit and body, then as it experiences different 'personalities' in mind, spirit and body, the Self will express doubts, suspicion and confusion. But as awareness grows around the Self, that awareness makes the Self realize that these personalities which present themselves on the stage of life are natural: they are the bodies of isms.

When the process of detachment and awareness starts, the Self can begin to balance these personalities in one person. This is equilibrium.

To understand the difference between Self and personality, think of the snake. There is light in the snake. Light here has the 'personality' of a snake. That 'personality' can appear in mind, spirit and body. If the Self is not aware, it can show signs of confusion and suspicion. The Self experiences creation in mind, spirit and body, because creation exists in mind, spirit and body. If the Self is 'caught' in pockets of light, it can experience a sudden materialization (of the snake, for example) in mind, spirit and body. These are delusions, hallucinations.

Both scientifically and religiously, it can be understood that creation came out of light (sound, colour and vibration). In creation there is totality: the physical has mental and spiritual counterparts. "When the Self, with awareness, is able to move with detachment in mind, spirit and body, it cannot be caught in the light spectrum. Light is the spectrum of total creation. When the Self follows light, it will be goaded into the spectrum of creation — and the cycle of evolution — until the Self can free itself from it with awareness."

Blindness — Maitreya addressed a group of Swamis on the nature of blindness and the ability to restore sight.

"Whatever is in front of you, around you, rest assured its roots are within you. Creation is within you. The roots of objectivity are in subjectivity and that subjectivity is you. When your karmas (your conditioned activities) are shocking, you want to shut them out, just as, if you catch sight of something unexpected, you close your eyes. The moment this is triggered, it has an effect on the physical body.

The moment you become aware, through understanding, that what you have seen is not dangerous, you begin to look. The awareness within you makes you look and you begin to experience a state of awareness which removes the fear. From within, something triggered the initial reaction. Those who know the art of triggering the organism from within can also trigger the pattern, from within, of sight. If you remove the state of shock the person will begin to see."

Maitreya asked the Swamis: "Is it important to you, restoring sight?" The Swamis: "Not to us, but to them, to the people; it inspires faith." Maitreya said: "Karma (conditioned activity) becomes Dharma (the way) through cleansing of mind, spirit and body. This cleansing is achieved through honesty, sincerity and detachment. If one is attached to creation this is involution, not evolution. This is why you must not be tempted by powers. You can do all these miraculous things but do not become attached. Be what you are. Your life will fall into the right perspective. The Self observes the karmas (activities) without becoming attached. Enjoyment is then possible."

CHAPTER THREE

FREEDOM, LIBERTY AND SALVATION

Freedom, liberty and salvation — Freedom operates on the individual level, liberty operates on the national level, and salvation operates on the spiritual level. All three principles evolve simultaneously.

Freedom — Freedom is essentially freedom from cyclic evolution. Although human beings are always in a state of evolution, the Self is immune from the forces of evolution.

Freedom and salvation — "I come to bring you freedom and salvation. What is freedom? To be able to move about at will. What is salvation? To be able to move about in mind, spirit and body at will. This is not a select gift only for gurus and saints. It is the destiny of one and all."

Freedom and possession — "Be what you are. Do not surrender your self-respect, your dignity to others. The moment you surrender yourself to some other self you become a zombie. Do not allow any shadow, even, to possess you. Your destiny is to be free.

"If the personality of an enlightened man falls on a child who is not yet prepared, what happens? The personality of that child is extinguished. The child becomes like charcoal. Apply this to many politicians and their children. The children get bogged down. They have no sense of freedom and are unable to express themselves. Therefore do not allow anyone to cast his shadow over you. A Master gives experiences, but does not cast his shadow."

Freedom and destiny — You are free only if you are able to guide your own destiny. This does not happen overnight. This is a science. It takes time.

Freedom and market forces — If you do not understand freedom and you preach it, it will create destruction. First you must understand what it is. Freedom is not the free play of market forces. Market forces have no 'eyes' — they are blind, therefore satanic.

In the spiritual world, spiritual power misused is destructive. Misuse stems from attachment. This is why Maitreya says: "Be detached even from spirit," (ie, spiritual powers).

Prisoners — The real prisoners are those who are in power. If you are free, open-minded, you have the power of awareness.

National constitutions — The constitution of every nation will ultimately be based on the three principles of freedom, liberty and salvation. No politician can defy the will of the Lord now.

Negative and positive currents — Ideologies can be thought of as either negative or positive currents. If you are attached to negative currents, they will destroy you. If you are attached to positive currents, the Self will be taken into unknown regions of mind, spirit and body, and it will be very difficult for the Self to 'come back', because there is no end to this process.

An example of a negative current is attachment to a particular political, religious or national sect to the exclusion of all other sects — a stance which necessarily creates opposition, strife.

An example of a positive current is attachment to meditation and allied techniques to the exclusion of all else, instanced by some yogis in the Himalayas, such that the heartbeat, body heat, etc, can be controlled. Even powers of materialization and dematerialization can be developed. Maitreya asks: "Is this salvation? No. Such a person is not free." This is why Maitreya teaches: "Be detached from My powers." If you are tempted, and you learn to do these things, you will not know how to control them and they will destroy you.

Jesus was also aware of human evolution and human destiny when he said: "Greater things shall ye do," but he also cautioned against allowing oneself to be tempted by these powers.

Creative energy — Poverty, disease and corruption are burdens that can be cured only by an upsurge of creative energy which has been released by the Supreme Being into creation. No one can understand 'how' or 'why'. But it can be experienced. "No one is bound to be a slave. The moment life begins to evolve in time and space (the 'becoming'), the goal is salvation."

Salvation — "Even by becoming immortal you do not achieve salvation. Salvation is achieved only through honesty, sincerity and detachment."

Energy and oppression — Whether you live in the East or West, if you are oppressed, remember that the forces of oppression are not inside you. If you allow these forces to possess you, they can destroy you. You are neither 'oppressions' nor 'terrors'. That is energy misused.

The Self witnesses it. The Self experiences it. If you are detached you experience it, but it does not destroy you. In the East, today, this energy absorbs you. This is the reason the Self experiences strangulation, loss of freedom.

In the West people are becoming aware of the values of life: freedom and liberty. But freedom does not mean copying one another, which leads to conditioning. Freedom is not buying a house or car. Freedom means awareness of the Self in mind, spirit and body. In the East, if you approach this energy intelligently it will not be able to create havoc and chaos in you.

Maitreya will change this energy by releasing new energies which will change the pattern of life.

"Oppression, compression, depression are in the mind." Ideology, as an example, conditions the mind. (One implication is that just as the West will have to give up the ideology of market forces, so in Eastern Europe old ideologies are being given up and doors are opening.) The danger is in giving up one ideology simply to embrace another. This is why it is important to understand what freedom really means.

Husband and wife/nation and country — The issues of freedom and oppression arise in both types of relationship (ie, in the individual and the broader social relationships).

Consider a husband and wife who were courting happily before marriage. After marriage they experience problems. When the energies of mind and spirit are trapped (bound, conditioned) they can go out of control. (This is the pattern of argument, mind to mind.) Through honesty of mind and sincerity of spirit, husband and wife create a space within. This enables the Self to control and guide the energies of mind and spirit, establishing a pattern of harmony.

The same sort of pattern can evolve in nation ('the husband') and country ('the wife'). Just as husband and wife, guided by the Self, do not break up the marriage, so nation and country do not destroy their constitution; instead, it evolves.

[Note: Maitreya is referring here, in effect, to the relationship between the state and the people.]

Space and peace — In married life, both husband and wife look for space for the individual Self. That space is sacred. The Self rests there. Space, in nation and country, is freedom, liberty. If that space exists, there is peace.

The West and democracy — If anyone says there is democracy in the West then ask what happens when you take away the pounds, shillings and pence (or dollars) from someone. Do they have the freedom to move about? Furtively perhaps, but the penniless do not have true freedom of movement and surely democracy must mean a freedom to do so.

China: Isms — Before the massacre in Beijing* the country had begun to open up, to reach for freedom and liberty because that is the destiny of the whole human race. But it is a mistake to think that anyone can turn the clock back. The leaders were trying to emerge from the ism of communism and then began to be afraid that they were losing control. The Chinese nation, however, has felt this urge to escape from the trap of ism and they will not be denied.

Isms are the life blood of the 'second nature' — the nature of illusion. It is only with intelligence that you can break out of it. That does not mean that you just escape from ism in order to seek refuge in intelligence. It is more than that, for it is the destiny of everyone to journey into light.

All the killings and events in China are the result of 'second nature'. Only intelligence can now wash the hands of blood and purify the self from ism. Those who cling to power are bound up in their particular ism — where they exist in 'me and you', 'good and bad', 'yes and no', 'yours and mine'. It is the destiny of everyone to taste intelligence and freedom.

The world's attention is focused on China. Politicians everywhere are saying: "Look, they've destroyed freedom and retreated into Communism." But Maitreya asks: "What will happen if the dark cloud that hangs over China suddenly becomes a white cloud of hope?" How will they react when the country's leaders suddenly announce that they believe in freedom and liberty for everyone and begin to bring in policies to support that belief? For that is what they have decided to do, once they have brought the national situation under control.

Ism is the mother of salvation and without it there is no salvation. "I need the thief and the saint to make My mission possible." In the same way, He needs the people who used bullets in China as He needs those who fought for freedom, for isms are inevitable processes of negatives and positives. It is only when you achieve detachment that a person or a nation becomes free of such opposites. (Jul 1989) [*Referring to the incident at the Tiananmen Square when the Chinese government killed the students indiscriminately on 3 and 4 June 1989.]

China: Freedom — Now that the dust is beginning to settle, the leaders are beginning to realize that the mass protests had nothing to do with 'counter-revolutionary' forces. They had blamed the students with their imported ideologies and were also fearful that foreign countries were behind a bid to foment trouble. They sent in the army to sweep out the threatening 'counter-revolutionary' forces, as they saw them.

Now they realize that there is a new spirit behind all these happenings. They are experiencing the same urge for freedom that drove the people and the students. This new energy is breaking open the shells of the mind, spirit and body to allow the Self to experience freedom.

Soon, Chinese leaders will begin to talk openly about this new spirit of freedom which is affecting the individual and the nation. They will also re-open the doors to the rest of the world and re-establish relationships and communications with other countries. They will have no choice — unless they want to starve and see their country lose its chances of developing its economy. We shall also see the situation reverting to the openness of some months ago before the protests began. Once again, the people will be able to talk freely about greater freedom in the media and elsewhere. (Jul 1989)

The pace of evolution — If you are enlightened and have reached certain stages, what will happen if you inspire someone who is less evolved to 'run'? That individual will be exhausted. If the process is accelerated it will destroy him. (Jan 1990)

Russia: Forces of evolution unleashed — If you 'mis-inspire' the people and unleash the forces of evolution in an unnatural manner, these same forces will move not only people but also the earth, mountains, sea, etc.

Mr Gorbachev now faces this difficulty in the Soviet Union. When he came to the West, he liked what he saw in the Western window and wanted the same. Mr Gorbachev has stirred the forces of life in such a way as to destroy social patterns. This leads to the disintegration of the habits of life.

If people feel that things around them belong to them, this becomes a new ism. If possessiveness is fostered, this leads to a process of self-destruction.

In creation everything is interdependent. If you claim property, husband, wife as 'mine', this will lead to confusion and chaos. (Jan 1990)

The past cannot be resurrected — As Maitreya predicted, the military has had to step in because Mr Gorbachev began to lose control. He has had to compromise with the generals in order to defend the state. He has had to show his authority when the Lithuanians threatened the state with their decision to break away. It is very important to establish that nations must not break up under the umbrella of freedom. Mr Gorbachev released the snake of freedom and now he has either to use the stick to put it back in the basket or kill it. People have been misled into trying to grab freedom; but, as with the snake, if you do that you will be bitten.

They are trying to resurrect the past and make it live in the present, but it cannot be done. It is like the person who can recall his past lives. He can point out the old places where he played as a child, describe the house, his parents, his widow. But what prevents him from being able to go back and claim the person and the life he had? The answer is birth. That is the barrier between our different lives. Once we enter through that door the past is behind us and no longer belongs to us.

So it is with nations. They cannot go back into history and dissolve the intervening years. Creation — existence — is balanced by wiping the past clean like a slate, offering the chance to write new experiences. Trying to live in the past destroys freedom, it does not confer it. Live in the present and look to the future. Sometimes we can look through a window and see the past but we cannot claim it.

Freedom cannot be experienced while we are caught in the conditioning of our mind, spirit and body. Only the Self can experience freedom. How can you expect a prisoner to enjoy freedom while he is still in prison? (Mar 1990)

Russia: Interdependence — It is the destiny of all people to be free. Freedom is a process of movement from one point to another, but one can only experience it with knowledge and wisdom. If freedom is snatched from another then it becomes destructive.

This is what is happening in Russia, where the Lithuanian government is attempting to snatch freedom. There can be states within states but in this world everything is interdependent — that is the basis of Maitreya's teachings.

Lithuania cannot demand the freedom to control its economy and its defence — all the states within the Soviet Union depend on one another in these two vital policy areas. To try to cut itself free can only be destructive. In many other areas of government the country can be granted autonomy.*

It is Mr Gorbachev's duty to try to hold the Union together, to put his foot down, but he is in a very dangerous situation now. He could be toppled at any time. He has had to move the army in but he is in a very tight position. Other countries will jump in with their own views. (Apr 1990)

[*After clashes with Soviet military in 1990, Lithuania became independent in 1991.]

Freedom is interdependent — Mr Gorbachev is in a very delicate situation. If you let loose a poisonous snake you need a stick to control it. Likewise, if you give people freedom and they end up on the rampage like wild animals, you need the police and army to control the situation. Mr Gorbachev has to appease the army as it is very important to his survival.

Those leaders in the Baltic states who are going to the West to seek support are leading their countries into difficult times. "The USSR consists of united states that are interdependent in such important areas as defence and the economy." They must remain that way — freedom is interdependent.

Western countries must not interfere or give support to those leaders trying to break away, or there will be international chaos. (May 1990)

Freedom is a right — Mr Gorbachev's presidential style will come to an end. The public will not accept it. From now on, the voice of the people will dictate the style of politicians and reflect the conditions of the country they represent. Mr Gorbachev will have to abandon his fondness for a Western outlook; that is not what his people expect of him. Freedom is a right of every individual. If freedom is compromised in the name of market forces it will only lead to problems. From now on, these market forces will be controlled by the people and not by the politicians. (Jun 1990)

The art of evolution — "You cannot transform a monkey into a zebra. To do so is undivine. You cannot undo traditions and cultures overnight; this is destructive. Everything has its own natural pace of evolution. Everything is subject to natural evolutionary processes. The so-called political, social and spiritual leaders must learn the art of evolution." If you talk about freedom you must learn what it is. If you dabble in religious, social or political leadership without knowledge, it will lead to chaos.

"Every spark in creation has its own distinct, separate evolutionary pattern which only the Lord Himself knows." (Dec 1990)

America — The same restlessness for freedom is happening in America. Many states are unhappy about the central control of the economy and are demanding more say in how money should be spent in their own areas. The drug situation is very bad in that country. It is also reaching a crisis in Japan and China. The effects are being felt worldwide as murder and destruction erupt wherever the drug culture takes hold. (Apr 1990)

India — The rule of government barely exists in India as state after state collapses into turmoil. People are trying to snatch freedom — and that can only lead to destruction and chaos. Now the governments of both India and Pakistan are trying to divert the attention of their people by getting them to rally around the possibility of a war over Kashmir. (Apr 1990)

Football: World Cup — Of course there will be incidents of chaos and violence in Italy, but that is not the point. The real problem lies in the fact that governments do nothing for the young in teaching them to be Self-aware.

The energy that goads young people into hooliganism is the same energy that sends people to pray in church. You cannot blame the energy, only the conditioning that prevents people being aware and free.

At a football match* there is a mood of freedom, and young people feel the energy pushing and goading them into bursting free of the conditioning in their lives. You can have 100,000 policemen around the ground and there will still be incidents. How can they control these people when their own leaders have done nothing to help the young to become aware? (May 1990)

[*Note: reference to the Hillsborough football stadium where 96 Liverpool football club supporters were crushed to death in a mass stampede on 15 April 1989.]

Freedom is movement — Just as knowledge and wisdom are in the domain of creation, so is freedom. Freedom means movement from one stage to another. You do not want to remain static. If you do, you will find the energies bursting, moving you into different directions. In order to guide yourself through obstacles, you have to believe in something and to fight for it.

In creation, freedom is never absolute.

Enjoy the blessings of life — "Be what you are. The entire creation is a Becoming of the Supreme Being of the Lord. Everything belongs to Him. It is the heritage of one and all to enjoy the blessings of life, which are freedom in creation and salvation in the Supreme Being."

Nations and countries (the people) are as interdependent as are the members of a family. The policies of nations and governments must involve the essence of equilibrium and of fairness, which will produce peace, harmony and happiness.

No nation, no country is superior or inferior to another. It is the duty of the government to protect and promote the welfare of the nation, and it is the duty of every individual to be who he is.

Life in America — "If you analyse American life you will find that the Self does not experience freedom. The Self is imprisoned, conditioned in the cell of egoism. Because of this, in America, the slightest quickening of the tempo of argument makes a man explode. This is why, in America, people live with guns and pistols."

Doctors and psychologists should "investigate this".

The American way of life, having not realized freedom, becomes a very destructive force. The Self is trapped, conditioned to such a degree that there is no freedom in mind, spirit and body.

This is why the younger generations, having failed to achieve freedom, having failed to realize the purpose of life, easily fall prey to drugs, alcoholism, etc, in order to escape from the doldrums they experience in life. American culture at present holds many dangers because there is no equilibrium.

One must be very careful not to allow oneself to be tarnished. "Be what you are. Do not try to be what you are not."

A boat without a rudder — "If you look across the world, you see killing and robbing in the name of freedom. This is not freedom, but a boat without a rudder going round and round."

Real freedom — When you experience freedom you will find that it is not outside but within you. You will know that real freedom, real security, real salvation is within you.

The moment you experience freedom from mind, spirit and body (ie from conditioning) you realize you are the eternal spark of the Supreme Creator. Each and every thing around you and within you belongs to the Almighty. It cannot be gained or lost. It is indivisible. It belongs to One and All.

Learn how to swim — A swami asked Maitreya: "How is it that in the name of freedom people have to suffer: people in Russia, Yugoslavia and other parts of the former Soviet Union?"

Maitreya says: "Before you jump in the river, you should learn to swim. Before you talk about freedom, learn to experience what freedom is.

"Whatever has happened in the former Soviet Union, in Yugoslavia and other parts of the world is not freedom. It is power-politics. A structure was destroyed and the Western world did not realize the consequences of failing to replace politics with a proper political system.

"It is like acting in a vacuum. What happens? Everything is powerless in a vacuum."

Institutions — "In this world, the moment anything becomes institutionalized it loses its divinity. Any karma (activity) which becomes institutionalized is undivine."

Anything and everything in creation is in its evolutionary form which is non-institutional, which embraces every station and department of life.

"In an institution, any activity (karma) which is without the rudder of freedom is like a blind man in the world, feeling his way but unable to see things."

"A station is where there are passengers, trains, many communications taking place. A department is where this becomes institutional. Institutions, stations, departments are important, but they should have their rudder of freedom in order to evolve."

Involution and evolution — If freedom becomes stagnant then the process becomes one of involution and you experience all the processes of destruction. People indulge in drugs and suicide. If freedom flourishes you experience evolution.

"You are born to be free. It is your common heritage. No one can deny it."

The only constitution — Freedom and salvation are the common heritage of one and all, through honesty of mind, sincerity of spirit and detachment. There is no constitution other than this. The time has come for every individual and nation to accept that the only constitution is to revere the will of the Creator.

Through honesty, sincerity and detachment the will of the Creator unfolds naturally in mind, spirit and body. In this way we respect the will of the Lord. This is the constitution of the New Age. The Lord is in the Self. The Self is in the Lord.

"I am in the Light. The Light is in me."

Have faith in the will of the Lord. Constitutions which have been tampered with for the benefit of the few while the people remain enslaved cannot survive. The constitution common to every country will develop in terms of the will of the people. This is the will of the Lord.

Meditate on light — Maitreya asks: "If you meditate on light, the alpha and omega of creation, where will you end up? In creation. You can experience psychic, spiritual, mental and magical powers. Does this lead to freedom and salvation? No.

"Why does no one speak like this? Because those who have meditated on light then need people around them, followers. When you are looking for freedom and salvation, why meditate on light? With the mind, you will arrive at the technology of light. With the spirit, you will develop spiritual powers. You can even do miraculous things. But this time, I have come to teach you freedom and salvation."

Service — "To serve even one individual is to serve the Lord Himself. In service you will never be lost. You will reach the path that leads straight to freedom and salvation."

Attachment to spiritual powers — "When you see My powers, do not become attached to them." When people become attached to these powers and try to develop them, they can become gurus, saints, yogis, etc. But this is not the meaning of salvation. Salvation is achieved through honesty, sincerity and detachment. You can go anywhere with these three principles and you will never feel fatigued mentally, physically or spiritually. You feel free within.

Infertility — Both birth and death are conditioned. Both are the result of the Law of Cause and Effect (karma). Suffering is also subject to this law.

Infertility means a woman cannot give birth to a child. What does the woman do? She goes to hospital for treatment in order to give birth. Infertility is not a disease or a deficiency. Instead, it is important to understand why one woman is fertile and another is infertile. The differences here are natural because, as evolution proceeds from one stage to another, the Self becomes that much more independent, free from commitments.

When you are on the threshold of salvation, everything leaves you. In the case of the infertile woman, nature has created opportunities around her so that she can learn to look within. "Look at saints. When they reach the threshold of the Lord, they have to leave everything behind. They give up a mundane life. This is done by the individual. But when nature gives you these conditions, they are natural. They are the blessings of the Almighty." This does not mean that fertile women are not on the road to salvation. But in the cycles of birth and death, each individual soul will come to the same stage.

Madness — A person who lives and behaves like a child is not mad. A person who is physically and mentally free, not conditioned, and able to express himself, is often branded as mad. Madness in this sense is not a disease. "Look at a saint. What do you find in him? He does not allow himself to be conditioned. He has the mind and heart of a child. But he is not branded as a madman because he has adopted a holy aura. But a person who has not adopted this aura, yet who behaves like a child, is also free from the automatic processes of conditioning. That person is also on the threshold of salvation. Conditioning does not take place in mind, spirit and body, and the Self can move around freely. These are natural qualities from birth. Whoever displays these qualities from birth is on the threshold of salvation."

The problem of one and all — Recently a highly evolved swami asked: "How can one say: 'Your problem is my problem'?" Maitreya had been explaining that the problem of one soul is the problem of one and all.

Maitreya said: "It is better if I show you in a vision. You can then tell me your own experience. Close your eyes ... now open them."

The swami saw a Master within and perceived himself as the source of all attachment. He realized he himself is an ism. He himself is the soul. He himself is destruction. He himself is construction. But when the soul witnesses, the phenomena change. The Master within each person does not participate in any acts of creation.

This is the path to freedom and salvation. When the soul practises that detachment with honesty and sincerity it becomes aware that it is not to be personified.

Awareness, which grows with detachment, makes the soul act with aloofness. The moment this happens the soul experiences equilibrium in mind, spirit and body.

"Sometimes you experience a momentary detachment. Like a cloud an emotion comes and passes away. If you detach from this emotion you experience equilibrium. But if you are attached you will lose it. Some are awakened by these momentary glimpses."

If the soul is detached, if it is a witness, it experiences wholesomeness in life. It is free to move around. It is not trapped in the web of creation.

These teachings are given out so that one can understand why one indulges in activities (karmas) which create hell in life — ie taking drugs and other self-destructive acts. All this happens because somewhere in life the soul experiences hopelessness, as if there is no purpose in life. This stagnation needs to be understood.

By practising detachment you are able to move in life freely. You will not then indulge in activities that lead from one point of destruction to another.

Salvation is not in religion, not in politics, not in philosophies or ideologies. It exists in practising the art of living with a strong sense of detachment.

CHAPTER FOUR

CAUSE AND EFFECT —
UNDERSTANDING ENERGIES

CAUSES AND EFFECTS — Perceiving Patterns

Violent human actions disturb the Earth's balance — On 12 July 1993 Maitreya's associate sent a letter to American President Bill Clinton. In the last paragraph, referring to Yugoslavia, Maitreya's associate pointed out that the forces which have been triggered and unleashed upon humanity, imposing murderous sufferings, "will now reverberate in terms of major earthquakes and disastrous floodings and aerodynamic failures. Let your generals and scientists now watch and analyse the happening".

Shortly afterwards there were floods in several parts of the world, among other natural disturbances; the event which the West focused on was the disastrous flood when the Mississippi River burst its banks.

The associate offered the information that Maitreya enabled a small group of people to experience these events vividly "as if they were there", in advance of the physical occurrence.

Maitreya's associate and a few others have written to a number of political leaders in a variety of countries, detailing these trends and events. The letters refer to Maitreya as 'The World Teacher' and more generally try to develop a wider understanding of the Laws of Cause and Effect, thus linking the violence of events such as those in Yugoslavia and elsewhere to subsequent natural disasters which can and do affect people not directly involved, but who nevertheless have to endure the consequences of a disturbed planet.

Knowing these laws enables Maitreya to foresee the effects of the causes we ourselves have set in motion.

Maitreya's communications (whether directly to groups around the world or indirectly through those who willingly assist Him) are designed to raise awareness of that for which we ourselves are responsible. A growing understanding of these laws will in itself lead to strengthened collective preventative action on the part of peoples and governments. (Aug 1993)

Spiritual law — Cause and effect can be understood as a major expression of spiritual law. It is illuminating to the extent that we identify causes and their effects correctly. It is important here to train oneself to perceive patterns. When a civilian airliner is shot down, it will be found that for no obvious reason one or two planes are lost. This constitutes a pattern. To understand that we live in a world of cause and effect creates self-awareness. (Jul 1988)

The oil rig explosion — There is a connection between the Iranian civilian plane shot down over the Gulf and the Piper Alpha oil rig explosion in the North Sea on 7 July. Responsibility for the slaughter of innocent people cannot be laid at the feet of the masses. It lies firmly in the hands of politicians, not just those who decide to wage war, but also those who supply weapons. Here the Law of Cause and Effect must be understood more clearly. The supplier of weapons generates causes whose effects eventually rebound on him. The oil rig explosion was itself an effect.

Maitreya asks: "Why take sides when innocent people die?" (Jul 1988)

Collective destructive thoughts — There will be massive explosions in a certain part of the world which will give rise to fantastic but inaccurate explanations of a variety of 'phenomena'. We do not understand, as yet, the results on the physical plane of our own destructive thoughts. The collective destructive thoughts of many (such as those generated during wars) actually become massive, energized thought-formations. These are causes. The explosions are the inevitable effects.

Maitreya is not a prophet of doom. Rather, man must take responsibility for his own thoughts, words and deeds. Thus he grows spiritually. (Jul 1988)

War in the Middle East — Forcing soldiers onto the battlefields and killing thousands of people creates devastating effects which can be measured mentally and spiritually. The atmosphere of the planet is affected in ways which are not well understood at present. Violent deaths affect those still living, in a variety of ways. There is a corresponding increase, according to Maitreya, in 'motiveless' murders and other violent acts.

The coming peace between Iran and Iraq, the outcome of important changes, is therefore significant. (Jul 1988)

Saudi Arabia and Great Britain — Saudi Arabia and Great Britain signed a major weapons deal on 3 July 1988. Once again, causes are being generated by both supplier and purchaser. Maitreya asks: "Against whom is Saudi Arabia defending itself?"

Oil revenues are being used to purchase weapons. One effect is that the oil wells will be depleted. Something will happen which will dry them up.

A new source of energy will be found and harnessed, such that the economics of oil will be profoundly altered. (Jul 1988)

Saudi Arabia — The King of Saudi Arabia is having second thoughts about the arms deal he recently concluded with Britain. According to Maitreya: "Oil is for prosperity, the good of the people. It is evil to use God's gifts to destroy one another." Information contained in these articles is also communicated via people working in India, Africa, the Middle East, etc. Therefore Middle Eastern monarchs also receive information and guidance, and are aware of the reality of spiritual law. It is possible the King may cancel the arms deal. (Aug 1988)

If "bounty is misused" (that is, the wealth from oil) the oil will no longer flow. The recent weapons deal Saudi Arabia signed with the UK represents an imbalance. This cause will generate its inevitable effects. "If you misuse that which is relative, it will exhaust itself." (Oct 1988)

Saudi Arabia will revise the terms of the weapons deal it concluded with Britain some months ago. Other purchases will be substituted for much of the weaponry. These revised arrangements will proceed in a low-key manner. (Nov 1988)

The drought in the USA — Natural disasters such as floods, earthquakes, droughts are connected, as responses, to human activities. These connections are not perceived at present, but will be increasingly perceived and understood as such.

As an example, Maitreya cites the drought in the USA. The indifference on the part of many to famine elsewhere on the globe is itself a cause that generates effects. Because the land in the drought-stricken area has become so dry that the soil is losing its cohesiveness, there will be a major landslide there. This is not just an effect of the drought. The drought itself is the effect. (Jul 1988)

Security forces and terrorism — Terrorist acts committed by security forces in the name of their governments are not distinguishable in spiritual law from non-governmental terrorist acts. These causes invariably generate effects that can be monitored. (Jul 1988)

Nuclear explosions — There will be more than one nuclear explosion. This will not be 'accidental' but rather, in terms of the law of cause and effect, the result of certain things which trigger the elements of nature. No energy, whether 'nuclear' or 'spiritual', is safe if the energy cannot be used constructively. Energy cannot be 'held on to' indefinitely. (Aug 1988)

The Middle East — Although the people are being made aware by the new energy, it is being blocked by political attitudes that cling to the past. This blockage is being flushed out in a wave of destruction.

Political and religious leaders are confounded by events. But out of this confusion will come an awareness that will strike the people and create in them an aura of expectancy.

People will begin looking for direction, guidance and understanding. (May 1990)

South Africa — In South Africa too, the energy is being blocked as the various groups find it impossible to give up power. Once again, there will be killing and looting. This negative energy, released in society, will eventually find its way into nature and the country will experience earthquakes. (May 1990)

Poll tax in Britain — With reference to the poll tax, Maitreya says that He "will not allow the British nation to become demoralized". A rich man can avoid a conflict with the lawmakers and pay this tax. A poor man necessarily enters into conflict through his inability to pay. Therefore, apathy, mistrust, animosity, hatred and violence inevitably arise. Thus lawmaker and non-payer undergo a process of destruction.

Spiritually and mentally, the effects are already rebounding on the person who generated the cause in question (that is to say, the lawmaker).

Therefore Mrs Thatcher will leave office. This is, again, not a prediction, but the fulfilment of the Law of Cause and Effect. (Oct 1988)

Afghanistan and the USSR — The Russians stepped into areas where they did not belong. Now they must face revolt at home. This is the action of the Law of Cause and Effect. (Apr 1989)

Cause and effect, and destiny — The more you become aware of cause and effect, the more you can take charge of your own destiny. It is important to generate right causes to obtain right effects.

Peace is free from cause and effect — Many politicians think peace is due to nuclear weapons. They are gravely mistaken. The so-called 'peace' that politicians are talking about is nothing but fear. They have translated 'fear' into 'peace'.

All these misunderstandings which have been generated are beginning to dissolve. Peace is free from cause and effect. This new understanding is dawning on the younger generation now. Peace is free of isms. Peace is free of oppositions between East and West, North and South. (Apr 1989)

ENERGY AND NATURE

Understanding energy — After the environment, the understanding of energy is the top priority in the world now. For the first time in the history of the human race, people will become aware of energy in their lives. Although no one knows where this energy comes from, or where it goes after death, all experience it during their lives.

In extreme cases, it is energy which goads a murderer to pick up a knife and kill another. Yet the murderer, unaware of that energy, wonders what forced him to act. In another extreme example, a yogi experiences a sudden surge of creative energy which pushes him into the unknown regions of life where psychic powers are available to him. But the yogi is not affected because his training helps him to remain detached. He is not possessed by the energy.

Without this energy nothing can happen, and without it none of us can fulfil our destinies. Just as humanity has become aware of the environment, checking food before we eat it, conscious of our health, so we will become conscious of this energy.

Once triggered, it can be guided and understood and used creatively. Triggered blindly, as in some scientific or psychic experiments, it will destroy. For instance, the energy that expressed itself in Hurricane Hugo and the California earthquake also expressed itself in a series of factory explosions around the world such as in Texas, where it was reported that a number of workers died and hundreds were injured. There were also factory explosions in Russia and China, but these have not been reported so far.

This pattern of violence can continue and people can suddenly go mad and kill, for there is very little 'space' between these happenings in accordance with the Law of Cause and Effect. This energy must be understood. Then it can be used to help the human race.

On an individual level this energy can goad the Self into situations in which it becomes trapped in the mind. But what is the mind? It is nothing less than the blueprint of creation. It is not personal. It is universal, like energy.

In spiritual language, energy is the Spirit while mind is the Holy Ghost. "It is like a ghost because it can appear in any form. It can be a human being, a snake, or fire." Anything and everything in creation is in the mind. If the Self is goaded by energy into the trap of mind then the Self will be caught up in the cyclic evolution known as Karma (cause and effect). But the Self has to undergo the experiences of the mind in order to evolve to the point of full Self-realization. The mind, of course, can act like God and control and manipulate the energy to achieve anything. But these psychic or magical powers can be very destructive.

When you enter the dominion of the mind, spirit and body, be detached and then you will experience freedom and salvation. "Carry out your duties with honesty, sincerity and detachment. A policeman who carries out his duties should not be judge and jury. He should be free from it all and fulfil those duties."

As awareness grows, it guides the Self which can then use the mind, spirit and body with intelligence. Balancing energy and environment is the key to salvation. In awareness there is no memory. Memory is only in the mind. All struggle and care is in the mind, never in awareness. The Self is neutral and free from suffering. Awareness protects the Self. Suffering, depression and craving for drugs are all states of mind. Awareness sets you free and allows you to enjoy life. (Oct 1989)

Inner space — Sitting quietly in your room, in your own home, you feel master in your house. Then people arrive and begin to argue and shout, making you feel ill at ease and angry until you tell them to leave. Afterwards, you feel exhausted and it takes a few days before you feel normal again.

Whenever you are involved in the hysteria of heated arguments and in a state of high emotion, you should realize that it is not you, the Self, that is distressed. What is it that makes people rush around in panic, fear and anger? Strip away all the names and what you have is destructive energy taking over. It is like a snake without eyes.

This force leads people into dark, unknown regions. It is the same energy that causes volcanoes, earthquakes, ship disasters and tragedies like Hillsborough. [Note: This energy may be neutral but, like the snake, if it bites you it will destroy you. It is the same for nations as for individuals.]

Everyone needs 'inner space' where there is no one directing you, telling you where to go and what to do. It is only here that you can be detached from this energy.

No one can lead you. You are born to be aware of yourself, to know the Master in yourself. Your inner space is sacred. It is where all things, all problems, dissolve. It is where you go when you tell others you are tired and frightened and 'fed up', when you want to be left alone to find your own space.

"You have been given that space so that the confusion and chaos around you will dissolve. You must never surrender that space to anyone, except your true Self. Meditation is really a journey back to that space to find peace and happiness."

Energy use and energy manipulation — There is a difference between using energy within its natural base of evolution and manipulation of energy. The latter leads invariably to trouble, because natural equilibrium is disturbed. An example of energy use would be a windmill, which uses wind power, while the 'controlled' underground explosion of a nuclear bomb is energy manipulation. The latter disturbs a balance in the Earth and ultimately can and does result in earthquakes. The recent earthquake in Burma which also affected neighbouring countries was the end result of underground nuclear explosions carried out in the USA, the USSR, China, Pakistan and India.

Human beings are linked to one another. The moment you have a thought it can, in principle, be picked up by anyone, anywhere.

Nuclear weapons are interlinked via energy and thought formation. If you play around with subatomic particles, the equilibrium of creation is disturbed.

The energy behind all acts of nature and all mental acts is one. When a negative current loses its "consort", positive current, it goes haywire.

Natural disasters are linked to men's actions. (Aug 1988)

Natural disasters — Earthquakes, floods, plagues, etc, are all interconnected in the sense that they are ultimates, end-points, of negative forces that are working themselves out on the physical plane. In certain parts of the world, coastlines and some islands will disappear. (Aug 1988)

Earthquakes — There will be a fairly severe earthquake in America soon. It will pass through the San Andreas fault. When disasters occur, on an international scale, people await a Second Coming. "The Lord has been here since the morning of time. When I am with you, there is no question of a second, third or fourth coming." When there is a calamity, the Lord is always with the soul. He gives it strength, comfort and bliss at that time, although with our minds we perceive only suffering. (Aug 1988)

[Benjamin Creme's comment: With regard to this earthquake predicted by Maitreya, I am informed that every effort will be made to restrict its effects to material buildings and constructions, so that the minimum loss of lives will ensue. This is the result of Maitreya's role as the Agent of Divine Intervention.] (Aug 1988)

Floods and earthquakes in the UK — The Thames will overflow and the Houses of Parliament will be flooded. The barriers which exist at present will lessen the effects, but will not be able to contain the flood. (Aug 1988)

A pattern of lesser floods in various towns in the UK will be observable, prior to the major event, the flooding of the Thames. There will also be an earthquake in the UK. The pattern of natural disasters around the world, as an effect of human actions, does not exclude the UK. (Oct 1988)

The flooding of Parliament will be the peak of the outbreak of flooding in Britain. People always thought Britain was safe from great natural disasters like floods and hurricanes. But Maitreya says nobody is safe. Everybody has a responsibility to look after each other. (Feb 1990)

Bangladesh — The floods there have a deep significance. Military rule there will not be sustained.* (Sep 1988)

[*General Ershad was forced to resign in December 1990. Parliamentary rule was restored in 1991.]

Hurricane Gilbert — Hurricane Gilbert, which devastated Jamaica and the Cayman Islands, made its way up the Yucatan peninsula in the Gulf of Mexico on 14 September 1988 and was heading towards Texas. It is the worst hurricane ever recorded, with wind speeds of up to 185-200 miles an hour.

The fact that it is heading towards Texas has a deep significance. Texas is one of the richest parts of the USA. In crises, people will be brought closer together and will help each other.

The causes of this hurricane go beyond the explanations of the weathermen. When Hurricane Gilbert subsides there will be earthquakes. (Sep 1988)

This hurricane is not, strictly speaking, a hurricane, but an energy which has been released. This energy will cleanse the world of destructive forces. The new incoming energy is bringing awareness and equilibrium simultaneously. Not only people but also nature will respond constructively. From now on, anything which operates by imposition of force will not survive. (Sep 1988)

The new energy — The widespread flooding of British rivers represents an act of purification by nature. When water rises, it means it has been energized. The new energy sweeping through our world will make the land more fertile, people will experience greater health and we shall see many diseases begin to disappear. People will feel at one with nature. (Feb 1990)

Earthquake in the USA — There will be a major earthquake in America which will enter the history books.* The energy that drove the recent Hurricane Hugo has not "disappeared". It lies waiting to erupt again, this time as an earthquake. (Sep 1989)

[*On 17 October 1989, the San Andreas fault in northern California had its first major quake since the great Loma Prieta earthquake of 1906. Much property damage occurred, but little loss of life.]

Underground nuclear testing — There will be a major earthquake in the USSR as well as floods. We can also expect to see a pattern of air crashes and crashes on land (such as lorries suddenly going off the road and train derailments).

These are not predictions but effects of causes man himself has generated — in this case, nuclear weapons testing in the form of underground explosions. Nuclear explosions disturb the elements of nature. The entire Creation is composed of atoms. If you disturb the pattern, the elements of nature, the weather cycles, and human beings themselves become disturbed. Since man-made items such as airplanes are equally composed of atoms, when these patterns are interfered with, crashes are inevitable.

People whose balance in mind, spirit and body is fragile can be tipped over the edge by the disturbance of atomic patterns. 'Motiveless murders' and sudden psychosis are the result. (Oct 1988)

The flu epidemic — Why (in December) is everyone suffering from flu? The scientists call it Asian flu but Maitreya says: "All this suffering is man-made. Man's inhumanity to man is creating problem after problem."

On the Vietnamese boat people: There is no law which denies people the right to escape and find future happiness elsewhere. How can Britain send them back to situations of disaster?

"America, along with Britain, created the situation in Vietnam and so they have to take responsibility."

"How is it that the flu affected Britain and not America? That is because there is a link between Britain and Hong Kong. Do not look for a virus in the atmosphere. All life is a closely linked pattern — disturb one thread and you disturb the others."

Britain had committed a crime against nature by interfering with the free will of others — the repatriated Vietnamese — but other countries also had to share the responsibility. Vietnam cannot be excluded internationally. (Dec 1989)

Hong Kong: Your home — "Never forget your home. Your first home is your body, where you return each morning after a night's sleep. Your second home is your country, where you were born. You must not break your ties with your second home."

The people of Hong Kong do not want foreigners to settle on their land — their economy cannot support them." (Nov 1989)

What culture can the people of Hong Kong claim to belong to? They are not Chinese, they are not British, they are not American. They are like chameleons. They have no home to run to. Hong Kong is their home. (Apr 1990)

China: Control by force — In China an attempt was made to make society more open, but the situation is now out of control. That which was controlled by force is being released. If you have been sitting in a cell, what would happen if you were set free? You might jump around, shout, etc. You might get involved in situations you had not anticipated. The reaction of the authorities is to regain control by creating more rules and regulations. But it is too late to control the situation in this way. (Apr 1989)

China: Destructive energy — The country's supreme leader Deng Xiao-ping is dying of cancer. The decision to send in the troops and massacre the students (who were demonstrating in Tiananmen Square) was wrested from him as he lay heavily sedated. The hardliners who obtained his consent did this so that Deng could be blamed for whatever happened. However, they will not be able to avoid the consequences of their part in all this.

The soldiers who went in shooting and killing in-discriminately in Beijing were drugged beforehand. They were unaware of this. The drug robbed them of any moral inhibitions and left them susceptible only to orders from their superior officers. Later they were horrified to discover what they had done and wondered how they could have carried out such brutal acts. This is why the army is now turning away from the hardliners. The will of the Chinese people will not be crushed, and the hardliners will be swept away.

As for the thousands of students and ordinary people who died as a sacrifice for the struggle for freedom, Maitreya intervened so that they felt no pain at the moment of death.

A huge earthquake will erupt shortly in China — larger than the Armenian disaster. This is because the same energy that sent in the soldiers to kill and slaughter will now erupt in nature. You cannot disrupt and disturb such energy with impunity. (Jun 1989)

China: Natural disaster — There are always warning signs before such a huge event. The energy of an earthquake is the same energy that lies behind creation. Disturb it, and it will manifest in different ways.

The slaughter of the students unleashed this force and when it can find no further expression in human affairs it will look for its expression in nature. First will come fire, setting light to houses and forests. This will be followed by sudden, huge downpours of rain, and then landslides. The inevitable and final outcome is an earthquake. (Jul 1989)

The flow of energy — The energy behind creation can never be possessed. No one can know the beginning nor the end of energy. If you attempt to possess it, it will destroy you. (Destruction does not necessarily mean physical destruction; it can also mean loss of mental or spiritual equilibrium as in the case of obsession, other forms of insanity, or undue emphasis on intellectualism at the expense of everything else.)

Energy must be respected with detachment so that it can flow fluidly in mind, spirit and body.

Mind, spirit and body can be disciplined in order not to be attached to energy, which becomes the medium, if used intelligently, for the betterment of life.

Cyclic energy — Energy is always cyclical. It will take you from one stage of evolution to another cyclically. Movement can be 'upward' or 'downward'.

Attachment/detachment — Attachment means energy is using the Self. Detachment means the Self is using energy. When energy uses the Self, the effects are destructive. An example is the energy used against students in China (the events in Tiananmen Square). That energy moved tanks and armour. Where has this energy gone? It does not disappear. It necessarily finds expression somewhere else. It will appear in floods, fires, earthquakes and other elements of nature. (Oct 1989)

[Note: Since the crushing of the student movement in China, there have been floods, violent hailstorms, and earthquakes measuring 6 and more on the Richter scale.]

Man-made disasters — After the winds, floods and hurricanes will come earthquakes. They will first hit China and then America, particularly in the border areas with Mexico.

Britain will experience landslides, followed by earth tremors rippling out from earthquakes in other parts of the world.

There will also be volcanic eruptions in countries such as Russia and Sicily. Canada will also experience its first volcanic eruption.

All this suffering is caused by man's inhumanity to man. The greed of those in power has condemned their fellows and nature itself. The environment has been polluted and nature has reacted.

Market forces have created social and natural havoc. People have been condemned to death, literally, in the name of profit and loss. Hospitals have been shut because they are not profitable, schools have difficulty in staying open. These institutions are essential for the health and well-being of society.

Spiritually and mentally, many people are bankrupt. They know only how to get up in the morning and go to work. They come home and go to bed. They have been conditioned by politics and religion and condemned to spiritual and mental imprisonment.

Everything around us has been created by nature, but disasters, destruction, depression and disease are man-made. The people you must demand an answer from are your leaders, those who have conditioned you and prevented you from enjoying a life of bliss and peace.

The energy which is wreaking havoc in the world now through storms, earthquakes and volcanic eruptions has been unleashed because man thinks he can do what he likes. He believes that if he has a healthy bank balance he has a healthy life. But greed drives him to destruction. Spiritually and mentally he is bankrupt.

We are seeing the end of the old age and the beginning of a new era. (Feb 1990)

Unusual events — There will be computer failures in the banking system. The Japanese stock-market crash will be preceded by computer failures. Some aeroplanes will be suspended briefly in mid-air. Trains will come to a halt suddenly. There will be renewed spaceship and UFO activity in the skies. (Mar 1990)

Earth tremors, a prelude — The earth tremors which recently shook China presage an opening up of that country, politically and socially. It is the same energy at work. The people will demand freedom. This natural force will transform both individuals and nation. This energy is also sweeping through Hong Kong and Japan. (May 1990)

Earthquakes in Eastern Europe — The earthquake which recently hit Romania and vibrated across Eastern Europe has not yet finished. Its effects will continue to be felt throughout the world as its energy ripples outwards from its centre deep within the Earth. It is like 'an act of God'. Eventually it will create a new environmental awareness, and new vegetation will grow which will balance the man-made ecological disasters. (Jun 1990)

Forces in Nature — Politicians have no understanding of the forces released in nature. There is a mischievous energy in nature born of the power of attachment. This energy has driven the United States to send arms to the Middle East. This energy, once released, must find its outlet. If it is not released through firing weapons, this same force will express itself in the forces of nature and we can expect more floods, earthquakes and other 'natural disasters' of various kinds. (Sep 1990)

Ideologies pollute — "Look at the world situation today. Everyone has fallen victim to ideologies in the name of religion, politics, civilization. Is it worth living this sort of life? The world has been polluted with ideologies. If the human race does not follow the path of justice, peace, happiness, grace, then nature will explode. If human beings (nations and countries) do not respect each other, the energies which are goading nations and countries to fight, and which are so vibrant in nature, will find expression in major disasters which are just around the corner now. You will witness major earthquakes, floodings, volcanic eruptions, aeroplane explosions."

"Everything you see happening in the world is entirely man-made." (Sep 1990)

Worldwide destruction — Massive worldwide destruction can be expected as a result of the warmongering in the Gulf. The energies of nature have been disturbed.

If one man is stirred up to fight and has no outlet he becomes depressed. If these energies are stirred up in hundreds of thousands of men, you create a disturbance of feeling on a massive scale. If it has no major outlet like a full-scale war (and Maitreya has forecast there will be no full-scale war in Kuwait) then all that unused energy has to go somewhere.

The energy will ripple out into nature, and, once let loose, inevitably there will be inexplicable crashes of cars, trains and aircraft. Then will come earthquakes, floods and finally volcanic eruptions.

It cannot be controlled; it must work itself through the natural world. (Jan 1991)

You cannot fool nature — "You cannot destroy the planet; it is the Lord's creation. You can fool your people but when you try to fool nature the music becomes very frightening."

"Do you want to fight a lion? Iraq is not the lion in this situation. But if you disturb the lion in nature it will eat you." (Jan 1991)

Earthquake, floods, landslides — There is going to be a very large earthquake in America.* Britain will suffer landslides, though not on a catastrophic level. The desert regions of Kuwait, Iraq and Saudi Arabia will be flooded by storms. This will make the movement of troops and machinery very difficult.

The Earth is moving, the energy released by the bombs and explosions of the fighting in the Middle East is now finding its way through Nature. This is the boomerang effect — whoever is responsible for releasing the violent energy will find it rebounding on them. (Jan 1991)

[*Northridge earthquake, 17 January 1994, magnitude 6.7 — the first earthquake to strike directly under an urban area of the US since the 1933 Long Beach earthquake.]

Cycle of destruction — A cycle of destruction has set into the Middle East, but no one is free from it now. It affects America and Europe (East and West) and the Far East also. The present fight in the Middle East is not, and will not lead to, a world war.

To impose the rule of market forces on other nations, as conceived at present in the European Community, would lead to a loss of self-identity in those nations. Life then becomes 'like a serpent without a head'. This type of imposition could lead to a world war.

"You are trying to sow the seeds of destruction, but you do not have to go far to understand the realities of life. Imagine two brothers. Each has a distinct identity. Evolving in this way, they will enjoy harmony in life. The moment big brother imposes his identity and personality on his brother, friction and fighting ensue.

"When you go to sleep, your identity is still preserved. It does not get mixed up with that of your brother. It remains separate, distinct. Your identity is sacred. If you play with it you will destroy yourself."

"All suffering is due to lack of respect for the Self. Human beings have failed to respect the Self. The moment you do respect the Self, you will enjoy freedom and happiness. The moment you practise the principles of honesty, sincerity and detachment, life ceases to be a struggle.

"When confusion, chaos and destruction have exhausted the cycle, you will experience emptiness, loneliness. This is a prelude to a peaceful, constructive life — a life of happiness.

"When you give up the futile struggle you will experience a life free of burdens. You will experience a lightness within you (ie, a lightness that comes when you are free of attachments). You will find newness, hope, happiness and absence of hindrance." (Feb 1991)

[Note: The teaching on detachment exists in the Vedic scriptures, in Islam, in Christianity. The principle can be applied by everyone.]

Animal qualities in war — When there is war, human beings will express and demonstrate every type of animal instinct and quality. Those who are destroying a country will experience vulture-type instincts and grab whatever comes to hand. There are no human qualities in these actions. "Look at the scenario of a dead cow in the jungle. All types of animals will devour it in half an hour. If your country is destroyed the same thing will happen."

"I belong to every individual and every nation and country alike. There is no 'high' and 'low'. If you have faith in Me, trust Me, why go out and take part in such destruction?

"Ask your leaders why you are doing so. They will try to compel the individual, either forcefully or by stirring up the emotions in the individual. They will try to play with your mind and spirit. Thus, Iraqis have killed Kuwaitis. Kuwaitis are using other nations to kill Iraqis. In both cases, after death, they come to the Lord.

"You, the Self, are sent into creation by the Lord, not because of any leader, guru or politician. And it is the Lord Who takes you back." (Feb 1991)

Elements of nature — If you play with the elements of nature now, nature will punish you, because nature is your second mother.

The elements will tame nations and countries, making them respect nature. You are visiting destruction on the planet.* Do the generals ever think about what is happening? Even learned people have not been able to influence them.

When you throw explosives on 'Mother Earth', the vibrations are set into the planet. Those vibrations will eventually create earthquakes, landslides and flooding.

The result of all the poisoning of the atmosphere will be sudden, extreme changes in the winds. The places where there was sunshine will experience heavy downpours and extreme conditions of cold. The result of explosions in the water is the disappearance of certain species of marine life.

When you destroy Mother Nature you destroy yourself. (Feb 1991)

[*Referring to the first Gulf War]

The Gulf War — The fighting may have ceased between the Alliance and Iraq but that is not the end of the story. The hunter thinks he has killed the lion but he is not dead yet.

"What about the elements of nature? They were not fighting against anyone." The planes bombarded bridges and buildings as if they were not alive, but a bridge is not lifeless, for the Lord is in all elements of nature. No one has the right to pump bullets and drop bombs into Mother Nature, either in the sea or on land. It is time to learn this, for the energies disturbed in nature are going to burst out in earthquakes and volcanic activity.

The armies are returning home but they were better off in the desert for they face enormous problems at home. These cannot be solved by bombs and bullets. The people need to be educated and given their freedom. The Western Alliance poured money into the Gulf and achieved nothing. Why didn't they spend it at home? (Mar 1991)

Whatever suffering exists on Earth is man-made. Man himself disturbs the pattern of evolution. "When you use high-tech instruments of war to destroy houses, bridges, etc, and destroy innocent life, you release the energy of destruction. This same energy affects the elements of nature." (Jun 1991)

The forces of nature have been massively disturbed by the war in the Gulf. The energy that exploded the bombs and bullets is the same energy that surges through nature, expressing itself in natural disasters. (Jun 1991)

Violence of war triggered a reaction — The disasters happening in the world — floods, earthquakes, volcanic eruptions — are the direct result of man's actions.

When we see starvation in Africa, the cyclones in Bangladesh, these have been created by the political mischief of America, Britain, Europe and the Soviet Union. When you disturb the pattern of evolution which embraces creation it disturbs the elements of nature.

But why should it be that the poor and innocent are the ones to suffer when wars are created by the manipulations of politicians? Those wars are destroying and damaging the innocent elements in nature — such as roads, bridges, water and the atmosphere. Those elements have nothing to do with the ideologies of the politicians who unleashed the violence. When these politicians use their intelligence to harm and slaughter innocent people, they are using the same energy that disturbs and harms those innocent elements of nature.

The violence of war triggered a reaction throughout the natural world and spent itself in disasters, famine and eruptions. The same energy that sends bullets and shells streaking across the battlefield also lifts up and hurls millions of tons of water upon the land.

What is the solution to the massive upheavals and tragedies taking place all over the world? Just as the politicians sent huge armies to defend the 4-5 million people of Kuwait to protect its non-existent democracy, so they should send armies to Africa where millions upon millions of people are suffering. Their suffering is a direct result of the mischievous politics of African politicians who have been given arms and ammunition by the West and the Soviet Union.

Where are the Europeans, the Americans and the Soviets now? Not in Africa or the Third World, because these areas have nothing to offer in oil or revenue. They call themselves the defenders of democracy and peace. But Maitreya calls them the Pretenders. They do nothing because there is nothing in it for them. It is not God who causes such calamities. The blame should be pinned firmly upon the politicians.

The answer has to be that the United Nations should send armies to protect the people of Africa and drive out the armies who are killing their own people. Just as they have created a safe haven for the Kurds in Iraq, the UN should create similar havens for the starving Africans. The United Nations must step in. They have no other option. (May 1991)

The UN, the seed of the World Parliament — "Famine is man-made. You cannot any longer say it is God-made. Now the developed nations, through the agency of the United Nations, must look after the welfare of the Third World. You will see many changes in the UN. The Secretary General will be changed. Younger blood will come in. The UN will become a powerful force.

"The United Nations is the seed of the World Parliament. This is a gradual process. It does not mean national parliaments will disappear. But there will be co-operation between world and national parliaments. The highest priority will be the environment; the lowest will be defence. Back-door deals to sell more weapons will not work in the long run." (Jun 1991)

MARKET FORCES

Commercialization, a new womb — In the last two to three years we have seen a reduction in the wars and conflicts taking place throughout the world as the superpowers withdrew from their policy of supplying arms to further their own foreign aims and interests. The energy which drives soldiers into battle and fills the air with warplanes has been switched off. But that energy cannot just disappear, it has to go somewhere. This energy has been roaming the world and suddenly it has found a new womb: commercialization, which has been created by market forces. The new creed of the superpowers has become the economy, which is the soul of commercialization, and this represents a serious new threat to the world, one that could even compromise human life.

The quality of commercialization is greed, and it will affect all nations. This negative energy which recoiled from the battlefield is a force without eyes or mind and will create a very hostile world. But although the politicians believe that commercialization is the future of the human race, they cannot control this energy.

This time the politicians will not be allowed to play with the lives of the masses. There is a counterforce growing which is emerging from the increasing awareness of the people. Examples of this are the stories about the contamination of food and environment and the demands that something urgently be done.

We are now seeing a new battle taking place which can only be won if the human mind can divert this negative energy. Only awareness will stop this force, and people will fight for survival if commercialization compromises human welfare and health. The situation will erupt like a volcano.

It is the human mind which has created this force and it can be changed by human awareness. Only Maitreya, however, has the power to turn this destructive energy into a creative force. Current events created by the drive for commercialization throughout the world are part of the pattern that will result in the major collapse of the stock markets.

Just as destructive forces had found a home in the fundamentalist ideology of commercialization, so it had found a weak spot in religious fundamentalism. The Ayatollah has no power to condemn. No one can judge another and sentence him to death. [Referring to the death sentence hanging over the writer Salman Rushdie.] People everywhere are recognizing that the Ayatollah does not have this right. (Mar 1989)

Water privatization — It is a time bomb. The elements of nature should never be privatized. If the politicians try to carry this out they will not succeed. Something spectacular will happen that will astonish the world. You cannot put profit before life.

Commercialization is more destructive than any nuclear bomb. (Apr 1989)

Brakes of life — How can it be that experienced train drivers pass through a red light? Something must have happened. While everything is working automatically and there is movement all around the person at the wheel, something within him stops.

The mind, spirit and body become aware only of stillness. That moment of standstill becomes the most important thing in his life — the moment when he suddenly becomes free from stress and strain. But these are the brakes of life and if they fail then the Self — free of mind, spirit and body — drifts helplessly like a ship without an anchor.

The brakes in life are important but they must not be too strong. The important lesson in all this is that we should learn not to overstress the mind, spirit and body, otherwise there will come a moment when the Self springs free without warning. It is like people who suffer a mental breakdown.

We must look for the pattern: three fatal train crashes in as many months. This is a warning that the destructive forces that drive the market forces of our economy will create graveyards. They must be controlled. This creed of commercialization is driving our society in suicidal directions. (Apr 1989)

Satanic forces — Market forces are the forces of wickedness, confusion and chaos, and their children are competition and comparison. Market forces are satanic forces. Market forces lead to 'mine' and 'more' (ie, possessiveness and greed) and there is no end to it. Market forces will bring this civilization, as we have known it, to the edge of disaster. (Dec 1989)

Japan: The stock market — The process which led to last year's stock-market crash* is being mirrored now in processes in Japan which will again lead to a stock-market crash. The way 'mega-giants' rob the health and wealth of individual nations does not come out in the media, because within governments everywhere individuals profit from this situation. "This has to come to an end."

After this crash, the first duty of governments will be to feed people with the right food. Their second duty will be to ensure adequate housing. Health and education will be the next priorities. Investment along these lines in other parts of the world will follow, and lastly, defence. In short, the crash will lead to a reordering of priorities. (Oct 1988)

[*Referring to the Wall Street Stock Market crash on 19 October 1987. The Dow Jones Industrial Index dropped 508 points or 22.6 per cent in one day.]

Japan — Japan now has one of the highest rates of suicide in the world. Drug-taking is rampant. Maitreya is appearing (in the form of visions) to many people in Japan, including several high-ranking politicians. Fellow politicians notice changes and are surprised. (Nov 1988)

The 'art of selfishness' — The impending stock-market crash is an outcome of commercialization. Commercialization means making money while others starve. The moment you are taught 'the art of selfishness' you cease to follow your destiny, which is to be aware of yourself. Those who cultivate rules and regulations that lead to nothing but selfishness eventually create a bad smell. This cannot be hidden for ever. When corruption takes place, people become aware of the smell, hence the process of disintegration taking place in Japan now. The press is no longer quiescent. The people are no longer complacent.

This type of culture (that created this state of affairs) will disappear. The end of commercialization is now at hand.

Here and there, there will be "pockets of gambling" to keep certain minds occupied, but in general the stock markets as they are now run will have no place in the new society. (Apr 1989)

[Patricia Pitchon noted at the time: The so-called Recruit Cosmos scandal in Japan, whereby a host of politicians were offered stock-market shares at preferential prices, as well as gifts, is causing a serious loss of confidence in Mr Takeshita's government.]

Tokyo stock exchange — As the new energy touches the stock market, the forces of greed begin to ebb. Those whose lives are involved in maintaining it and making money will lose interest in the system and all it represents.

As the energy drains away, so the stock market will begin to collapse. (Jan 1990)

Crumbling economic systems — The present economic systems are crumbling. The Japanese economy has cracks in it; and it will come to an end. It is clear now that pure capitalism has come to an end. It has no future whatsoever. The economy, education, the environment — everything — will be placed within the context of global social democracy in which everyone participates.

Communism also is coming to an end. (Mar 1990)

Market forces have devoured Japan — Market forces have devoured Japan. In market forces there is no justice. "The soul of market forces in Japan is the stock market. The day it is extinguished the whole body will collapse." In Japan and Hong Kong, which have surrendered to market forces, many are spiritually bankrupt. Market forces have ruined family life there, where even mothers gamble.

If you are shackled in this way in life, the energy goads you to breaking point. The only outlet found there is the martial arts. But the pace of life in Japan and Hong Kong is almost suicidal.

The Japanese are sitting on a time bomb. The destruction will be far worse than in any Western country. (May 1992)

Japan: Corruption, family disintegration — Japan is entering a phase where much corruption, the darker side of Japanese life, is opening up and will bring to an end the era of more and more money-making. There is much family disintegration even in Japan (due to the pressures created by excessive competition and daily struggle, themselves the products of an excessively commercialized world).

Market forces are the antithesis of freedom and salvation. (Sep 1993)

Japan: Self-sacrifice — The Japanese are capable of self-sacrifice. This is why they have been successful. But it would be destructive for them to forget their roots. This means they should not forget their Oriental (spiritually based) way of life.

Mrs Thatcher: Market forces — Mrs Thatcher, the British Prime Minister, will retire from office soon. She has done great damage to the morality of the people. They have been made to suffer because of her destructive policies. She does not understand market forces. Market forces, like phenomenal powers, are not to be followed nor submitted to. They are to be used with right motive and detachment. If you cling to them, they will corrupt you. Whichever direction political and economic leaders fix, if they obey market forces alone they will simply be enticed into the unknown. To be extreme is to be destructive. Her powers are drained. Her 'wheel of fortune' has turned against her.

In the time of Jesus he told the poor not to pay taxes. Rules and regulations made by institutions or governments that demoralize individuals will result in the fall of these institutions or governments. Maitreya will not allow the demoralization of the people to continue in this way, and instead will create a different situation. An example is the poll tax in the UK. Many individuals will be unable to pay this tax. This crisis will lead to the downfall of the government.* (Jul 1988)

[*Margaret Thatcher resigned in November 1990.]

Mrs Thatcher: Dark forces — When Mrs Thatcher supported a united Europe based on market forces she was only interested in creating more wealth. But she did not pay attention to the dark side of these market forces. It is this dark side which results in countries losing their identity and their sovereignty. Now she is experiencing the effects of these dark forces and is trying to change her approach.

A nation's identity is sacred and if politicians try to manipulate and exploit it for their own ends, a country and its people become prostituted, morally, physically and spiritually. (May 1990)

Euro-culture — Politicians are sitting on a time bomb if they try to create a Euro-culture through market forces. Every individual, nation and culture should retain its own identity.

If, in the name of market forces, the identity of a country or the personality of an individual is compromised or sacrificed, this could only lead to chaos and havoc, even war. Politicians are playing with dangerous, dark forces. These could be the seeds of a Third World War, if unchecked.

Ask any politician if he is prepared to sacrifice his own identity in the name of the French, the Germans or any other international personality. Of course not. So why is he trying to draw nations into an international cartel at the expense of their cultures?

Politicians will not have a free hand in shaping the destinies of nations. These same forces can throw a person off his well-trodden path.

"When the races themselves cannot get on together, how can you force the nations to get on together?" (Jul 1990)

East and West — Market forces do not bring freedom and salvation. It is futile for Eastern Europe to copy Western Europe, or for the East in general to copy the West. Cultures differ, and the differences must be respected.

In the USSR, for example, Mr Gorbachev will find that Western-style capitalism cannot be imposed. The attempt to do so will create such havoc that the military may well move in.

The problems creating friction between East and West Germany are huge. Western-style democracy (as practised at present) cannot survive because it allows market forces to rule excessively. This could be the seed of another war. (Apr 1991)

Social consciousness — Old political systems are coming to an end. In the new systems, even market forces will be based on social consciousness. Market forces will not be 'in charge' of social consciousness. Social consciousness will guide market forces. (Mar 1990)

The essence of market forces — The current creed adhered to internationally is that of market forces. "Market forces mean one surrenders. The Self is made to surrender to the unknown forces of life with a view to maximizing profit. Market forces generate possessiveness. Possessiveness can only be cherished with attachments. Attachments can only be maintained by passions in life.

"The essence of market forces is greed and separatism. The more one is attached to these forces, the more they create cells of imprisonment. This leads to spiritual bankruptcy and mental disequilibrium.

"The mental body or pattern is controlled by the brain on the physical plane. When the mental body experiences disequilibrium, the brain is affected and is not able to control the physical organs."

Referring to the so-called 'mad cow disease' affecting British cattle at present, "The poor cow, in the name of market forces, is being fed with chemicals to generate more and more food. This creates disequilibrium in the mental body of the cow and affects the brain. As a result, many physical organs are unable to function."

The same pattern applies to human beings: the baby's natural food is milk, but when children go to school, market forces influence even the children's diet. Girls at 12 or 13 look physically mature but the mental body is often in a state of disequilibrium. The same applies to young men. This process of continuing disequilibrium creates difficulty later. To escape disequilibrium people resort to drugs — creating further disequilibrium.

"Market forces in the West create wealth at the expense of millions of people dying from illnesses originating in chemicals in food."

Maitreya will no longer allow unbridled market forces to prevail among the nations.

The market will exist, but balanced by social democracy. Market plus social democracy maintains equilibrium. (May 1990)

No nation without individuals — Without individuals there is no nation. The individual must become 'number one'. That individual is your Self. The more individuals become aware of who they are, why they are, the more market forces will be tamed and used for the betterment of mankind. Then market forces will not rule nations and countries. (Apr 1991)

Market forces create a giant — You should never allow market forces to rule life on planet Earth. If you do this you create a giant. What does a giant do? It keeps on eating, day and night, regardless of whether it is hungry or not. Market forces should not govern the life of the individual; they have a place, but will have to fall into a perspective where the individual remains sacred. (Jun 1991)

Taming of market forces — We shall see the taming of market forces which have become the creed of so many politicians. They have deprived people of their health and wealth but the people are awakening now in the name of humanity. The bounty of the nations will be shared among everyone. (Jan 1992)

World collapse — Not only large financial institutions which are tumbling into bankruptcy; the whole world is becoming bankrupt — mentally and spiritually. The world is going through a huge crisis and all the medicines have been tried and failed. The tumour has to burst open before the healing can begin.

The world is in such a chaotic state that it could happen at any time. The politicians and the generals can do nothing to stop it — everything they have tried to avert disaster has failed.

The Tokyo Stock Market has been turned by the politicians and businessmen into a giant monster serving only a culture of greed. Now it is crashing like everything else. Even the United Nations is being forced to serve the interests of the strong and the greedy. Only charitable institutions, like Oxfam, are caring for the weak and the needy; governments are too caught up in killing and destroying.

Scientists have become like witches — brewing up new creatures through genetic experiments to make money.

Crime is on the increase throughout the Western world. Look at the faces of the politicians; they have no sparkle. What is happening is beyond their comprehension. The world is like a volcano waiting to erupt — in fact it is only a matter of time before it bursts open. (May 1992)

CRIME AND VIOLENCE

Crime in the cities — Cities are the places where "crime combustion" occurs. People are hooked on drugs, sexual violence, murder and other crimes. This process of combustion brings the dirt up to the surface. The prison population is growing and will revolt. Neither the police nor the military will be able to control this situation adequately (ie, the crime situation as a whole). In the extremity of such a situation, both sides, in fact, cry out for help. Then Maitreya will act. This process has already started.

Eventually, certain judicial reforms will take place. Minor or petty crimes will not lead to prison sentences. When world tension begins to decrease, when the principle of sharing begins to be implemented through a variety of social, economic and political reforms, people will feel less threatened and crime will decrease.

There is a growing awareness that redistribution of resources rather than wealth creation is the key issue. (Apr 1998)

Prisons — The prison population is exploding. It is possible that there are more people in prison in Great Britain, for example, than official figures suggest.

Recently, Maitreya visited the prison population (at a so-far unnamed place) in Great Britain. He gave the prisoners certain experiences in order to make them realize that they have possibilities other than simply rotting in prison.

It is common knowledge that, due to overcrowding and lack of a variety of facilities, many prisoners spend 23 out of 24 hours a day in their cells. Even in such conditions, an experience of spiritual illumination is possible. (Jun 1988)

Prison crisis — As mentioned before, the situation in prisons has reached crisis-point. The difficulties reported at Glenoacle Prison on 21 July 1988 are but a glimpse of conditions in many prisons, not only in the UK but around the world. It is not only prisoners but also prison officers who are revolting at these conditions. Prisoners everywhere have a strong desire to free themselves from excessive rules and regulations and are increasingly able to express things which they could not do in the past.

Army personnel, too, will increasingly revolt against governments around the world. They, also, are affected by the urge to be free from arbitrary rules and regulations and ideological control by those in power.

Maitreya is giving prisoners all over the world experiences of Himself such that they will discuss their experiences and this will become known. (Jul 1988)

Drugs given to prisoners — At present, a type of drug is being given to prisoners whereby the prisoners, when they are released, do not even remember what crime they have committed. Such people become harmless (a positive effect) but also mindless (a negative effect). It is a mind-numbing drug and people become zombies.

This method of social control means that the person who has taken this drug is no longer in control of himself. He cannot be taught self-awareness. This is happening now, but future effects could be even more serious. These drugs may well reach the open market and become available like Smarties. Then the masses will yearn for these drugs (that is to say, for an experience of oblivion). This issue needs in-depth investigation and debate. (Jun 1988)

Rules and regulations — What is happening in the prisons in the UK will have its rebounding effect in the British Parliament, the seat where rules and regulations are made.

Psychologically and spiritually, corruption has set in, in such a way that politicians hide their face. Likewise the judiciary.

"If you throw a pebble into a pond, it creates ripples. The ripples are there because the pond has accepted the pebble. But the pebble rebounds if the water of the pond is frozen. The pebble is thrown at a particular speed. It will rebound at the same speed.

"If you try to put the mantle of whatever rules and regulations you make on the mind, spirit and body of the prison population, there will be a 'rebound' effect which will affect the 'seat of origin'." The effect will be psychological and located where those rules and regulations were made.

Psychologically, the mantle-makers (in terms of rules and regulations) will have to wear this mantle against their will. The mind is therefore wearied. To run away from this situation, the mind seeks refuge in drugs, alcohol, unlawful sex. This causes the downfall of the individuals concerned. Notice the connection between lawmaker and recipient. Hidden laws of nature are at work here. This truth was known in the past. This is why the disciple was always so fully trained to accept the knowledge and wisdom of the guru. A Master can control this. But how can politicians and educationalists, who have no control over their own destiny, control the destiny of others? (Aug 1988)

Negative forces — Wherever the negative forces are found, in human beings, in nations (in the form of corruption, drugs, violence, etc), they will be found to be growing like a tumour. When the tumour is hard, it cannot burst open. When it does burst open, the pus runs out and the tumour eventually disappears.

In the case of violent crime, the vibrations of mind, spirit and body are disturbed. The Self realizes it is imprisoned. In society as a whole, the attempt to emerge from bondage results inevitably in these disturbances as a prelude. The Self is imprisoned in the web of the mind to the extent that there is no purpose left in life. Crimes are committed in a confused state of mind. The mind has taken over the Self. The Self is not the perpetrator of these crimes.

Although prison is the only alternative for violent and dangerous criminals at present, this condition cannot be cured by sentencing people to prison. Not all people, however, are in prison for violent crimes. Many who are in prison are not criminals.

An energy has been released in the world which counteracts these negative forces. The trend will be for the prison population to decrease. (Sep 1988)

Food for the body — The science of nutrition is developing, and, likewise, harmless drugs will also be found which will help to calm the nerves. People will commit less crime and the prison population will be reduced.

Appropriate food for the body contributes to awareness so that the Self and the body can work together.

The elements of nature will respond.

Changes in prisons — Maitreya says to prisoners: "Society condemns you, yet I am with you." The prison population will begin to feel that they are not forgotten. Even prison guards will begin to feel the sense of openness and will expose what is happening behind closed doors. The public will be informed, and this will result in beneficial changes.

Revolution in prisons — No one can control the revolution taking place in Britain's prisons. The government was warned in 1982 that the situation would explode.

If it thought that by sending in more men the situation could be contained, then it was misled. The prison population has become aware of who they are and what they are. They are no longer prepared to put up with the inhumane conditions and treatment that they have endured for so long. Eventually, government policy will turn to building more open prisons containing educational centres to teach prisoners to value both themselves and life itself. (Apr 1990)

Transformation in prisoners — In prisons transformation is taking place. Those who commit crimes will not be deprived of a human environment and the awareness of prisoners will grow. They will understand better the processes of mind that led them to commit crimes. To give prisoners an environment that is like a jungle creates poison, havoc. Maitreya says to prisoners: "Don't lose faith. Don't lose direction. I am with you." (Jun 1991)

The armed forces — Around the world, the situation in the armed forces is akin to a 'human time bomb'. People will revolt against army service. Imprisoning ideologies lead to destruction, but "anything created in the name of Self-realization will last for ever and ever". (Jun 1988)

The armed forces are needed for protection, not aggression. Army personnel in America, Central America, Sri Lanka, Russia and Afghanistan are questioning their role.

A soldier is the same as any saint. He is prepared to sacrifice his life for the nation. We need soldiers for defence. "If a snake or tiger is in the room, you need the bullet. But if the tiger is tame, do you need the bullet?" (Oct 1988)

Soldiers bewildered — Soldiers around the world who fought and killed are now bewildered and look towards the political leaders who ordered their actions. They are asking: "What next?" But their leaders have no answers; it is the end of the road.

A sense of frustration and betrayal is arising among the armed forces of many countries as they face the prospect of unemployment. It is becoming a matter of concern to the politicians who realize that it is an enormous threat that they will have to face. In order to avoid that as long as possible, a number of leaders are creating false wars. But this will not work, for the time is soon coming when such large numbers of soldiers will no longer be needed in the world. (Jun 1990)

Duty — The duty of a soldier, a policeman, a Pope, are all equally divine. (Jun 1988)

Cause of drug addiction — Politicians' contributions to this problem consist of television advertisements. Again, a proper analysis of cause is required.

Drug addicts are suffering from spiritual starvation, from extreme self-alienation. Life becomes purposeless and people want to bring their lives to an end, committing slow suicide via drugs. There is no substitute for dealing with a person's internal world. If life has no meaning, then 'meaning' must be restored. For this to happen, it is necessary for the person to experience himself differently, to experience a sense of his own worth. Once that happens, he can grow in self-awareness.

Maitreya is training disciples in techniques of self-awareness. Some of them are already employing these in connection with treatment of addicts. Many more are going to be called to this task. (Jun 1988)

Drugs — When resistance is created in mind, spirit and body, life becomes meaningless. To escape this, people take drugs, and then become addicted. Only when the Self is freed from tumour-like isms can this problem be solved. This can happen only when the Self is given self-respect. The art of communication is an important part of this process. If communication flourishes within a family, the family is happy. Similarly, communication must exist between different parts of a nation.

Drugs destroy the family unit, and hence society. By deploying additional policemen and meting out stronger punishments you cannot solve the problem.

In the past, government policies here [in the UK] and elsewhere which deprive people of adequate housing and livelihood lead to a loss of self-respect and to an existence which becomes meaningless. Those who feel they have no place in society will resort to whatever form of oblivion — ie drugs — rescues them even momentarily from this loss of meaning, identity and purpose. Witness the streets of

Washington or New York. "It can happen in London." (Jun 1989)

Nourishment — Even when the Buddha became enlightened He was told that His first duty was to energize His stomach — in other words, to be properly nourished.

If people are so straitened in life that they cannot even eat properly, they will lead desperate lives. They will sell their bodies, steal, and end up in prison. If you deprive people of any future in life, deprive them of nourishment, they will end up on drugs to help them to forget their desperation. And from drugs it is not far to crime, even murder.

The politicians alone are to blame for the desperation of these people.

Drugs: Power of environment — The massive threat posed by drugs cannot be solved through fear of the law. Strong policing will be needed to crack down on the organized gangs of drug producers, but it is not the answer to the individual drug user.

If you offered £1 million to someone to fly in a plane that was due to crash, he would obviously turn it down; the same if you offered him a drink of deadly poison. But when it comes to drugs — which have the same eventual destructive effect — somehow people shrug it off as not really threatening them.

It is the person's mind that deludes him into believing that the threat is so far off that it cannot really hurt him — he will be able to give up drugs long before there is any danger. Therefore it is the mind that must be addressed and that can only be done through creating Self-awareness — and that can only be achieved through Self-experience. Self-awareness embraces the mind, spirit and body and creates instantaneous harmony in all three.

How can this be achieved? Not through the fear of laws, or by preaching ideology. The only effective way is through a person's environment. If you create a neat, clean and tidy environment, it creates a neat, clean and tidy way of living.

It is through the power of the environment that you create Self-awareness. When an individual enters a church he feels peaceful and tranquil; the Self experiences this, and the mind is no longer in confusion or turmoil. Living in the bleak, depressing conditions of a run-down council estate, a person's mind will be desperate and reach for drugs to find escape.

That is why the environment should be a high priority among the country's leaders. "Clean your environment and your life will respond to it." If there is no stress or strain in your surroundings, then there is no need for drugs, for within the human body is the most powerful drug known to humanity — detachment. And that can only emerge and happen within a sane, clean and peaceful environment.

Addiction — One of the Swamis close to Maitreya recently said that he was concerned that the streets of Britain were experiencing an increase in drug addiction and quoted the example of New York where six people a day die from violence related to drugs.

Maitreya told him: "Everybody is addicted to some sort of drug. How can you stop it? Not by restricting people's movement, or extra police or more prison cells. The only answer is developing detachment in mind, spirit and body. You must become free from any ism — for that is the deadliest drug. It is like a sponge — it absorbs illusions like water and engulfs the Self." Emotion, too, is a powerful drug. The only way to be free from this trap is through intelligence which can be developed through awareness.

Unlike our mental conditioning, awareness is free of anger, fear and other emotions.

When helping drug addicts it is no use telling them not to take drugs, or sending the police to arrest them. The only way to transform their lives is by teaching them "Be what you are".

They should be taught to practise detachment, even while they are still taking drugs. The next time they take drugs, they will find themselves a little reluctant about continuing their habit until eventually they will realize that it is the body that is being injected with drugs, and not the Self.

Maitreya himself has been helping drug addicts. Some time ago, in America, Maitreya showed his disciples the figure of a man who lay collapsed on the ground. He was 78 years old, a millionaire who had turned to drugs in despair after the death of his wife. He had now reached the point of suicide by injecting himself with an overdose. But because the man had, in his past, done many good deeds, they should help him by giving him an experience.

Maitreya turned to a Swami and said: "Cure this person with a ray of light", and that is what the Swami did. The conditioning of the man's mind was dissolved. Then his body responded and he came to. He had forgotten about committing suicide and thought that he had simply fallen down. He has never taken drugs since because the conditioning is no longer there.

Through awareness and then detachment, habits of all kinds will fall away like leaves in the autumn. (Nov 1989)

Drugs are isms — Drugs are neither good nor bad. It is how you use them and why that counts. It is not the Self that takes the drug, but only the body. The Self is trapped somewhere within it, feeling pain or withdrawal.

If you analyse the difficulties and problems of life, the appetites and emotions, these all have a drug-like effect in the way that a person speaks, thinks or acts. "Without drugs of some kind no one could survive in life. They operate not only on the physical level but on the emotional and spiritual planes. The drugs are the isms in their various forms.

"If you can teach a person the art of Self-realization, whereby they can move freely in and out of the mind, they will not need drugs." Scientists have already been taught by the Space Brothers how to use the technology of light to dissolve drug habits by targeting specific areas of the brain. These methods are already being used in hospitals in China and Hong Kong where drug addiction has become a massive problem. (Nov 1989)

119

Shooting of terrorists — By shooting, "do not think your problems are solved. You have achieved nothing. You have done away with a physical obstacle but you have created a spiritual problem" — the spiritual equilibrium of the person who did the shooting is disturbed. Within his lifetime, that person will undergo such trials and tribulations that they will make life negative, meaningless. Such people, to get rid of disturbing thoughts, either commit suicide, end up in hospital or resort to drugs and drink.

Just as a rapist is taken over by destructive forces, "when you open fire you are also taken over by this type of force" and the Self is knocked out. [Maitreya was referring here to the incident in South Africa on the occasion of the Pope's visit when South African units opened fire on a bus that had been taken over (with its civilians, including nuns and children) by a group of terrorists in Lesotho.]

Such killings are not undertaken with tranquillity of mind.

When the mind is peaceful, tranquil, graceful, 'killing' does not happen. "When you have a human form, why sacrifice the Self in the name of certain ideologies, inspired by politicians, religious leaders, etc? When the Self falls prey to the powers of mind, spirit and body, you lose your free will. These powers will goad the Self to commit acts against its will. You become a slave to conditioning." (Oct 1988)

Terrorism and revenge — To avenge someone is an indirect action (that is, on someone else's behalf). To take revenge is a direct action.

Terrorism and revenge are not equivalent terms, because terrorism has its roots in the differences between haves and have-nots. (Sep 1990)

The genesis of violence — Throughout the world, governments are faced with seemingly intractable problems. But in many places they are not being dealt with appropriately. A growing barrage of rules and regulations is not the answer. The only way to deal with any problem in life is to understand how it came into being. The moment you know its process, you can reverse it. "When you know its birth, you can know its death."

Any problem requires analysis along the lines of how, when, where, why and what. Such an approach yields results.

A practical example is the problem of growing violence among young people in the UK. The reasons offered for it include poverty, unemployment, boredom, etc. Recently, however, youths rampaged through a number of towns in the prosperous southeast of England and thereby shattered stereotypes. These young people are comparatively affluent, employed, etc. In the words of one sociologist writing for a London paper, these events "blew all the indicators".

The bemused reaction in government and academic circles alike is a dramatic illustration of inadequate analysis and its ensuing dangers. The domain of the problem cannot be limited to the riots themselves, because the solutions will then be 'reactive', that is, they will deal with effects, rather than causes. To understand the genesis of violence it is necessary to get a much more detailed, overall picture of the pattern of the lives of these young people in order to assist them so that energy, wrongly directed, can be channelled constructively. Rules and regulations per se will shift the problem to other locations, but cannot solve it. (Jun 1988)

Crime in the UK — The UK is afflicted now and will continue to be afflicted for a time by waves of crime. The same energy which affects the elements of nature also affects human beings. This energy flushes out negative forces. It then creates a state of alertness in individuals and will create a new phase of life. More and more people will revolt, because old habits, centuries-old codes imposed on the mind, must be broken. People in schools, colleges, hospitals, etc will not accept imposed solutions.

The prison population is mounting. Additional rules and regulations will lead to destruction. The armed forces and the police will be shaken. The government must first learn to feed the nation with right food; next it must provide the right environment (adequate housing, etc). Then it must refrain from dogmatic interference in education. Then, crime and drug problems will decrease.

Spending billions on nuclear weapons is a process which will be coming to an end.

Awareness is a God-given gift. No one can take it away from you. It cannot be controlled by rules and regulations. (Oct 1988)

UK: Violence will increase — Havoc is sweeping through the country as new energy flushes out old ideas, old patterns of thinking. It will become so destructive that neither the politicians, the army, nor the police will be able to control it. We will see more violence, chaos and confusion. Individuals in Britain are beginning to feel like robots, imprisoned by the increasing rules and regulations in their environment.

The politicians need new policies; the old ones have failed. When they (the politicians) lose their old habits of thinking they will begin to learn awareness and know how to create harmony. As the energy sweeps away the old, awareness grows like a small flower day by day, bringing equilibrium and balance into the community. (Apr 1989)

Motiveless murders — [Patricia Pitchon noted at the time: Recently in the UK thieves doused four people with petrol and set them alight. Two of them died. There have also been a number of seemingly motiveless stabbings, etc. Violent crime increased in the UK last year (1988) by 17 per cent.]

Dousing people with petrol is a (horrific) expression of the havoc which has been created in the temples of the Lord (that is, in mind, spirit and body). This is due in part to the aura created in society by the divisions between rich and poor. This creates a grab/steal mentality. If the rich behave selfishly and the poor are goaded into struggling for their life and livelihood, havoc ensues. Who has created this state of affairs? Politicians must bear some responsibility here. (Apr 1989)

Northern Ireland — There is no smoke without fire. If you choke the smoke off there will be an explosion. The same Law of Cause and Effect is now working in relation to human beings. The government's attempt to stifle the voice of those who are angered — for whatever reason — by passing rules and regulations will cause murders and explosions no army can stop.

It is the duty of the government, the trustees of the people, to make sure the feelings of all the people are represented, not choked off. Otherwise, they are not acting in the name of democracy, nor are they acting in the true name of government. (Oct 1988)

Thoughts are energies — Examine the case of a person who picks up a knife and stabs another. Was he aware before he became a partner in this process? What made him pick it up?

The moment he becomes identified with a loose yet powerful thought whose energy compels him to commit such an act, he is lost. These thoughts are energies akin to ships without rudders, because the thoughts are not tied to awareness.

The Self, through awareness, can control these energies. If it abandons awareness, it becomes prey to these energies.

Awareness is the light of life. Anything done outside awareness leads to destruction.

All thoughts which lead you to selfishness lead you away from awareness. Yet in awareness there is no burden. You remain meticulous, immaculate, pure. There is gracefulness, peace and happiness. These are the blessings of the Lord. (Apr 1989)

Forces out of control — [Patricia Pitchon noted at the time: Recently so-called 'motiveless' murders have continued to occur, and to engage the attention of the press and the public, particularly in America.]

Mind, spirit and body are full of energies. If they go 'haywire', they can make a person go mad, or turn him into a beast. In fact, the Self has no control over these forces playing around mind, spirit and body when violent acts occur. There is no communication between the Self and mind, spirit and body. "I have come to teach you salvation. In awareness lies

123

salvation. In awareness you can control the energies within you. Only in awareness is there equilibrium." (Apr 1989)

Nuclear energy, thought energy — Nuclear energy can be created even by an individual of his own free will. Yogis can do it. Take as an example an extreme winter. Some children have few clothes yet they survive. In mind, spirit and body they have created energy. We often speak of instances where adults have also 'braved the cold'. It is because they have decided they will, and they can. In fact, they have created energy: thought energy.

How is it that some people can walk through fire or lie on a bed of nails, yet the body is neither burned nor pierced?

The preoccupation with 'nuclear' energy is only for politicians who say: "Give me the power, so I can rule."

Spontaneous combustion — Spontaneous combustion is also a case of energies 'going haywire'. In your 'second nature' (which means when you are identified with mind, spirit and body), the energy is controlled by mind, spirit and body. But when this energy is not controlled, a person can literally burst into a blaze of fire.

Murderer — A Swami asked Maitreya: "What happens with a murderer? Does God guide him?" Maitreya gave this example: "If you are sitting on a settee and there are mosquitoes about, what do you do? You swat the mosquitoes and kill them. Ask yourself what the energy behind you is. Did you feel any pain, any regrets? You swatted a mosquito; the mosquito died. There is no thought formation in your mind. When the energy goes through you, you strike.

"The same occurs with a murderer. The murderer is sick, which means he is out of balance. Equilibrium in mind, spirit and body would enable him to express that energy in another way. The person in equilibrium experiences a state of freedom within. He will not commit murder."

Murder is in the mind — "When a murderer is executed, the physical body is punished, but can you punish the mind? It is the mind, not the physical body, which is responsible for the act. You think you have destroyed the cause of the murder by destroying the physical body. The problem has not been solved. Once dissociated from the body, the mind still has to run the course of its mental life. It acts as an invisible force and comes into contact with another mind in a physical body, and compels it to commit an act of murder. Suddenly a man goes berserk and kills a number of people." Maitreya says to scientists, psychologists and doctors: "Try to investigate this problem."

Even if you multiply the prison population you will not solve the problem if you do not attend to the minds of prisoners. It is important to make the person understand the environment and the Self. Self-realization (a gradual process entailing non-identification with anger and other destructive emotions and ideas) brings equilibrium in mind, spirit and body. When the mind is still sick it can do mental harm beyond the walls of the prison. (Dec 1990)

POLITICS AND POLITICIANS, RULERS

Politicians — Politicians are realizing that this nuclear age is defunct. They have exhausted their knowledge and wisdom and do not know which way to turn. It is not soldiers on the battlefield, scientists in their laboratories or children at school who are bankrupt. It is the politicians. Politicians are dividing in order to rule: the rich are richer, the poor are poorer. They will become accountable for each and every task. If you do not change things, they will be changed for you by mutation.

Political dogmatism — The idea of politicians as 'masters of the universe' is coming to an end. Now politicians are realizing it is the will of the people which is important for the happiness and safety of society. It is so sacred that those who interfere with it will face the graveyard. (This means death in the form of heart attacks or suicide, or mental illness.)

To betray the will of the people sets in motion a dangerous process: when you betray someone, something recoils within you. It is the withdrawal of the Self from mind, spirit and body. This recoil is very destructive, leads to mental strain, and in extreme cases even to suicide or murder.

To believe dogmatically in market forces, for example, is to believe in forces of destruction which are like a snake without eyes let loose. Market forces divide: some will be happy, others will be unhappy. This creates contradictions and chaos.

Politicians face the consequences — What does it mean when a dog howls in the early morning? It means death. Why do you think there has been such a pattern of dogs going mad and biting people? It all signals the fact that those politicians who refuse to obey the will of the people are having to face the consequences. "When a child is called home by its parent because it is time and that child refuses to come, then it has to be dragged home. Soon we shall see politicians 'being dragged home' — in Iran, in China and elsewhere." (Jun 1989)

The politicians have been using their position to accrue material wealth and have used the forces of law and order to maintain their position of power. These tactics used to be employed by the kings of old. Now politicians behave like kings in the name of the people. They have used their position to create an elite class of power and wealth while others have been deprived of food, health and education, and left to kill themselves with drugs.

The principle of impartiality — Mrs Thatcher, the British Prime Minister, will not remain in power for long. The simple policy of dividing and ruling, whereby the rich have become richer and the poor have become poorer, has serious consequences. An example of this is the contentious poll tax which is Mrs Thatcher's biggest test.

Mental, spiritual and physical laws can be obeyed and respected, but they can never be controlled. "If you attempt to control these laws, they will destroy you." The key criterion here is impartiality. (An impartial law is one that applies equally to all; a law that favours the rich and discriminates against the poor represents a departure from the principle of impartiality, and an attempt to control rather than respect lawful principles.)

This applies in other fields also. For example, if you were to know the law of materialization and you tried to manipulate it so that its effect favoured one person as against another, it would destroy you. Laws must be applied without these distortions.

This is why detachment is the significant factor in life. (Apr 1989)

Complacency and the judiciary — In Great Britain, the judiciary is independent of the executive, but individually, judges are not free of complacency. Many of them live in a privileged atmosphere such that they are unable to understand the nature and the needs of the masses of people. To be unconnected to the realities of life is to have no vision. Thus even sentencing policy is affected.

When people move in this mental atmosphere of complacency, they are essentially cut off from their real selves and fall into a monotonous routine — that is, 'the same old thing' day in and day out. Life is movement, but complacent people are, in effect, in an arrested condition. The mind, therefore, seeks new peaks of experience, which can and often does lead to a variety of forms of corruption and perversion. Thus complacency is ultimately self-destructive, and whole societies can be destroyed by it.

Corruption — Where there is wealth, there you will find complacency and that is the source of corruption. Choose any politician and you will find that he is vulnerable to this dark side of nature. As power and wealth corrupts, the first step always lies in sex. The ultimate step is drugs and suicide.

A nation's leader — The time of domination by politicians is over. How can a nation's health be supervised by lawyers and accountants who become MPs? It should be left to doctors and scientists.

A nation's leader should be one who can unite a country through diversity, not stand to one side and, while confusion and chaos reigns, say they will not interfere. Mrs Thatcher is not a leader. She allows situations to develop which set families against each other. (Jan 1990)

To lead — To lead the people one must be a true, honest and sincere disciple of the Lord. Otherwise it is very difficult, because there is a split personality in the individual all the time which creates moodiness, ups and downs.

The imposition of ideology — [Note: The following refers to a sharp labour conflict which the British government, seeking to change long-standing work agreements, has suddenly precipitated in a section of the UK dock industry.]

Two months ago no one gave a second thought to the situation in the docks. Suddenly the government has turned the spotlight on them in order to win public sympathy. It is a new target. The dockers, however, are used to the old system. If you really want to teach people that there is a better way you can only do this by making them aware, by showing them what direction changes should take, how much, and how fast they should happen.

To bring in sudden legislation like this can only create disharmony and confusion. If you cut people off from their past in this way you leave them rudderless. They have to start all over again fighting old battles. You cannot impose your ideologies on people through the forces of law and order. This is what the government did with the miners; but this time they will not succeed. (Apr 1989)

Privatization — The privatization of the country's assets (such as health, education and water) for profit can only release destructive forces. You cannot play with the forces of life. The biggest test facing the government is the poll tax which symbolizes the imposition of political ideology on the people. (Apr 1989)

Britain: Vacuum — If politicians go against the forces of evolution, they will create resistance and conflicts which will build up until they explode. This explosion is followed by a loss of power and in the ensuing vacuum, as in other countries, isms dissolve, leading to consensus and to evolution again taking its course. Maitreya is teaching people to observe these processes. (Jun 1989)

UK: Political scandals— A big scandal is in the offing, one that could destroy the UK government and shake the foundations of the Conservative Party. There is so much corruption, chaos and sexual misdemeanour taking place in Conservative circles that when news of it bursts upon the world the nation will no longer have any faith in such a closed system of power as represented by these politicians.

The scandals involve every level, from the Cabinet right through the Conservative Party. It also involves members of the judiciary. Desperate attempts are being made now to try to cover it up, but the scandal will reach a crescendo and burst into the media within months. The Conservative Party represents conservation of power. "You cannot conserve power. You must be detached, respect energy, and allow it to flow through mind, spirit and body." (Nov 1989)

New energy — The poll tax cannot work. It is a scheme by politicians to control the people. It is like a time bomb. Those politicians who support the poll tax will be finished because the new energy is creating a system of politics that reflects the voice of the people. (Jan 1990)

UK: Financial scandals — The revelation about the big gun for Iraq is only the tip of an iceberg of a huge scandal of selling arms to warring nations. This involves big business interests with governmental complicity. Mrs Thatcher's government has known about the Iraqi deal — and others — from the beginning. Once again, market forces are behind this exporting of arms and ammunition to countries like Iraq.

The wealth of the nation has been drained away to overseas banks. This wealth has been taken left and right by big business with the encouragement of politicians. The country is suffering because its wealth has been plundered. The poll tax was created to find the money necessary to deal with the huge economic problems faced by social services, education and health. It is time for the politicians, and these businessmen, to let the nation know what has happened to its wealth.

The wealth of a nation should remain with that nation. Anything extra should be used for the welfare of neighbouring nations. Nothing can stop the exposure of the financial scandals which have undermined the country's economic health. (May 1990)

UK: Diversion of attention — The politicians are afraid that current policies, which have ruined families, created cardboard-box houses and deprived youngsters of hope for the future, have created negative political effects. If the attention of the nation is not drawn elsewhere the people will become aware of failures at home and will start questioning the policies of the politicians. Politicians want to focus the attention of the people on the Middle East in order to stay in power.

"No one need fear, because I am with you. Without the Lord, there is no creation. It is the heritage of one and all to experience the Lord's creation and enjoy the blessings of life, which are peace, bliss and happiness in which there is no fear." (Sep 1990)

Cause and effect — "If you have forced someone out through trickery, you will be forced out by the same process. Mrs Thatcher was goaded into an extreme position on the poll tax by various politicians in her own circle. Extremism destroys. The poll tax was not her own idea, but when it backfired, the treachery started. However, the politicians in question have not won the battle. They have not solved the problem."

The sparkle in Conservative politics will disappear. The new British Prime Minister, John Major, is a stepping stone to a Labour government. But Labour without capitalism cannot succeed. Both are important and must play an equal role. Labour will have no landslide victory.

When Mrs Thatcher was leaving No.10 Downing Street, she had a spectacular experience. Within seconds she composed herself. "Among politicians she believed in herself. This was her outstanding quality."

Maitreya has given Mrs Thatcher an experience which can lead to a transformation. Conservative politicians may seek her advice. She would then play a role in uniting the nation, transforming educational systems, and she could be inspired to look after the handicapped, pensioners and the poor.

She has made a sacrifice no politician in the present circle has made.

Likewise, in Russia, Mr Gorbachev has made many sacrifices but the pace of change cannot be forced. "Imposed transformation is undivine. Transformation from within is always permanent." Thus, the military will try to take over, but behind closed doors. They will allow freedom, but to dismantle everything overnight is self-destructive. Things will evolve at a slower pace. (Dec 1990)

Political hypocrisy — Power does not bring happiness. Politicians and leaders who have failed to understand what awareness is in life cannot lead the masses. Man's 'second nature' (ie his conditioned nature) can evolve into awareness through honesty of mind, sincerity of spirit and detachment. But if the environment (the circumstances people find themselves in) fails, the 'second nature' is like a blind man walking the streets.

Bosnia is a tragic legacy for political leaders West and East, and for the United Nations Security Council. They have failed to protect the innocent, leaving the conscientious few to venture into the war-torn arena to feed, shelter and nurture the people. Defenseless people here, in the estimation of all these leaders, are worth less than the oil wells in Kuwait. Present-day politics are sheer hypocrisy. (Sep 1993)

The danger of empty minds — An empty mind is the devil's workshop. If you have no job, if you cannot take care of your body nor meet your responsibilities at home by taking care of your family, then mind and spirit cannot evolve. Governments are creating policies which lead to the suffering of the people.

In Washington, for example, the people (committing violent acts) on the streets are not the culprits. The government has to look after the welfare of the nation. But what do politicians do when they are in office? They acquire a nice house, a nice car. (Apr 1989)

Corruption in judicial system — The present judicial system will also end as the corruption of the judges is exposed to the public. "How can one person judge another, tell them what they should not do, and then go ahead and do it themselves?"

Very shortly there will be a number of shock stories about corruption among the judiciary and parliament and a number of politicians will be forced to resign.*

"Wherever there is complacency there is the seed of corruption, chaos, confusion and ultimate destruction." (June 1989)

[*Patricia Pitchon noted at the time: While Maitreya is referring to a current situation in the UK, we have little doubt that these events can also be expected elsewhere.]

Political game — In the past, when political leaders could no longer control the masses, they resorted to war. That is no longer possible, so today they have found a new game to play — that is the political game of chaos and confusion. (Jul 1989)

Middle East — The Middle East demonstrated a confrontation between the energies of destruction and creativity. Meanwhile Maitreya warned the politicians: "You cannot play with the planet or the forces of nature."

Mr Shamir, the Israeli Prime Minister, has already been given an experience from which he is still shaking. Maitreya revealed to him his own violent terrorist past under British occupation and asked him: "Are you still a terrorist?"

American politicians, also, would "have to face the consequence of their actions" because they have supplied guns to Israel and kept quiet when they should have intervened with criticism. "All those who indulge in the act of warfare either by word or by deed face the most shocking experiences of their lives".

So traumatic would those experiences be that some politicians would turn towards the darkness of political oblivion.

"This time," says Maitreya, "make no mistake. No war can be won on any frontier."

As for Terry Waite*, he will be in no danger. Fulfilling Maitreya's mission, he will always be under His protection. (Aug 1989)

[*Note: The Church of England envoy who was taken hostage while negotiating for the release of those already held captive in Lebanon.]

The French Revolution celebrations — [On 14 July 1989 France celebrated the bicentenary of the French Revolution with great fanfare. The French government spent about $80 million for this occasion. At the same time, members of the seven richest nations, the so-called G7, met in Paris at an economic summit where the environment became a top issue.]

Why is everyone becoming 'green' now? Awareness of the environment is the first step in Self-realization. Individuals are becoming environmentalists. (This begins with concern for what one eats, drinks, breathes, etc.)

Politicians think the world is their oyster. Yet all the ideologies have failed and will continue to fail. Individuals are going to produce changes.

As for the Revolution, "it was made by people long gone. They suffered. The present generation is not interested in the past. Why fan the fires of the past?" Politicians are attempting to control the people. These celebrations were not for the poor, for the people. Had the money been spent on basic needs — food, health, education, etc — it would have been money well spent. (Jul 1989)

Voice of the people — We begin to hear the voice of the people; they are beginning to realize that the politicians have failed them. The young, for instance, have no faith in politics, religion or philosophy — they just want to get on with each other and their own destiny.

People who are forced to live on the streets, or are finding it hard to pay their mortgage, are saying that we did not elect these politicians to live like this.

The young people say: "I was born in this country, deprived of milk as a young child, forced to eat fish and chips and sandwiches, and then, at the end of my school life, told there is no job for me. A house is beyond my reach." "What sort of life am I going to lead," they ask. They are told "You are on your own, this is a democracy where everyone has the freedom to do what they want. Why don't you try abroad?" But of course when they go abroad they are told by the people there that they don't want strangers coming into their house.

Social structures must undergo fast changes, for the divisions in our society are created and sustained by the politicians. The world is not wicked — only the rulers are wicked. They only know about looking after personal power. (Sep 1989)

Rulers — Those sheikhs and sultans who syphon off the wealth of their nations into overseas accounts, and fail to look after the welfare of their people at home, are not fit to be considered rulers. The will of the people will deal with them, for the will of the people will decide their countries' constitutions. This is particularly true of Saudi Arabia. The ruling Royal family has to go; their time has come. There is no longer any place for them because they have betrayed their people's faith. (Sep 1990)

Evolution of awareness — The power of the sheikhs, kings and sultans has been broken. The days when the people of Middle Eastern countries were treated like slaves has come to an end. The people are demanding government by the people, for the people. The evolution of awareness in the human individual is spreading throughout the world as people begin to realize their heritage and their destiny. The seed is growing into a plant that will flower and give fruit to the younger generation. (Sep 1991)

Peace or terrorism — This is a testing time for Britain, America, Saudi Arabia and Israel to demonstrate whether they are on the side of peace or terrorism.

They have to face up to their responsibilities, particularly in the light of the roles they have played in their relationships with Iraq and Iran. (May 1990)

Middle East diplomacy — Middle Eastern countries are running out of arms and ammunition, time and friends. They are all desperately seeking support for their causes. Iran, Iraq and Israel are trying to entice international backing but the price they will have to pay is the release of hostages.* Meanwhile, Britain and America are playing dubious games in the name of diplomacy and this must stop. Their people are aware of the processes of peace, and demand that they respect their wishes and open the doors to negotiations and talks that will lead to the release of the hostages. (May 1990)

[*Several hundred foreigners were captured by the Iraqi government as hostages.]

Power of awareness — The reason Saudi Arabia concluded a huge weapons deal with the UK (in 1988) is that the leaders wanted to scare the masses at home. "You cannot do this. People are becoming aware. Awareness is so powerful it could even make creation disappear. It is the destiny of the individual to have this power of awareness from God. No politician, no religious leader, can control it."

In Israel, politicians are trying to gain the support of the masses by whipping up emotions of fear. Many older people, who have seen so much, do not want this situation to continue. Mothers do not want their sons killed in war. Maitreya says to Shamir: "Whatever you have plotted, you will be ousted."

Whatever is happening in the Middle East, whoever is doing it, whether Arab or Jew, they will have to pay the price. (May 1990)

India and Pakistan — It is not the people of those countries who are fighting, but the politicians. In Pakistan, Mrs Bhutto has no power. Power remains in the hands of the generals, who are still in command. The politicians in India have no power to rule the country. Politicians in both countries are trying to wield power through creating confusion. They urge their people to fight in the name of patriotism to distract attention from the massive internal problems affecting both countries. This situation may last four to five years, such is the mentality of the politicians. (May 1990)

No real enmity — There is no real enmity between peoples. Animosities arise out of the ideologies of political and religious leaders. A leader who cannot respect the human race, morally and spiritually, is not worthy of the name.

"The world does not belong to politicians. You cannot afford a war. He who is humble, who respects the will of the Lord, will always say, 'I am the servant, I am the messenger' — never 'I am the leader'. This is true of Rama, Krishna, Buddha, Jesus and others.

The time has come for money to be spent on the welfare of the nations. Every nation, every country, belongs to the people. "Those who divide God's health and wealth in the name of ideology are themselves corrupt." (Sep 1990)

Northern Ireland — Those who are patrolling the streets are saying: "We cannot kill the people because of political ideologies." Politicians in Northern Ireland are bankrupt. They are 'the bees in the bonnet', employing the dark forces of 'divide and rule' to govern the people. Yet soldiers are experiencing the senselessness of their role. People are beginning to feel interdependent. (Mar 1990)

Northern Ireland: Politicians — The politicians are in a state of panic. They know the people are now becoming aware. There are thugs who call themselves politicians and espouse 'hard-core' politics, but their ideologies have failed. The people in Ulster have been awakened and are getting together. Exploding of bombs will come to an end. Maitreya says to the politicians: "You are fighting among yourselves but you are hurting others."

[Brian James noted at the time: The voice of the people is insisting that talks continue and that a solution be found which will end the sectarian violence of that unhappy province.] (Jun 1991)

Superpowers — Politicians who inspire war in the name of ideology or religion will fail. "Remember, everything you see around you is changing. Everything that you don't see is the seed of what is to come." The American and the Russian people must become aware of the purpose of existence. Politicians who sacrifice the aspirations and security of nations to balance their own failed political ideologies will not succeed. The energies which are wasted in the pursuit of their policies will rebound through the elements of nature, in the shape of floods, earthquakes and volcanic eruptions.

Russian and American politicians have failed to fulfil the aspirations of their people. Their economies are weakened. How can they call themselves superpowers? America's economy is in shreds and morality is almost non-existent. How can you call it a superpower? (Sep 1990)

The West — The people of the West have also been betrayed by the politicians. When Maitreya came as Jesus Christ [by overshadowing Jesus for the last three years of his life] He taught that everyone should love their neighbour as themselves. Politicians are not immune from this teaching.

"No one can understand Me, but they can experience Me. I am your defender and sustainer. Your destiny is to inherit the wealth and health the Lord has bestowed upon you. Look within and then look out. Fear no one."

Defences — You need a stick to ensure that the deadliest snakes do not bite you. Every nation and country must have defences. But you must make sure that the human race is not eliminated.

Serve as servants — The politicians must serve the nation and country as servants, not as masters. The moment you act as a master rather than a servant, egoism becomes an evil force which eventually kills the individual. "In the Lord's creation, one acts as a disciple and not as a master. The moment you act as a master in the Lord's creation, the doors of His Supreme Being are closed. The moment you act as a disciple, a devotee or a servant, the doors of the Lord's Supreme Being open."

Therefore, realize that the policies of the nations and countries should be imbued with the principles which bring individuals, nations and countries closer harmoniously and not through fear. Anything and everything done in the shadows of doubt, suspicion, confusion and fear will cause the process of evolution to degenerate. This means 'involution'.

Respect tempo and temperament — This time, politicians and other leaders will not be able to repeat history. This means they will not be able to read the history of the past and formulate their actions accordingly. In a nutshell, this time it is the people who, with their awareness, will make the politicians respect the tempo and temperaments of the people.

Peace and war — Peace and war are two sides of the same truth. The truth is that if you respect the energies which control creation, you will experience peace. But if you disturb them it leads to war. Learn to respect the energies of creation. Do not fight them. The political message of this truth is: peace is where people have the basic necessities of life. Where these are non-existent, there is war.

So the politics of 'rich and poor' have no place in this new age.

Any politician who thinks that capitalism, under the banner of democracy, is the answer to modern problems is as ignorant as are the generals, the soldiers, who are made to fight on the battlefield. They do not know what they will achieve by killing people.

Politics, vast changes — The present-day politics which consist of nothing other than ideological warfare are undergoing vast changes. They are being transformed into the politics of Self-realization. Look around the world, and you will see that many politicians are slipping into oblivion. (Nov 1990)

Politicians and double standards — "Politicians have double standards. When the leaders themselves have lost the way, what have they to offer? They are like zombies: psychologically, spiritually, mentally finished." (Apr 1991)

Corrupt leaders — There are many scandals involving the judiciary and religious organizations as well as the worlds of commerce and banking. How can these leaders demand law and order when they are so corrupt themselves? It is like the relationship between a guru and a disciple. If the guru is cunning, how can you expect the disciple to develop in an honest and straightforward manner?

The people will realize that their so-called leaders cannot be trusted with power. What sort of future lies in these hands? The days of many leaders, political, religious and commercial, are numbered. Some will commit suicide while others will just disappear.

In the New Age it will be the poor, those who have nothing, who will celebrate the arrival of fresh hope and a new purpose in life. (Jul 1991)

Racism — As political systems around the world die, tribalism and racism appear, "like lice leaping off a dying animal". We are seeing it in South Africa and Yugoslavia and in a short time it will affect some European countries as well. It happens because politicians cannot solve the problems of their changing societies and so the people take the law into their own hands. This always leads to destruction. (Jul 1991)

Diversity — The culture of creation is diversity, which is the basis of every nation and of every religion. Try to remove those differences and you only provoke destruction. This is why the drive towards Europeanization in the cause of trade and commerce is so dangerous. Once you open the floodgates, the water will spread everywhere. It will be out of control and the politicians won't know what will happen next. If you try to undo creation you will bring about havoc and danger. You must respect the laws of diversity to maintain harmony and peace. (Jul 1991)

The younger generation — The younger generation, and ordinary people everywhere, expect politicians to set an example, to serve the people with honesty, sincerity and detachment. No leader is attending to his duties in the right fashion at the present time. Instead of fulfilling the will of the Lord, they are merely fulfilling their own desires. This way lies nothing but confrontation, confusion and chaos. "It is the destiny of nations and countries that you are playing with. What are you doing for the younger generation? Nothing. You want them to walk in your footsteps, but there is a gap growing between the older and younger generations. Society will not be what the older generation is hoping for. It will be completely different."

Nuclear weapons — Whenever politicians fail to hold the masses they try to create confusion and chaos. What made the politicians begin to dismantle nuclear weapons? It is awareness which changes the person. Politicians have been made aware that nuclear weapons are not the answer. They will keep a few for basic defence "in case the snake becomes violent". (Aug 1991)

The art of politics — The art of politics is the art of reconciliation while respecting diversity. Those who play with power and life, who are attached to greed and ideology, end up by making war that destroys life. When a leader refuses to respect the realities of life, then accidents, sickness and death await them. We shall witness this process of ill health among many politicians.

This ill health also awaits the gurus and spiritual leaders who are not guiding their people as they should. Life is immune from isms; no one has the right to control the lives of others. Life is immune from past, present and future.

Germany — The sudden rise of right-wing extremism has come about because of the desperate plight of millions of unemployed people. However, it is not a political philosophy that will survive because it arose through the failures of the present politicians.

When a person has no work and therefore no money, no means to care for himself or his family, he is bound to revolt. The politicians were eager to take over East Germany for their own ends, but since then they have done nothing. They have allowed industries to collapse and unemployment to escalate. It is instinctive for people to fight to protect what they regard as their country and so the natural enemy to them are foreigners. The younger generation in particular are demanding that the rights of their country be defended. This is nationalism and should not be branded as fascism.

The politicians have used this situation to maintain control. The young are forced to move towards an ism. They are crying out for their rights.

The same pattern of reaction is happening in Britain where unemployment is destroying the harmony of so many people's lives, particularly the young. (Mar 1992)

A gradual process — A gradual process of unfoldment is taking place. Maitreya is appearing increasingly to more people, especially to politicians, who are puzzled. To them Maitreya says: "If you ride the big wave of your ideology and then land with a thump you will realize you cannot rule the masses with ideology. You cannot play with the lives of people."

"If you run after power you can derail yourself." (Apr 1992)

Contact with the people — Politicians cannot continue to bombard people with legislation and nothing else. A better way to rule must include real contact with real people. The needs of the people have to be addressed. Only then can they be educated in terms of self-respect, which leads to self-awareness. The values of the individual must be safeguarded. At present, there are few mechanisms of communication between leaders and the people. Nevertheless, contact 'on the ground' is necessary. If real needs are addressed, corruption will decrease, and the prison population will fall.

The true crisis of communication exists not only here in UK, but also in America.

No oil interests — Why is it that the United Nations is taking so long to intervene in Yugoslavia and the Eastern bloc to help put a stop to the suffering and dying? Why are they showing no interest in Somalia or the Third World?

Why didn't the American, British and other Western powers send in military forces to stop the Yugoslavian army from slaughtering innocent people? It is because they could not see any gain in doing so, unlike their need to protect their oil interests in Kuwait. They only evaluate humanity on a material level. (May 1992)

A civil war — The war in Yugoslavia has been called a civil war but this is really the butchery of humanity without even the rules of war. (Aug 1993)

RELIGIONS AND RELIGIOUS LEADERS

To the bishops — "The struggle to become bishops, etc, should end. Do not say you are becoming a bishop in the name of Jesus, when in fact you are doing it for yourself. Since you are not doing this for the Lord, the Lord cannot be with you."

Religious leaders — "Those who are supposed to spread My message and are in a position to serve the people have used their position to obtain personal comforts instead. What they have not wanted to do, they will have to do now."

For example, on 14 September 1988 the Pope was forced to make a brief, unscheduled visit to South Africa. His plane was diverted there due to bad weather. The Pope had wished to avoid a visit to South Africa. Causes beyond the weather forced the Pope to land in South Africa. South Africa is as much "a part of the Lord" as any other country. The way forward is not through confrontation. The effort must be made to seek agreement. Other situations will arise now such that the Pope will find himself "walking with the people". (Sep 1988)

Slums — Slums where human beings are made to live will be washed away. Churchmen will no longer simply sit in their churches. They will realize it is their duty to help house the people. (Jul 1988)

False prophets — False prophets are those who, surrounded by pomp and circumstance, protected by bodyguards, deny themselves contact with the people. A simple life, with the people, would make this unnecessary for the messenger of the Lord. The true messengers are those who work on the ground, with the people, eating with the people, healing and helping the people. The others have departed from the example of Jesus.

Who clings to power — Politicians are baffled because they cannot control the people with ideologies. But those who cling most to power are the religious authorities who believe 'there is only one way to go to heaven'. Yet how do these religious leaders live? What is their lifestyle? Perhaps that of kings: palaces, jets, bullet-proof cars. Krishna lived in a hut. This is true divinity. Likewise today, Sai Baba (an unequalled spiritual teacher in India) sleeps in a small room, in a simple bed.

The people who are frightened are those who are attached. There are religious leaders who are more attached to 'spiritual' power than politicians are to temporal power.

The Churches — The bishops and archbishops are having their old certainties shaken by doubts. The old biblical stories of the virgin birth and the resurrection are suddenly being questioned by them as they undergo experiences from Maitreya. They do not want to make it public, though, (apart from the UK Bishop of Durham, who recently openly expressed his doubts) in case they upset the politicians and members of their flocks. (May 1989)

The nearest and the furthest from Me — Maitreya points to the empty churches and observes that the young people are not interested in the old ideologies of their elders. He teaches that the moment a person gives up his brand of ism he will be free. "He will find that I am within him for I am free of all ideologies." Churches, mosques and temples will become meeting places as well as centres where those in need can be helped by others.

Fundamentalism and dogmatism are coming to an end. That time is quickly passing. "I have come to teach you not to cry out for Me. The gurus and religious fanatics cry out for Me and the end result is that they never know Me. You are not born in sin, as they insist on telling you. For I am with you and you are with Me."

"The nearest and dearest to Me are the people who do My work without reward. But so is the thief. Why? Because he does his work without knowing what will be its outcome. He has to fulfil his basic needs and so acts in the only way that he can. He does not set out to do anyone harm. He does not cry out for Me."

"The furthest from Me are the saints and gurus who have given up all the duties and responsibilities of life. They have closed their minds to the realities of life, and every day and night search for God, wanting to know Him, to find out where He lives, somewhere in Heaven. Outwardly, they appear sane and peaceful. Inwardly they are in chaos, crying inside in their desperate search for God."

Animal instincts — In the animal world, the stronger rule the weaker. Although the total sum of creation is in the human being, you can have the anger of a tiger; you can go around killing people. Saints think they have conquered their animal instincts, yet when they go into unknown regions they realize they are not immune.

Sai Baba stories: 1 — [Sathya Sai Baba is an internationally known Guru or spiritual teacher living near Bangalore, South

India. He has several million devotees around the world. Many see Him as a Divine Incarnation or Avatar.]

A party of American scientists, including a top nuclear physicist from Harvard University, visited Sai Baba in India.

They met Baba and said to Him: "We have read many books about you and heard many stories about you. You are called a divine being. If you are, then you must be able to do anything — such as making a rainbow in the sky. If you can do this, we will be convinced."

Baba smiled at these people, looked down and then raised His finger and said: "Look up."

They did and there was the rainbow shining in the sky. This happened in front of thousands of people who were also there to see Baba. What happened to these scientists? They became humble.

They are ready to come forward and talk about the truth they found. But the question remains: why do these things that Baba does in India not receive coverage in newspapers and the media elsewhere in the world? The answer is that the newspapers and magazines are controlled by people who are motivated by market forces. Stories about Baba are not important to them. (Feb 1990)

Sai Baba stories: 2 — There was a sick man who came to Sai Baba to be healed. He and his family joined thousands of others at Baba's ashram at Prasanthi Nilayam. For three days and nights they waited. The husband grew worse, but Sai Baba assured the man's wife that "everything will be all right". Then the man died. His wife and daughter continued to wait.

In the heat the body began to smell. Health officials appealed to the wife to let them remove the body but she refused, saying: "If He is God then He can bring him back to life."

At last Sai Baba appeared and the wife and daughter fell at His feet, weeping. Baba said: "Don't cry," and then He went into the room with the body and closed the door, leaving the women outside. A few minutes later, the door reopened and

Sai Baba called them in. Inside the room they found the 'dead' husband sitting up in bed, laughing and smiling.

If such a resurrection happened in the West, what would the reaction of people be? They would ask: "Where is God?" (Feb 1990)

Religions, the rungs on a ladder of evolution — The relation-ship between the Self and God is personal. This relationship is the process of becoming. A person's faith and trust in a religion or a philosophy are like the rungs on a ladder of evolution. As a person grows, so his beliefs change.

The relationship between the Self and God never changes. That is where the Supreme Being resides. The Self experiences that Supreme Being, which is eternal, in his heart.

Religions are the rungs of the ladder and he who is on the lowest rung can only experience what is in that sphere, but what you experience is not important, for only the heart is eternal.

Writers, philosophers, saints, swamis, priests and gurus are all standing on various rungs of the ladder and whatever they experience they should not try to impose on others. That is un-divine. They should not be obsessed by their beliefs and experiences, for if they cling to them they will be destroyed.

The religious Scriptures — The Self moves into and out of the mind, spirit and body at will and experiences the beauties of nature, beauties which until now were experienced only by yogis, saints and gurus. Traditionally, people believed that only through the sacred books of the Koran, the Bible, the Gita, and by living exceptionally good lives, could they qualify for such experiences. Not any more. As the Self learns to move through the mind, spirit and body these beautiful experiences can become a daily thing.

Religions have created strife, have conditioned people. This is coming to an end. From now on, schools, colleges and universities will help people discover where thoughts and ideas come from, that we are all connected to the Almighty and that we do not need scriptures to experience our true Selves.

Do not create barriers — "Do not give the people the impression that you are holy. If you do, you create barriers. You create in the mind the division between holy and unholy things. In creation, all is relative. What is good for you may not be good for others. If you parade yourselves as holy you are saying 'Only the good go to heaven; the bad go to hell.' "

Do not mislead others — Religious leaders, gurus and saints the world over are aware of Maitreya's question: "What have you done to distort the truth?"

They have no answer to this charge, for they have continually misled the people about the truths contained in the Bible, the Koran and the Bhagavad Gita. They have used their ideology to please their political masters and those who control market forces. Maitreya's message to them is: "Be what you are, and do not mislead others."

His message to ordinary people is simple: "Look within yourselves and you will find the true master in your heart. Ignore the emotional prejudices generated by the so-called spiritual leaders; they will lead you nowhere, except to self destruction.

"No one has the right to kill in the name of spirituality." "To know Me is to realize Me. There is no sacrifice involved of any kind."

Religious dogmatism — Jews from the Soviet Union, attempting to settle in parts of the Middle East, must not disturb the balance of power or create another time bomb between Arab and Jew. Israeli politicians are being made aware of these dangers and are now changing their policies to make sure that peace is preserved in their country and surrounding states.

Religious dogmatism, particularly in Iran, will lose its hold on the people. Many in that country are questioning the spiritual leaders who inspired them to fight a war in the name of their religion: "Why are our so-called enemies helping us now in our earthquake crisis?* What sort of leadership have you given us?"

Deep, fast moving changes are beginning to sweep through the Islamic states as the people become aware and realize that orders from above are false and misleading.

"To realize Me involves no sacrifice. One has to experience whatever is in creation. To understand and experience Me is the destiny of everyone. The gurus, saints and religious leaders who talk in terms of sacrifice to realize the Lord are not speaking the Truth. To know Me is not to sacrifice one's self. To know Me is to realize one's Self."

Those Middle Eastern teachers who tell people to kill, kill, kill in the name of Allah are totally misleading their people. God does not need sacrifice. He does not need pleasing, or charity or compassion. He does not need people to be 'good'.

God says: "I am neither good nor bad, this or that. I am everything. Why have heaven and hell? Enough is enough." (Jun 1990)

[*Referring to the help extended by Iraq to the Iranian earthquake victims.]

Understanding Islam — "Allah made it very clear that you should work together, share together. This is a basic principle in the Koran. If you have anything in excess, share it among your fellows, who are your brothers and sisters."

Another important principle made clear to Muslims is that no interest on capital should ever be charged to anyone.

"If you do this, you will defile the Islamic faith and you will destroy the individual, the country and the nation. This is the root cause of sufferings and evils in the world. If the Koranic principles are observed by individuals and nations there is no seed for war.

If the wealth of nation and country remains within the country, the nation enjoys health and wealth. But if you take the wealth abroad your brothers and sisters suffer because there is no material wealth, and this leads to chaos and ultimate war.

"Be what you are. If you are a Christian, be a Christian; if you are a Jew, be a Jew; if you are an Arab, be an Arab, but do not try to impose on yourself a foreign personality because if you do that you are destroying yourself."

Islamic fundamentalism — Islamic fundamentalism has awakened in the Middle East. There is no place for it in politics, for the people can be enslaved by this ideology. It will give them no freedom; it is no solution to their problems.

"I bless the poison and the nectar with equanimity. I am on the side of neither Yes nor No. I do not participate in situations. When you are at the bottom of the mountain, what do you see? You see the diversities of the mountain. But when you view it from the peak, everything looks the same. You are not goaded by religion or politics, for you view all with equal detachment." (Mar 1991)

Working together, sharing together — Whatever your leaders are doing to you, to your nation and country, eventually they will have to admit that they have wasted precious time, and they will have to work together and share together.

When people are exhausted, when there is a lull, when there is despair, argument subsides. People recognize futility and look for God's guidance. Then they will try to rebuild their lives. These are cyclical happenings in life.

Do not teach with attachment — If you teach with attachment you create a 'forced' enjoyment of habit and ritual. "When you see Me, you will know I am within you and the struggle will end. Even if you are living in a cottage you will not envy someone living in a palace."

Religious leaders — The Pope should stand up and speak out against any war in the Gulf. He should remind the politicians about the teachings of Christ — to love one's neighbour as oneself.

Similarly, Muslim religious teachers should question why Saudi Arabia, the defender of Islam, has called in foreign armies to fight to fulfil the desires of politicians. (Jan 1991)

The duty of spiritual leaders — It is the duty of spiritual leaders, including those in the Church, to help politicians realize the truth: life is about implementing spiritual values. Individuals are becoming dehumanized in the name of politics.

Joining the club — "By joining 'the club' you cannot achieve freedom and salvation." However, both political and religious people say: "Either you join my club, or you are out."

CHAPTER FIVE

HISTORICAL PERSPECTIVES

PROCESS OF MIDDLE EAST CRISIS (1988-1993)

Iraq — There has been so much suffering in that country. It is time for Hussein to step down. If he doesn't do so voluntarily someone else will make sure that he does. It is inevitable.

Anyone who rules by force will be removed by force. (Apr 1990)

Kuwait — The Iraqis will pull out of Kuwait. Kuwait will then be returned to the people, who will decide on the formation of the government. The time of Royal dynasties, running the country for themselves, is over. The new Kuwaiti people's government will be a model for the Gulf states as well, for the time of sultans, kings and sheikhs running those countries as their own playthings is at an end. There is no need to worry about the Western hostages in Kuwait for they will come to no harm.

In future the oil as a resource will not belong to any one country but to the world. President Saddam Hussein has been given a clear signal that it is time for him to step down. If he does not, he will be pushed. (Aug 1990)

Saddam Hussein's action in invading Kuwait did not happen out of the blue. The Western powers and their Middle Eastern brothers gave Saddam billions to fight and kill Iranians. These same people withdrew assistance from him and eventually refused to raise the price of oil so that his economy would suffer more. Iraq's economy was in turmoil. "An inevitable process is at work here: if there is no food in the house you will go elsewhere to get it." When Saddam Hussein asked for help to restore his shattered economy at home, those who had supported him should have helped. (Sep 1990)

Even now it is not too late to avert disaster. If an international package is organized to support the economy of Iraq, a mystical power and force in nature will make Iraq withdraw totally and unconditionally from Kuwait. Thus, without firing another bullet, without taking another hostage, the same ends are secured.

Maitreya's message is: "Work together, share together. If you make your neighbours starve, the time will come when you must face equally serious problems."

Your first duty in life is to feed your physical body. To starve it is the biggest crime in life. "I am with everyone. When you fight, you fight Me." (Sep 1990)

The Gulf crisis, a milestone — This is a milestone in the history of humanity. The crisis has brought countries closer together in a bid to resolve the threat of war created by Iraq's invasion of Kuwait. Until now, politicians everywhere doubted that they had the ability to co-operate on such a scale. Suddenly, they realize they have the potential to bring about changes in the world by acting together.

The top priority from now on must be a sharing of the world's resources and wealth. At last an international will has been generated that will not allow the peoples to die of starvation. (Sep 1990)

Saddam Hussein — The Iraqi leader is not as bad as he is painted by the Western media. He is a man with a generous heart and for that reason he was inspired to meet the hostage children face to face. Immediately things changed for the hostages. He was made aware of the vulnerability of the women and children and that is why they were released. He is also being made aware that it is against the sacred law to invade another country. He is being told that he must leave Kuwait without further destruction. He will quietly hand Kuwait back to the people.

Hussein is not alone in receiving experiences. The American generals in the desert were feeling very excited — 'high', as if on drugs — surrounded by all their arms and ammunition. They felt as if they could conquer the world. On the other side of the border the Iraqis knew that the American forces were more powerful. But one thing strengthened them. They knew that if America invaded Iraq they would be defending their country and for that they were prepared to die. The truth for them was that, in order to preserve their identity, they would be ready to sacrifice their lives.

The Americans, however, were only there to preserve their oil supplies. A high-ranking general was suddenly made aware of this and he began to think that this war, if it came, would not bring happiness or peace but only destruction. He began to talk to his fellow officers and men. He said that, in the interests of humanity, they should act sensibly and not be too hasty. These comments soon reached Washington and began to cause panic. This led to Mr Bush calling Mr Gorbachev. Suddenly, there was a backing away from the brink of war.

The Masters are keeping a careful watch on the Gulf situation. Their presence is affecting people and events. (Sep 1990)

[Note: We are informed by Maitreya's associate that President Bush has sent an envoy to Maitreya informing Him that the Americans do not want war, and presumably asking for His advice.] (Oct 1990)

Soldiers are puzzled — The soldiers facing each other across the desert front line are puzzled now. They are beginning to feel a sense of futility in all this warmongering. The war scenario is being created to divert people from the huge problems at home caused by the failure of the politicians. The people of Iraq and Kuwait do not want to fight because they do not have the means to survive.... "When they asked for help, they were turned down. So the Iraqis stole to survive." They had asked for $2,000 million but were refused. "How much more in money and human misery is the resulting crisis going to cost? A hundred times?"

"There will be no war as a result of the corruption and deceit of the politicians because I am among you. So far I have been acting behind the scenes, with My hands concealed, in order to give room to those in authority to change their ways and to serve the will of the people. But now the time is imminent when I will have to raise My hand so that people can converge on Me and look towards Me for guidance." (Sep 1990)

Members of family — Middle Eastern countries are like members of the same family. There can be fights between brothers and sisters, but they are temporary. Afterwards they will get together and forget their differences. In such a situation, the Americans will be 'the odd man out'.

In the United States, the fear is that if it does not retain direct or indirect control of Middle Eastern oilfields its whole economy will sustain various setbacks. (Sep 1990)

Arab culture — The process of haves and have-nots in the Middle East continues, but it only came to the forefront against the background of outside cultures penetrating the fabric of the Middle Eastern way of life. Maitreya says: "An Arab is supposed to be an Arab, with an Arab culture, an Arab background. The masses remain Arab. The rulers lead a double life. This means that at home they show they are Arabs. Abroad they identify with non-Arabs. This process guarantees a type of aura which makes one fall apart.

"Look at the Sheikhs. They tell their people they defend and nurture their countries with the Arab way of life. But what have they done?" The wealth of the nations has been spent on arms, on personal luxuries and investments abroad, while the masses struggle for existence. The conflict in the Middle East is not the result only of Saddam Hussein's actions. It was already in the offing.

Maitreya says to these rulers: "It is time for you to go. Government will be by the people and for the people. The wealth of the nation is for the nation. If the nation is deprived of its health and wealth, it will rise up."

Maitreya has made it clear to various Middle Eastern rulers that although they have tried to involve the Americans, the consequences spell disaster. Even if war takes place, there will ultimately be no sultans, emirs or sheikhs continuing to rule as they do now.

Everywhere, the politicians are frightened. The people will begin to ask questions about the billions spent on arms, which should have been spent on the people. (Sep 1990)

The Gulf crisis — Western politicians talk of defending democracy, but there is none in the Middle East, only totalitarian states ruled by kings and sheikhs. The Saudis and the Kuwaitis are having second thoughts as they begin to realize the consequences of a war with Iraq. Put simply, there would be no more kings and sheikhs. Instead, they must sit down and think about spending their wealth on their own people.

Maitreya is appearing before many influential people in the Middle East to inspire them. This is leading to powerful voices coming out in favour of a settlement. The United Nations must not be used to paper over cracks in the alliance; it should not become a political tool. Its role is to look after the welfare of the peoples of the world.

Shortly, you will see the Saudis shaking the hands of their Arab neighbours, the Jordanians, Iranians and Iraqis, in the name of Allah. America has to realize that Kuwait is not another Vietnam. A completely different solution is called for. No one can afford a war in the Middle East. (Oct 1990)

Maitreya will intervene — President George H. Bush has realized that ideological warfare in the Middle East will not solve anything. He has been made aware of the facts, namely that there is no democracy in any of the Middle Eastern countries. He has been made to realize that the will of the people must form the constitution of any country and thus his support of sheikhs and kings is doomed. If he continues to support them, a fight is inevitable. In fact, a fight is just around the corner. It could break out at any moment. But it will not be a full-fledged war because of the intervention of Maitreya. The moment the American and British people become aware of the casualties, the fighting will have to cease and the politicians will have to answer for their actions.

President Bush has also been made aware that Israel, too, has nuclear and chemical weapons and that they intend to use them if they are attacked by the Iraqis. Maitreya asks the UN what action they are going to take regarding these weapons. (Nov 1990)

The United Nations — The UN resolution to sanction military action against Iraq has been brought about by politicians whose self-interest and ambitions are creating chaos and confusion instead of peace. Their actions will be self-destructive. The UN has been converted into a political football game.

Maitreya has given a warning to the assembled armies in the Gulf region that they should look to their sophisticated weapons and make sure that they function. The chances that many of them will prove deficient are high. Ordinary people have been made aware of the reasons for preparing for this war. There is only one — oil. (Nov 1990)

Hostages — Many influential public figures from the West who have travelled to Baghdad to appeal for the release of hostages* have been inspired to do so by Maitreya Himself. (Nov 1990)

[*The Iraqi government freed the first 100 of the British hostages on 10 December 1990 after four-and-a half months, and the rest of the 400 followed later.]

The Sheikh of Kuwait — The Sheikh of Kuwait sat in his Saudi Arabian palace, wondering how to goad the Americans into attacking the Iraqis and get them out of his country.

Suddenly his brother appeared — except that it was Maitreya appearing through his brother's form. Maitreya asked him what he was going to do with the billions of dollars he had invested in America. Surely it should be spent on helping his countrymen and his brother Arabs. The Sheikh answered that, yes, he had been wrong not to have used the money in that way.

Then Maitreya asked him why he had not lent President Hussein the $2 billion he had asked for before the invasion. "Yes," answered the Sheikh, "that was a mistake. I lost my country."

"Why not offer the Iraqis double that — $4 billion — to leave your country? You could even go to the Saudis and ask them to come forward with a loan as well, as it is obvious they do not want a war," suggested Maitreya, speaking as the Sheikh's brother.

The Sheikh thought that this was good advice but believed the Americans would not trust Hussein to fulfil any promise of withdrawal. If they left, what was to prevent the Iraqis from invading again?

"In that case," said Maitreya, "we should ask the Arab League to resolve the problem. They would act as arbiters to ensure that any treaties were kept." The Sheikh thought this was an excellent idea.

He was somewhat taken aback when he later spoke to his brother who denied ever having had the conversation. (Nov 1990)

President George H. Bush — He does not want a war in the Gulf. His actions will not match his words. Everything will be dragged out to avoid a final military confrontation. (Dec 1990)

Middle East — Rapid changes are taking place. For the first time the Saudi royal family is having second thoughts about the Gulf war as they realize that it will threaten their position. Once the people become aware that they have been led into fighting their brothers and sisters to preserve the status of sheikhs, kings and sultans, they will turn against the rulers.

Palestinians will have their homeland. Lebanon will be reconstructed. Throughout the Middle East there will be a new atmosphere of brotherliness in Allah, in Christianity. Politicians have sensed this new atmosphere and are now prepared to sit down and resolve their problems. (Dec 1990)

Defence is not attack — Some resolutions on the Middle East which have been passed by the Security Council of the United Nations have been fostered by egotistic warmongers.

The military will be told: You are important. You can defend the sacredness of your nation. This is a divine duty, the will of the Lord, not politics. Therefore, the soldier who serves respecting the will of the Lord fulfils his duty. This is indeed a different thing from warmongering. Defence is not attack. (Dec 1990)

Given the large quantity of arms and ammunition amassed in Saudi Arabia, the soldiers are training day and night. The minds of the soldiers are at war, and their physical bodies are moving with the mind. Maitreya asks: "The day war does not take place and the armies are sent home, do you think all the soldiers will return home in a sane state?"

Some men will go berserk, fall prey to a criminal mentality; they will find themselves killing and shooting people in the street.

Having fought, under orders, they often fall prey to depression and other mental effects when they return home. They are changed by the karmic effects of the actions in battle.

Any fighting in the Middle East will be brief. (Dec 1990)

Threat of war diffused — The threat of war in the Middle East is being diffused. Politicians are wondering how this has happened. Everyone will try to save face by sitting round the negotiating table now. There is no other way out. (Jan 1991)

Political survival — The politicians know that if there is a war few of them would survive politically. This includes President George H. Bush. "Are you prepared to face catastrophic destruction?" (Jan 1991)

Frightening scenario — Those who can look intelligently ahead see a very black future in the aftermath of a war:

- Kingdoms and sheikhdoms would come to an end.
- Survival would become very difficult for millions of people. The destruction would make parts of the

world a dark place for 40 to 50 years because of the poisons released into the atmosphere; the planet would become much hotter.

- Life in many areas would be killed off.
- There would be widespread famine. (Jan 1991)

The role of scientists — Scientists are advising the politicians who are now thinking twice before taking action. There is a terrifying scenario in the minds of scientists and some politicians who are working very hard behind the scenes. (Jan 1991)

The Gulf conflict — The world's politicians and leaders (including Saddam) have been whipping up the emotions of their people to follow and support them on the battlefield of Kuwait. But when that conflict ends, the people will realize the chaos and suffering this warmongering has created and deep disillusion will set in.

Once this happens there will be no hiding place for these politicians from the anger of the ordinary people. They will want to know why they have been lied to and misled into such destruction.

Meanwhile, the world is experiencing extremes of weather as a direct result of the violence taking place in the Gulf.

The atmosphere is going 'haywire' over the deserts of this region and we shall see extremes of heat and cold with very wet and windy climatic conditions. (Feb 1991)

After the Gulf conflict — After the Gulf conflict there will follow a peaceful scenario. Eventually, even Israel will make peace, for they will have their right to exist recognized by their Arab neighbours. They will live as brothers and sisters and the Palestinians will have their own homeland.

In the West, Christian principles will be awakened by Maitreya and we shall see the end of the grip of market forces. People will begin to work together and share together. (Feb 1991)

Syria — Why do you think the Syrians have dispatched their troops to the Gulf? "It is not to fight brother Arabs but to make sure that the Israelis do not take advantage of the situation by annexing even more of Jordan." (Nov 1990)

Iran's new role — At the beginning of the Middle East war, when people were involved in fighting and heavy bombardment, no one wanted to play the role of peace broker. Then a major spiritual leader of Iran, an old man, heard a voice urging him "to awaken the Islamic constitution in the name of Allah". He heard this twice. He looked around and saw no one.

Then Maitreya appeared to him, dressed in white, and told him: "In the name of Islam, let there be peace." The Iranian spiritual leader spoke to his colleagues and inspired them. Now the Iranians are speaking both to the Iraqis and Americans.

The Iranians are discussing the Palestinians' problems. Maitreya reaffirms that the Palestinians will have their homeland and the Iraqis will withdraw from Kuwait. This will be done with dignity. You will find that the Americans and the Iraqis will shake hands; each will return home.

The American government is not a warmonger all the time. But to achieve peace, there must be a place in politics for human dignity.

The Iranians are working under the inspiration of Maitreya. The Iraqis will respect their efforts, as will the United Nations. (Feb 1991)

The West and the Middle East — "The nature of the person cannot be changed; it is given by the Lord. The Constitution of Islam has been awakened in the Middle East. It will become a very strong force. There is no room for Western politics in the Middle East." America and Britain cannot impose solutions. It is time for the West to leave the Middle East. "Serve your own Western homelands with honesty, sincerity and detachment. Only then will there be peace."

Maitreya says to the Western politicians: "Look after your own nations. Observe the changes around the world. You

cannot teach prosperity abroad when there is none at home."
(Mar 1991)

Saddam Hussein — Saddam Hussein recently experienced a
powerful vision of Maitreya. He was sitting in his bunker when
Maitreya appeared to him and told him that from now on he
must work for peace in the Islamic world.

The President agreed that he would work for peace as long
as it could be achieved with justice. We will see things change
now; President Hussein will talk about peace in the Islamic
world. The whole pattern of events is changing.

Once the President agreed to work for peace, Maitreya told
him: "I will lead you." We will see steps being taken to
achieve a peaceful settlement. People will begin working
together in the Middle East in such a way that will surprise
everyone.

Maitreya also made it clear to Saddam Hussein that every
nation is sacred and that he must hand Kuwait back to its
people. (Feb 1991)

Maitreya appeared (again) to Saddam Hussein and asked
him: "What have you done?" Saddam replied: "Allah forgive
me." Maitreya said: "Had you respected the Constitution of
Islam, this would not have happened." Saddam asked: "What
can I do?" Maitreya replied: "The time has come for you to
stop the war and get out of politics."

Maitreya says: "I will defend the people. I will guide the
people." (Mar 1991)

The Gulf war: no victor or victory — Maitreya has said that
there is no victor or victory in the Gulf war.
Soldiers, too, are suffering. (May 1991)

The Kurds — The aggressive act of Iraq has in fact awakened
the people of that region. Already the power of the spiritual
leaders of Iran has been greatly weakened. The people have

become aware that wars are futile and are not carried out for the benefit of the people.

Saddam Hussein is genuine in his treaty with the Kurds, granting them self-rule. The Kurdish state will flourish.

It is a prospect that is already disturbing the Iranians and the Turks who do not want to see a successful, independent Kurdish state. They will try to foment trouble between the Kurds and the Iraqis, but they will not succeed. (Jun 1991)

Arrival of democracy — We will begin to see the arrival of democracy: government by the people for the people. The sheikhs and sultans are being exposed to this new force and it is only a matter of time before they give in or are swept away. (Jul 1991)

The process of change within Iraq — Swami: "Master, when the war took place in Iraq, with the consent of the United Nations, a lot of destruction set in. Even the elements of nature have been disturbed. There is also no clean water. Why did things stop at a certain point? They could easily have got rid of Saddam Hussein. Surely, without someone's intervention, the war would not have stopped then. It was not difficult."

Maitreya: "Both sides were in the wrong. The opposer was wrong and the defender was wrong. But I am making both of them realize that I am looking after one and all. They got rid of arms. What is important — the arms or the life?"

Politicians made a blunder in terms of the extent of human suffering.

Maitreya asked Saddam Hussein: "For whom did you do these things? For yourself?"

Hussein: "I am doing this for my people."

Maitreya: "Are they suffering, or are they happy?"

Hussein: "They are suffering."

Maitreya: "You did these things because you wanted to rule them."

Hussein: "There is something within me which makes me do these things. I want to be out of it."

Is there any newspaper reporting at the moment that Saddam Hussein will step down? No. Yet Iraq is preparing government by the people, for the people. And Hussein is going to step down gracefully. He realized he had within him the personification of being a ruler, which goaded him. Now, he wants to practise at the feet of the Master.

"Look at the UN. Has anybody reported this [ie the process of change within Iraq]? If this is reported, all evil designs will fail. These designs include the division of Iraq into four parts. This will not happen. The identity of a nation is sacred, just as the identity of an individual is sacred. In your lifetime, your identity will never be tarnished." (Nov 1991)

Saddam Hussein — Shortly, the President of Iraq will be forced to step down and allow the people to take charge of the country's destiny through democratic elections. It is time for him to obey the free will of the people.

Since that free will is abused, events will occur which will force him to obey. (Jan 1992)

President Saddam Hussein is no longer the man portrayed in the Western media. He has had more experiences of "Allah" and says that he respects His wishes and that he will turn the tide of events towards peace and brotherliness. (Mar 1992)

Saddam, a figurehead — The Middle Eastern countries are spiritually bankrupt. The Saudis and the Kuwaitis promised their own people democracy, government for the people, by the people, so they do not want to get involved in another war against Iraq, for example.

Saddam's days in power are numbered. His power is monopolized by people around him; they have him as a figurehead. Very smoothly, he will step down. All Middle Eastern governments are struggling to survive. (Jul 1992)

Iraq and Iran — Despite the fact that this war has dragged on for seven years with, apparently, no end in sight, a compromise will be reached between these two countries.

There are spiritual leaders in Iran who are beginning to seek solutions that will lead ultimately to a less harsh religious climate, and to peace being restored. (Apr 1988)

Terry Waite — Everyone will be heartened by Maitreya's forecast here. Mr Waite, who was kidnapped in Beirut in January 1987, will be freed soon. (Jun 1988)

The release of Terry Waite — Despite the fact that the shooting down of the Iranian airbus by the Americans contributed to a delay in the release of hostages held in Beirut, Terry Waite's release is imminent. (Oct 1988)

Middle East hostages — The focus now is on Terry Waite and his fellow hostages. Very soon, they will be released. They are on their way out of captivity. Maitreya reminds us that Mrs Thatcher has done nothing for them; she has only sat on the fence. The British government should have engaged in diplomatic talks with countries like Iran and others, and not relinquished their responsibilities on the grounds that they do not believe in dealing with terrorists. But Maitreya is demonstrating that we should not always be dependent on politics for peaceful coexistence. Humanity is greater than politics. (Feb 1990)

[Note: Terry Waite was freed by the Islamic extremists on 18 November 1991, following the release of other fellow hostages who had been released in August and September.]

The Effect of the Gulf Crisis on Israel

Israel — The generals are beginning to say that the politicians have misled them.

Maitreya is giving experiences to many political and religious leaders around the world, particularly in areas of conflict such as Israel. (Sep 1989)

Soldiers — In Lebanon, soldiers are realizing the war must end. Both Syria and Israel must (and eventually will) withdraw to their own borders.

Recently an Israeli soldier patrolling the street in the occupied territories raised his gun when children began to throw stones. He was about to fire when suddenly he saw his own face in the face of the children. He wondered whether he was hallucinating. The children disappeared. He walked back to his colleagues and said: "I don't want to fight any more."

Soldiers in Israel are telling their officers: "Enough is enough." Maitreya says: "You cannot fight. You must sit together and respect each other's boundaries, personality and right to exist as a nation. Everyone has a duty to respect these duties and responsibilities."

Maitreya is making soldiers realize they are fighting a futile battle. The day is not far off when politicians will sit together and sort things out, as is beginning to happen in South Africa. This process of reconciliation is gathering speed. (Mar 1990)

[Note: Israel pulled all its troops out of southern Lebanon on 24 May 2000, ending a 22-year military presence there.]

Russian Jews — It is a myth that hundreds of thousands of Russian Jews will settle in Israel. Most Russian Jews will remain in Russia.

Some intellectuals will go, because Israel needs intellectuals to guide the nation. If Israel renounces those politicians who are creating chaos, it will prosper. Every people will have its nation and motherland. This is true for Palestinians also. (May 1990)

An effect of the Gulf crisis — The crisis over Kuwait has created a healthy situation in international politics in which the winds of change are blowing away old attitudes and dogmas. International pressure, for instance, will force the Israelis and the Palestinians to find a solution to their old conflict. As a result, there will be created a homeland for the Palestinian people. The Israeli government will have no choice but to agree to seek such a solution. (Aug 1990)

The USA and President Bush

The US general election — Maitreya's comments about the US general election on 9 November 1988 are: "Landslides are finished now." The winning party will have a small majority. Left and right, liberals and conservatives, will be brought towards the centre now. The energy of equilibrium which has been released in the world will maintain a balance between right and left. "To have a harmonious state where you can enjoy peace and prosperity, you have to observe the centre point."

This applies to any act in life. In any station or action in life, follow this principle and enjoy peace, prosperity and happiness.

Many miracles will occur in the USA, such as healings and visions of the Lord (experienced by people in prison, psychiatric institutions, educational institutions, the armed forces and political circles). Politicians will suddenly change their tone. Positive feelings will spread.

People are initially silent about such experiences. At first, they are taken aback. They hold that experience as sacred. They will speak only to those who can understand it. But as "the aura of communication develops" and people become able to communicate with each other, an ever-widening circle begins to hear about these experiences. People will speak openly now. (Nov 1988)

Mr George H. Bush — He has declared another war — this time against Colombian drug bandits — in order to attract public attention to himself to show he is still the US President. Mr Bush was warned about the problem of drugs on the streets of America back in 1982, when he was Vice-President. Why did he not do something about it then? This latest war is between politicians and drug barons — in other words, it is about power. (Sep 1989)

Broken promises — President Bush's broken promises not to increase taxes will create national friction which will lead to more unemployment and drug problems. Individual state authorities will press for independence from central government control. (Jun 1990)

A Democrat to become the President — The President knows his days are numbered and is using the UN and the Gulf crisis to win popularity. A Democrat will become the next President of America. (Nov 1990)

President G.H. Bush — Despite his so-called victory in Iraq, the President realizes that at home he has failed to solve the massive social and economic problems of America. With another election coming into sight he will try to divert the American public's attention. (Oct 1991)

General Colin Powell — The Commander-in-Chief of the US Army will soon resign. This is because of an experience that his young grandson has had of Maitreya. One morning recently the General's grandson came to him and asked: "What did you gain by killing the poor children of Iraq?" According to the associate, the General was stunned by his grandson's question and went to his wife demanding to know who had put him up to it. She had no idea, and said she was sure it wasn't his school. General Powell then asked his grandson why he had asked such a question. The child told him that at night he had seen a man in a white cloak who had played with him and talked to him. He said he felt as if he was living in heaven. Then he told his grandfather: "I could see babies being killed and hurt by the bombs and their mothers running and screaming. That's why I asked you the question."

Maitreya had given the little boy a vision of what happened in Iraq in the name of democracy, said the associate. At the moment, General Powell is undergoing a painful process of self-questioning, but soon he will step down from office. He will become a firm believer in Christ and spread the teachings in whatever way he can. (Oct 1991)

UK: Fall of the Thatcher Government

Mrs Thatcher — Despite Mrs Thatcher's recent statement in a London *Times* interview that she would go on to a fourth term of office, Maitreya repeats that she will leave office and make way for "younger blood". The man who will take over as Prime Minister at that point "will be working to heal the wounds she has created as a result of her policies. He will galvanize the country to bring it 'towards the centre'." (Nov 1988)

Cabinet reshuffle — Mrs Thatcher's reshuffle of her ministers shows the same instinctive reaction to danger as a chameleon — she simply changes colour. In the case of the Department of the Environment, the change is to a more sympathetic, greener-looking politician than the previous incumbent who was creating much hostility in the country. But it changes nothing. All her policies have failed. We still have politicians who have been brought up on the idea that life is about divisions, yes and no, good and bad. But life is not like that. All the colours have to be in harmony.

This divisive art of politics has come to an end and a new one that respects harmony, will soon succeed. How else can you explain the emergence of the Green Party with such devastating success in recent elections? Once despised, they are now receiving much attention as they bring urgent issues to public debate. (Aug 1989)

Political priorities — Mrs Thatcher has been made aware that she cannot solve the problems of the people by the pursuit of market forces. There is little point in spending money on hospitals which should be spent on education. If people are made fit enough to face life through a proper education they won't end up sick in hospital or locked up in prison because they cannot cope.

She has become isolated; her political philosophy is obviously failing her now. There is no place for her in the new political atmosphere which is dominating the world. (Feb 1990)

Revolt — Mrs Thatcher will not survive the revolt against the poll tax. There will be confusion and chaos. People will take to the streets in crescendo. Government will be brought down by the poll tax; it has no way out. No amount of manipulation will make any difference. The boat is sinking for the UK government. She exists like a robot in the political world looking left and right for support. In the new political systems, Mrs Thatcher has no place. The new mode will not suit her thinking. (Mar 1990)

The poll tax will eventually be withdrawn and replaced with a combined property- and income-related tax. (Apr 1990)

The British leadership — Mr Major, the new British Prime Minister, will not last long. The people around him are too devious for him to survive. Mr Major is a simple politician compared to the grey-suited men who manipulate power behind the scenes. His election is a stepping stone to a probable Labour victory in the next General Election.

When they realized that the boat was about to sink, the "men in grey suits" decided to ditch Mrs Thatcher, but Mr Major's 'honeymoon' period as Prime Minister will be short lived. The failures and failings of the policies inspired by the right wing of the Conservative Party continue.

Mrs Thatcher has always been true to herself, has always believed in herself, and that was her strength. The boat is sinking, and even with her sacrifice it will continue to sink.

Meanwhile, the Labour Party cannot afford to be complacent. The successful party will have to present a policy that blends the best elements of socialism and capitalism. There has to be equilibrium between the two.

As a result of an experience given to Mrs Thatcher as she stood on the steps of No.10 Downing Street for the last time, we shall see a different woman in the future. (Nov 1990)

Spending on the war — The UK is spending £13 million per week on weaponry and soldiers in the Middle East. If this amount were spent on the homeless, the cardboard boxes they are forced to live in on the street would disappear overnight. (Dec 1990)

Public protest — As the (Gulf) war deadline approaches, there will be public protest and revolt. In the UK, people will refuse to join the war effort and there will be calls for politicians to resign. (Jan 1991)

Treason — "You cannot destroy nations through ideological warfare. It is treason not to defend your own country, but it is not treason not to fight for others in this situation." Maitreya says to the politicians: "You can fight, but I am the defender of the people."

As the deadline (to go to war) approaches, politicians will 'hide'. To 'hide' means to go quiet, to avoid public statements. (Jan 1991)

Conservatives will lose — Mr Major will not survive in the present hostile atmosphere; the quagmires of politics are so thick and smothering. He will be replaced. This 'takeover' will prompt an election. This time, the Conservatives will lose. Nevertheless, Labour cannot win outright and the Liberals cannot win on their own. The Liberals flourish because they are not straightjacketing the nation in fixed values of life. The Tories have straightjacketed the haves; Labour has straightjacketed the have-nots.

The have-nots have remained on, and below, the breadline. What exists now is a confrontation. Politics is the art of uniting diverse cultures, beliefs, modes of life — not of destroying them. (Sep 1993)

Mr Gorbachev and the USSR

The USSR — Maitreya has appeared to leaders in the USSR. The Russians and the Americans will agree to destroy nuclear weapons. This process, as we know, has already begun, and will continue. (Apr 1988)

Mr Gorbachev — An attempt will be made on Gorbachev's life and he will survive it. The problem here is the pace of evolution. To force the pace of life in society is dangerous. "In the process of being open, do not dig up the past. Let bygones

170

be bygones." In the USSR, people are "opening the graveyard" of those who have died. This process invites trouble because the forces that created those past conditions are being invited back. Therefore chaos and struggle ensue. There are representatives in the armed forces of the USSR who are watching the situation very closely. Gorbachev is in a delicate position and ultimately he will be replaced. The best way forward is to harmonize the opposing forces (which can be called positive and negative); you then create energy. There must be an attempt to reach a consensus; thus both forces lose their unnaturalness. Whatever is natural remains. Otherwise, you replant the seeds of destruction. The difficulties inherent in this process can also be observed in Poland. (Aug 1988)

The opposition waits — Recently Gorbachev replaced much of the 'old guard' in government. By excluding the old guard you do not do away with the opposition. This opposition now waits, "like a snake", for the opportunity to create some havoc. "Exclusion is not freedom." It is necessary to include, to persuade, to debate and to discuss. Despite the fact that Gorbachev will ultimately be replaced, the process of glasnost, of openness, though somewhat slowed down, will nevertheless continue. (Oct 1988)

[Note: 19 August 1991 a coup was attempted by various members of the Soviet government who disliked Soviet leader Mikhail Gorbachev's move toward more democratic policies. Gorbachev survived.]

Unleashed consumerism — The Russian capital now has to contend with hooligans and drugs. To unleash consumerism, to permit an excessive struggle for possessions, leads to destruction. Russia wants transformation, but to force the pace creates more problems.

A much broader consensus that will clarify aims will eventually lead the USSR out of its present difficulties. (Nov 1988)

Soviet Union: Growing confusion — The Soviet Union is facing a growing crescendo of corruption, chaos and confusion, much of which is not being reported. The people are being freed from the bondage of the past by the policies of openness. However, it is like letting a deadly snake loose from a basket.

True openness does not lie in trying to copy the West. Despite democracy are they any happier? Is there less violence and confusion? True happiness lies not in democracy or communism, but in an awareness that is free of any ideology. It will not be long before Soviet politicians change their minds about the current thinking on openness. (Apr 1989)

The three aims — "I have come to teach three things in life: honesty, sincerity and detachment." If Mr Gorbachev had applied these, the process of change in the USSR would have been gradual, and the interdependence of the various regions would have been emphasized. (Jan 1990)

Opening of Soviet society — Mr Gorbachev has been 'helped' to open up Soviet society. It is a time to do away with the rigidities of communism, and he will have his way. There will be a lot of confusion behind closed doors. Eventually Mr Gorbachev will go as nationalist strife, for which he will be blamed, increases. He allowed the 'deadly snake' of freedom loose from its basket before the people were ready. It was the right thing to do, but at the wrong time. (Feb 1990)

Unleashing freedom— Mr Gorbachev is now experiencing the problems created by unleashing freedom within the country and they are weakening his position. Freeing a state within the Soviet Union is not freedom. People may call it nationalism but they are deceiving themselves. It is a road to selfishness and destruction. (May 1990)

Soon, the Baltic states will get their independence but will agree that defence and the economy be controlled by central government. (May 1990)

The republics — The republics will be granted the freedom to manage their domestic affairs; only defence and the economy will be left in the hands of central government. Mr Gorbachev will abandon his idea of copying the Western approach to solving his problems.

China, Japan, the Soviet Union and Eastern Europe are undergoing fast changes which will create stability and security in the world. (Jun 1990)

Internal problems — The Soviet Union faces enormous internal problems. If the leaders do not resolve these problems they face massive revolutions within the country. There would be the creation of states within states. Chaos would reign, the strong would dominate and persecute the weak; it would be like a lawless Wild West, where the only law would be the gun and the word of the rich man. (Oct 1990)

Anarchy — Mr Gorbachev now realizes his mistake in believing that he could thrust 'freedom' on to the Soviet people. There is a possibility that the Army may have to move in to prevent widespread anarchy. The situation is chronically fraught with public disobedience which only the military will be able to control. (Nov 1990)

Mr Gorbachev will be ousted — He will be ousted. The Soviet leader has failed to understand the true meaning of freedom. This did not simply mean opening up Soviet society to market forces, for these by themselves lead only to destruction and the dehumanization of people. (Dec 1990)

Gorbachev — Gorbachev has completed his work; he has fulfilled his role. He will go gracefully at the appropriate time. He will keep a ceremonial or symbolic position. (Aug 1991)

Nuclear weapons — Russia will not have the power over the control and use of the Soviet nuclear weapons. This will be administered by a central authority under the leadership of Mr Gorbachev. (Sep 1991)

Boris Yeltsin — The present Russian leader, Boris Yeltsin, will be replaced. Both the CIA and elements in the Russian military want him to go. He is viewed as dangerous and in some ways akin to Stalin. He is trying to rule dictatorially in the name of openness.

Gorbachev will be inspired to remain available for a post related to the newly created Commonwealth of former Soviet Republics. This post may well include overseeing aspects of defence and the economy. (Dec 1991)

Politicians — Politicians are grabbing power as the former Soviet Union states struggle to establish their identities. Politicians are like leeches, but their days are numbered. One day, Mr Gorbachev will be brought back and given presidential powers to supervise the areas of defence and the economy for the new Commonwealth. (Mar 1992)

Ukraine — Political leaders are playing a dangerous game by persuading the people to vote for independence. The Ukraine has never been a nation; it has always been a state within a state, and that is how it should remain. There will be no true freedom for the people because this move for independence is simply a game played by the politicians for personal power. (Dec 1991)

Russian vacuum — In Russia there is a vacuum. Anything can happen to reverse the whole process. Politicians are propounding ideologies but people want to experience. (Apr 1992)

Yeltsin will be removed from his present position. He cannot fight the machinery of opposition within Russia. With "masked faces", elements of the old regime will come in through the back door. It will not be the old communism, but socialism with a blend of capitalism, modelled on the current pattern of political and economic evolution of China. "If a person has been born in a jungle and you take him out of his environment into 'society', you can change him over years but not overnight."

The countries of Eastern Europe will find a way of evolving more in line with their own values and not by trying to be carbon copies of Western-style democracies. There will be, eventually, a better balance of socialist and capitalist elements.

In Russia both Boris Yeltsin and the forces opposing him will have to work together. The politics of confrontation will have to give way to the politics of food, shelter and protection for the Russian people. Boris Yeltsin cannot rule by force and decrees. Many in the military are behind him only up to a certain point. Boris Yeltsin has put his faith and trust in the armed forces but there is a law in creation which will compel him to give up rule by force. The moment the armed forces realize that these are nothing but dictatorial attitudes their support will begin to fade away.

At the end of the day the representatives of the people and the government itself will give priority to food, shelter and protection, which will be the politics of Russia. The same scenario will begin to develop elsewhere, including the West. (Sep 1993)

CHAPTER SIX

TRANSFORMATION UNDER WAY

EQUILIBRIUM — New Energy

Editor's comments:
Students of the Alice Bailey Teachings will know that, according to the Master DK, when Maitreya announced, in June 1945, His decision to reappear, He was from then on overshadowed by a Cosmic Entity, the Spirit of Peace or Equilibrium. This great Avatar works through the Law of Action and Reaction, which are opposite and equal. The effect of His energy, working through Maitreya, is to harmonize and bring into equilibrium, the prevalent discord and violence — in exact proportion to their manifestation today. Thus we will enter (are now entering) an era of peace and stability, of mental and emotional poise.

The changes in the world scene outlined in these pages by Maitreya should be seen, therefore, not as magical acts on His part, but as the scientific working out of this Law. It is for this reason that Maitreya is able to make precise forecasts of these events. (Aug 1988)

Earth's rotation — A decisive change has occurred in the rate of the Earth's rotation. The speed of the Earth's revolution has slowed down. In consequence of this, the forces surrounding the planet have been made to slow down. These are not 'blind' forces but the effect of men's activities. This momentous event occurred at the end of July (1988). As a result, there will be decisive changes, both in the short term and in the long term, in the Earth's atmosphere, in the air, on land and in the seas. Some have already begun.

This can be understood as the 'turn of the wheel' which marks the end of an era (ie the Piscean age) and the beginning

177

of a new era (Aquarius). "The wheel governs all creation. When it turns, no one can escape transformation." (Aug 1988)

Reversal of destructive forces — Destructive forces (the effects of human behaviour) are being reversed in such a way that they will become constructive. "This planet will come close to the Lord." Naturally, this process will occur gradually during the whole Aquarian cycle, but some changes are imminent and observable.

A certain number of natural disasters, such as floods, earthquakes, etc, are inevitable. This 'end of an age', however, is not one of cataclysmic destruction. It is a matter of degree, and the portents of doom generally offered are exaggerated.

Human suffering during this process of adjustment is inevitable, and in suffering the destructive forces are released from their natural pattern and dissipated.

Through our own free will we can lessen distress by responding with alacrity to human need. (Aug 1988)

Warming of the Earth — Changes in weather patterns are already occurring and will continue as a result of the Earth's warming. "Even mind, spirit and body will be changed."

The Earth will be full of food, and no one will be able to understand the process fully.

It will be found that, in Ethiopia, the soil will bring forth crops. The countries suffering drought earlier on will now get water. The necessities of life will be on hand. (Aug 1988)

New energy — A new energy has pervaded the planet now. It can be called the energy of Vishnu, the preserver. Scientifically this is the energy which creates equilibrium between positive and negative currents.

We will see a new equilibrium — a change of pattern in the way the rivers and the land will give forth sustenance.

In countries flooded at present, such as Sudan and Bangladesh, when the floodwaters recede there will be new forms of vegetation.

Civil wars in Sudan, Ethiopia, and even Northern Ireland, will subside. In Northern Ireland the issues will be resolved locally and some form of local parliament will evolve. The British army will pull out of Northern Ireland.

More and more people are responding to this new energy, becoming aware, realizing life, becoming free.

No politician on Earth will now be able to repeat past history. Rule by force will disappear. The politicians will become the servants, not the masters, of the people.

Governments round the world will be spending more money on the welfare of the people (on education, medicine, sports, etc) rather than on destructive weapons.

The nations right across the world have been filled with this new form of energy which creates self-awareness, which leads to equilibrium and therefore to mutual respect. (Aug 1988)

The sun has been brought closer to the Earth — in a particular way (symbolically speaking) — in order to energize it. This will help people live closer to nature. There will be greater harmony between the plant, animal and human kingdoms. Nature will respond positively in terms of new vegetation, new food. Because of greater harmony between nature and people, people will be happier. To disturb the environment is to disturb your own nature. (Aug 1988)

The ozone layer — There is no hole in the ozone layer. Imagine you are holding a tennis ball in the dark, and you shine a torch on it. If you bring the torch closer, the light will be on the surface of the ball, but behind the ball there is darkness. Likewise, the sun "has been brought closer to the Earth", symbolically speaking — its radiation has increased — but "behind" the Earth there is a circle which remains in darkness, where light does not penetrate. This is the so-called "hole" in the ozone layer. Although we think of light as travelling in a straight line, the rays of the sun do not fall in a straight line onto the Earth.

The 'hole' is not caused by the use of chlorofluorocarbons. Nevertheless, it will be beneficial to ban these sprays. Constant use of hair sprays eventually kills skin cells (on the scalp) and this has a detrimental effect on skin cells in other areas.

Skin cancers are not increasing due to the 'hole' in the ozone layer. They are increasing simply because people expose their skin excessively to the sun. (Oct 1988)

[Note: Nevertheless there is more active ultra violet radiation since the Earth has moved minimally closer to the sun.]

The weather — Enjoy the warm weather, the early spring and the blossoming life around you. It has nothing to do with holes in the ozone layer or the 'greenhouse effect'.

What has happened is that the pace of the Earth's rotation has slowed down and the Earth has moved closer to the sun. This is so that there can be more vegetation to feed the world.

It is not only people who have enjoyed the mild winter and the warm spring. The animals and the plants have also enjoyed it; not only that, they know that something good is happening. God is the one who cares — it is only man that destroys, poisons and kills through ignorance. Only the politicians, with their ideologies, are frightened because what they calculated would happen is not taking place after all. They wanted to lead the masses by terrifying them with stories of doom and disaster. As this warmth and blossoming continues, people will learn to open up their hearts to the elements of nature, and they will begin to look after one another.

"The tenets of God's Kingdom which is to come, and for which every Christian goes to church to pray, is here now on Earth." One effect that we will see is the disappearance of a number of species of animals that breed in the colder zones of the planet. These will evolve on to a higher plane. (Apr 1989)

Unusual weather — The frequent gale-force winds which have become a pattern over Northern Europe are pushing huge blocks of ice towards the North Pole. The milder weather will melt the ice. The water at the pole will become energized and then flow through the seas and rivers in a gradual process which will alter plant and animal life. Some species will disappear or become more rare. Of the latter, monkeys are one species that will become rarer. (Mar 1990)

The long hot summer — It is not the depletion of the ozone layers that is creating the sunny days enjoyed in Britain and elsewhere, but Nature. When scientists become clever enough to play with genes and genders, they think they can play with Nature. But Nature controls creation and no scientist will ever have that power. People can learn to understand the laws of evolution and use them creatively, but they cannot control the destiny of creation.

The days will continue to be sunny. The environment is changing and we can expect to see certain species of animal and plant life disappear. Particularly vulnerable are long-distance flying birds which are affected by weather and changing climatic conditions.

More food will be grown for the Earth's population and people will become healthier. We shall see less crime, chaos and conflict in society, both on the physical and psychological levels. Fast changes are taking place since the planet moved closer to the sun.

Politicians have no idea what is going on. They will only do the right thing if they listen to the voice of the people. (Jul 1990)

Exciting times — These are exciting times. Even in the next few weeks, a new awareness will be observable. This is a turning point in the history of mankind. People will be talking of peace, of living together in harmony. In this new era, the people themselves will come to the fore in all walks of life. They will express themselves through aid. They will express their political, religious, social and educational needs.

Religions, political systems, ideologies are "rungs of the ladder" which are necessary in order to "reach the roof". Once you have reached the roof you do not need them.

Religions are important; but they will be transformed in such a way that they will be teaching the truth.

National governments will still be with us in the long term; but responsibility will increasingly be carried by the united nations of the world. (Sep 1988)

Energy of Equilibrium — When the energy of equilibrium is brought into play, nothing is immune from the transformations which take place. Monitor these two processes:

(1) Judicial systems round the world are undergoing rapid change;

(2) Ideological struggles are beginning to decrease between East and West. This process will also take place between North and South.

These are not predictions, but the fulfilment of law. (Oct 1988)

Drug-taking will decrease — Drug-taking will begin to decrease. Politicians will be surprised; spiritual workers will be thrilled. People everywhere will begin to experience a sense of inner happiness. (Oct 1988)

Disasters before calm — We are seeing a dramatic climax in the number of disasters taking place around the world. Then will come a period of calm — the violence and destruction will come to an end.

As people gain awareness their guilt will recede and they will realize that it is not the Self that is causing all this mayhem. This has been created by an outside force of destructive energy which has sucked them into the storm of chaos and confusion. (Apr 1989)

The new feeling will be like rising in the small hours of the early dawn when you are surrounded by a sense of tranquility and calm. So it will be when you are able to experience the realization that you are not the creation or the universe but a completely separate spark, able to witness God's work taking place with serenity. You will feel free and light. You are not this or that, you only experience life. There is no blame in it. (Apr 1989)

The universe and creation — What is the difference between the universe and creation? The universe is the Being — it cannot be explained, it is there. Creation is the becoming of that Being. It is always in the process of changing, day by day. It is evolutionary.

Creation has now been energized by a new force, the constructive force that is being felt around the world.

It is changing everything: people, nations and nature. It is creating an intense sense of freedom, not only in countries like Russia and China but also in the West.

The old energy of destruction demonstrates its power in Hillsborough, the Middle East and on the battleship Iowa.* It is an energy that grips hold of people, dominating their mind, spirit and body. Against awareness, however, it is powerless and recedes. (Apr 1989)

[*A turret of the US battleship Iowa exploded and 47 of her gun crew were killed.]

The new energy and the younger generation — It is the younger generation which is experiencing the effects of this new energy and this gives them the strength to change the old systems which have imprisoned people. The young know where the power is: it is not in the bullet but in the heart, which is the source of light. Life comes into the body with light and lies in the heart. The body is able to function while the light is there. That is why Maitreya says that whoever controls light controls life.

The new energy affects everyone — Everyone is being affected by the new energy pouring into the world. Those who believed in political, religious and philosophical systems have become disillusioned because they have failed to bring peace, prosperity and happiness. You can only solve the problems of the world with a sense of realism that is not clouded by ideology or market forces.

There is no peace in the world at this time, all is confusion and chaos. But all is not doom and gloom. It is a new age. Today the voice of realism is found among the young people who are free from ideology, philosophy and theory. They are realistic about life and meet it as it comes.

No one can resist this new energy. It is taking nations and individuals by surprise. "Look within and you will find that I am within you, guiding you always."

The message is that there are many changes taking place within the universe, changes which are dissolving all sorts of negative energies.

"Do not be afraid or upset. I am with you now. I have come to help you realize that the mind, spirit and body are the temples within which you realize Supreme Being. You are not these, for the Self is above them and teaches Itself how best to use them." This is a vibrant time. Everyone is experiencing a growing awareness.

The old modes of life — The new energy is dissolving the old modes of life around the globe. It is no longer possible to replace new modes with old ones, although there are political leaders (for example, in China) who would like to do so. (Jan 1990)

Visitations from outer space — A new energy is making the people of Russia, China and Eastern Europe aware of their heritage and freedom, and also that life exists not only on Earth but elsewhere in the universe. They have been experiencing many visitations from outer space by Beings of more developed civilizations. This phenomenon will become increasingly and openly discussed throughout the world.

Energy through wind and wave power — Scientists are learning to develop energy through wind and wave power. They are also devising methods of conserving energy from human bodies and living entities, both vegetable and animal. Dependency on oil and coal is short-lived.

Nature — Environmental changes for the good are taking place. There will be increased growth in vegetation which will save millions of people from famine, especially in Africa. Why are these changes suddenly taking place? It is because Maitreya is now moving about Creation.

Equilibrium — If there is no equilibrium, wars, famine and natural disasters will take place. If there is equilibrium, the same energy can create happiness, enabling people to live and share together.

The mystery of life — Life is mysterious; it has a pattern and a non-pattern. The mystery of life will be experienced by nations and countries, for example, around Christmas. People will feel the presence of the Lord within the entire creation. The essence of being a nation and country will be experienced for the first time. That essence consists in looking after one another.

SOCIAL REGENERATION — Education

On an individual level — Children will be able to express spiritual insights through their behaviour, thought and speech which will surprise even religious leaders.

In brief, despite the fact that there are many localized wars and areas of so-called low-intensity conflict around the world, we can look forward to a period of increasing harmony.

Opening of centres for young people — In Britain, Maitreya has made himself known in various ways to religious and political leaders. There are deep divisions in society, but these divisions cannot heal unless they come out openly. The social, economic and political ferment Britain is experiencing will eventually produce a mellowing of capitalism and there will be a balanced blend of socialism and capitalism.

Aspects of Maitreya's mission in Britain will include the opening of certain centres which will attract young people and families. The aim is, first of all, to treat these youngsters in a way that will generate self-respect and build trust. Thus equipped, they will be helped to find jobs. The banking sector will eventually offer help, and teachers, doctors and politicians will visit these centres and study them for guidance. (Apr 1988)

Self-respect, the foundation stone — Maitreya has emphasized that social regeneration must centre on the family unit. Self-respect is the foundation stone of social renewal, and without it nothing can be built. Those who will be working in these centres will be asked to take up this task, either directly by Maitreya or through disciples close to Him. These workers will be trained by Him, and it is their experience, thus guided, which will equip them for the task. "Nothing will be imposed from without. Everything will flower from within." Thus, the individuals working in these centres will be inspired but not compelled, and their way of working will include simple and direct teaching and the ability to make contact with people in a meaningful way. Inertia, stagnation and despair will give way to hope and the desire to follow one's own destiny. Workers at these centres will also be inspired by Maitreya to help young people find jobs. But an inner process of developing self-respect and the awareness that ensues from it is the necessary prelude to success.

Pilot projects have existed for some years in the Asian community in London, in India and in the Middle East, and are meeting with good results.

Eventually this approach will spread from Britain to other countries. Professionals in different walks of life will visit the centres and learn from them.

Voices in the mind — Sometimes, at a tender age, a child hears voices in the mind. Doctors may brush this under the carpet and diagnose the 'illness' as schizophrenia. What happens is that sometimes, due to certain conditioned activities (karmas), the windows of the mind open up. If the incarnating entity is not mature enough to control those voices and images coming through the mind, then it is taken over by those forces, whose vibrations are in the mind.

"Do not say there is only one voice within you, the voice of which you become conscious. There are multifarious voices and images in the mind."

Some jivas (incarnating entities) are able to experience these while very young.

"By injecting drugs in mind, spirit and body you do not solve the problems. Temporarily the person is made numb. But the person is not 'cured'.

"The only way to close those windows of mind and spirit is to become conscious of who you are and what you are. Let the individual self become aware of who he or she is. The moment the Self becomes detached, the windows begin to close. These are the realities of life. Human society must learn to respect them."

The pace of consciousness — Never quicken the pace of consciousness. Even if you know how to quicken the consciousness of a baby, it should not be done. Let natural growth take place, and the mind will be in a state of equilibrium.

There is a common and universal cry in the mind and spirit of people around the world. Conditioning is such that one tends to lose faith and trust in life. Mind has been conditioned by ideological warfare, by the failures of various gurus and leaders.

Britain will develop an art of civilization — Britain is going to develop an art of civilization in which there will be justice and peace. People will be more open and the politicians will respect the will of the people. Great Britain will be the 'rising star' among the nations.

It is an evolutionary process. Look at the younger generation: it is healthy, strong, open-minded, wanting to keep its own identity, adventurous, not war-mongering. "Never say the younger generation depends on drugs. Drugs have been forced on some of the younger generation by the failures of politicians. It is wrong to say the younger generation has no sense of direction. This is nothing but whitewash. The leaders have failed.

"When you look at the children, you are inspired by their grace, peace and happiness, because their mind, spirit and body are free from isms. Go out and look at the faces of the children. This is a special generation."

The young will rebel — The young will rebel against the ideologies of old, whether they are imposed on them by politicians, religious leaders or intellectuals. And their demands will have impact. The surge of young voices is already being heard in Africa and the Middle East. In Iraq the younger generation is now talking openly about democratic representation and freedom. It is even being sanctioned by President Saddam Hussein himself.

Young people want to see constitutions that are by the people and for the people. They are tired of the old nepotisms of family, party and ideology. How is it that Western politicians encourage the Eastern bloc to create democratic constitutions and then preach a different sermon in Europe? Does it make any sense? No, of course it does not, and the young can see through it all.

Even children are beginning to challenge the adult world as they respond to the energies of the New Age. In every country, children of soldiers are questioning their fathers about the morality of killing others in their name. In Northern Ireland the children of IRA gunmen are telling their fathers: "What you are doing with bullets and bombs is wrong." The days of violent confrontation between the IRA and the British Army and the endless tragedy of sectarian violence are coming to an end. Children everywhere are saying that they want to see friendship, humanity and goodwill throughout the world. (Oct 1991)

Cult followers — The younger generation today are becoming cult followers of pop stars, actors and actresses. This is dangerous. It does not bring happiness. In this way you threaten your own identity. The same occurs if you follow gurus and saints.

Maitreya says: "Even though I am you and you are Me I make it clear to you that if you follow Me, you do not know who you are. If you know the Lord is with you, you do not run after Him."

To the younger generation — Maitreya says: "Your Bible, your Gita, your Koran, your scripts of life, are within you. You alone will experience this and realize it. Those who tell you what to do are themselves indulging in acts which will lead nowhere but to cyclic evolution and involution.

"The same thing can be explained in the simplest language, in terms of the baby playing with toys. One moment he creates a bridge, another a house; thus pleasing himself, he thinks a new thing has been created but does not yet realize it is still a toy.

"The same baby, having grown up, realizes that toys are toys and therefore does not play with them.

"In the same manner, gurus, disciples, prophets and saints play with the toys of creation. But the moment they realize they have grown up (which means that they themselves have evolved into 'the image of the Lord') they do not play with creation.

"The Teaching of Maitreya — to be honest in mind, sincere in spirit and detached — helps the Self to move into creation and not play the role of guru, saint or prophet, but with humility to respect, revere and obey the Divine Will which governs Creation.

"Therefore you will experience freedom in Creation: freedom in Oneness and Manyness; freedom in Unity and Diversity and ultimately salvation which comes from the Supreme Divine Will.

"When you reach this stage in life, there is no difference between the soul and the Almighty, in which there is no beginning and no end."

Giving up 'divide and rule' — "The approach of 'divide and rule' in the family, in the community, in the nations, will be extinguished for the first time."

Within the family, harmony will grow between children and parents, man and wife.

Key changes in the family — The early signs of important social changes which will set their seal on the 21st century should be sought in the changing relationships within the family which are occurring now. Now, before the baby is born, the parents start talking to the baby in the womb. The baby is capable of responding. When the baby is born, the art of communication between mother and baby continues and grows. There is no question of the mother 'imposing' her views on the child.

This is a new process and it is happening all over the world now. If there are contradictions between mother and child, the child questions the mother (that is, "Why do you do things like this?"). The mother explains and the contradiction dissolves. The first questions arise from the children, in complete innocence: there is nothing fixed in the mind, and the parent responds. Because of greater awareness in the family, politicians will lose control of the way they run things today: by divide and rule. The 21st century will witness a new form of society. Awareness is growing from the centre, the individual, the family.

Even in the educational system, great changes are taking place now. Children will offer things completely out of the unknown — not from textbooks. The changes are coming from the children.

Families and nations — "There is no difference between a family and a nation, a country." It is the art of communication between parents and children which creates a pattern of peacefulness, gracefulness and harmony. It creates all those values of life which contribute to the evolution of people. Where communication exists, awareness becomes the constitution of that family. Awareness is not ideology. Likewise, "if you want peaceful coexistence on planet Earth, do not bring in ideologies".

Through better communication, big power blocs of opposition will dissolve. Maitreya asks of governments everywhere: "Why make such a plethora of rules and regulations?" This is how people become ill, demoralized. Any government whose life-blood is ideology will not succeed in bringing about peaceful coexistence.

The art of communication — If you force your viewpoint on someone else, it creates a sense of burden. This occurs in the totalitarian family, and equally, in the totalitarian nation. To pile on rules and regulations — a process of addition, or a process of multiplication (a rapid form of addition) — tilts the scales. There is no equilibrium. The problem cannot be solved merely by a process of subtraction. The weight decreases, but the problem persists. The way forward is through division, which means learning to exchange views and developing the art of communication. Freedom lies in the art of communication. This creates harmony, equilibrium. This results in true democracy. Referring to politicians around the world, Maitreya adds: "By sitting within your four walls you cannot hope for the good, when people have not got either right food or a decent place to live".

"Where the people's voice is not heard, there will be revolution." This is not prediction, but an instance of the law of cause and effect. Where there is suppression, repression, this force will collide against a growing awareness in the people.

Husband and wife, and nations — What maintains equilibrium between husband and wife? It is trust. Trust is a process. It brings happiness. When there is trust between nations, there is peace.

Trust will exist only where there is honesty, sincerity and detachment.

If you are honest with yourself, sincere with yourself and detached, you can trust the one to whom you lend a large sum, because you are detached from the loan itself.

Education without morality — When your teachings are devoid of morality you bring destruction. Without morality the forces of life dry up and become a type of solidified ism. Morality is the water of mind, spirit and body which cleanses them of isms. Morality brings fragrance into life. If there is no fragrance, you feel everything is 'dead'. Isms are a disease. Morality protects the forces of life and prevents them from becoming isms. Morality generates self-respect which, when it is present, prevents self-abuse. Does this require courts or police forces? In the UK, the Education Secretary is now going to develop education on the basis of profit and loss (ie what industry needs); he will create human robots.

"What has happened in New York can happen here in London. In New York people have a life-pattern which is fast in a mechanical way; mind, spirit and body feel the fetters of life. A tiresome routine is experienced. The escape is drugs.

Children — The attention of governments will increasingly be centred on the welfare of children. More funds will be found for their nourishment and care. In various countries (including some in the Middle East) there will be a Minister for children. The voice of children will be heard even in parliaments.

The shackles of life — The values of life given to children through the educational system must never be imposed in the name of traditions, philosophies, religions, etc. If they are, they become shackles in life, and in time they become time bombs, which means they can explode.

Education and faith — In many countries, there is strife because representatives of different faiths disagree. This creates crises in the educational systems. Maitreya says to every mother and father: "Look in your garden. Admire the beautiful flowers. The garden is beautiful only when there is diversity. In creation there are seven colours. If one colour is missing, there is no light. You are not here to take or reject faiths. You are here to experience all seven different colours. Thus your knowledge and wisdom will be increased.

"If you do not understand Christianity, how can you criticize Islam, Hinduism, Buddhism, Judaism or other religions?"

"Parents are right from one angle. Young children depend on them for guidance. But later, schools are in many ways responsible for their welfare. Here one should not impose religions or ideologies. It is only when a person can use his freedom that he can choose his direction. Until then you should not close your eyes to the other colours in life. Do not make decisions about the other six colours."

Teachers cannot control classrooms because the leaders themselves are unable to understand what life is about. They are only good at unleashing market forces and turning individuals into robots in factories.

Now, responsible intellectuals will come forward, not just those who do not know how to live, who are ruled by the ballot box and ideology.

Indoctrination — To indoctrinate a child is un-divine. To impose ideologies on anyone is un-divine.

Education — The minds of children at present are stuffed with facts and figures. How can the Self experience peace and happiness? However, "in the name of the children everything will evolve".

Changes in lifestyle — Changes are taking place which will lead to people altering their lifestyle, less towards work and more towards leisure and recreation. Sports will thrive and as people become healthier there will be a shortening of hospital waiting lists. The West's educational institutions will switch their curriculums towards a more practical approach that will be useful in everyday life. People will be made aware of technological advances.

Religion will lose its ambiguous, mystical teachings which will be replaced by the philosophy of human realization. "Life is to be enjoyed."

The art of survival — Change will take place in our educational institutions which will teach people the art of survival, not just in the material world, but also to inspire them in mind and spirit. Education in the future will be free of ideological and religious bias. It will create fullness and wholesomeness in the individual.

Religious authority — The older generations have been taught: 'Come to the temple. Give a donation and you will be free.' Children do not run after God. The children of today often do not go to churches. Why? There is an awareness in them that 'The Lord is within'. "God is not in the sky. God is in the heart." Although He is in reality everywhere, individuals are becoming aware that it is possible to experience the Lord in the heart.

Maitreya's message to religious leaders is: "Do not create fear in the minds of innocent children. Fear is poison." This has been the way of religions until now. Maitreya teaches the swamis around him: "I am with you. If people have not attained to certain truths in life, give them these truths freely, but do not claim them as your own." "The same Light you came from exists in the snake, in the mountain, in water, in fire, etc. If the same Light is common to all these, how can you say 'this' is more important than 'that'?"

Realization of this truth creates a sense of unity, of harmony. "Since it is the same for every human being, if you come to know this truth, will you then compare? Or try to dominate one another? You will not. Instead you will respect one another."

The Christ — No one has a hold on the Christ. All the great religions are undergoing rapid changes now. In the case of Christianity, there are divisions; people are questioning, challenging. Christianity, along with the other religions, is undergoing a process of purification, in that individuals are going to experience, for the first time, that Divinity is not "outside" but situated simultaneously in the heart and in the universe, in all of creation. The Self is now beginning to experience its own, distinct identity. The One who sustains the Self and makes Him aware cannot be limited; He is universal.

Religious structures are cracking — When something cracks open, the essential remains. All are in the process of questioning; therefore religious structures are cracking. Those who cling to old forms will create division after division. These forms will eventually disappear. This process is inevitable. There is no contradiction in the different religions.

Religions have been trapped through words and slogans to vie with each other. This will disappear. The essence will remain. When one prays to God with honesty of mind, sincerity of spirit and detachment, the Self experiences salvation.

Hindus, Christians, Muslims, Jews and Buddhists will all experience Oneness.

New temples in the New Age — New temples dedicated to religions in the New Age will be opened soon, beginning in Montreal and followed by London, Kenya, Mombasa and India.* They will be centres not just for religious faiths but for the arts and sciences. These temples will be unique because they are the symbols of the fountains of wisdom and knowledge sought by poets and scientists. The temples will begin to unify diverse faiths. It is still important that there are different faiths and beliefs, for without diversity there is no unity. "As the Self is unified in Me so it retains its separate identity." (Feb 1990)

[*Note: These processes, as of 2005, have not yet started.]

Prince Charles — Prince Charles will be a "true king". He will not be sitting in his palace; he will be with the people, with the nation. He will inspire respect right across the political spectrum. He is taking a constructive interest in society now. His actions will create greater unity and a common approach to life. He will be the true defender of the nation and the country. (Oct 1988)

The royal family in the UK — Many members of the royal family in Britain will begin to speak out on behalf of the people. The barriers to this approach "will disappear overnight". Prince Charles will "moralize the nation so that the blessings of God's kingdomship will be experienced collectively by the people."

The role of monarchies round the world will change now. Monarchies will be "positively active now". (Nov 1988)

The language of the heart — Teach the language of the heart. "The language of the heart is where the Lord lives." In individuals, and even in nations generally, you will find there is a difference in tone of voice. Some tones of voice are nasal, others are more melodious and appear to come from the mouth rather than through the nose. The nasal tone does not come from the heart. It is not the breath of the heart; it comes from the mind and specifically, from certain parts of the brain. If you speak the language of mind, you have confrontation, contradiction. The mind is a machine and can be dangerous. This gives rise to violence in society.

You will find that the Welsh and the Scots speak the language of the heart. People in Africa speak the language of the heart. In the West Indies and in America there is greater variation, and minds are confused in many cases.

The English are at a 'crossroads' in mind, spirit and body. They move from heart to mind, from mind to heart. But the Self is not caught in the mind. This is why they "change with the seasons". This is a chameleon-like protection, and this ability to change with the surroundings makes for good diplomats.

[Note: Maitreya is not singling out individuals here; he is speaking only of general trends.]

The heart — The heart is never tarnished or touched, it is the seat of the soul. It is the mind that leads us astray. Peace, bliss, happiness and grace are the qualities of the heart. "By tuning into the 'feelings of the heart' you are able to experience your natural innocence, that innocence you had as a child. Do not 'visualize' the heart. For that is only the mind seeking to find the source of light with a torch."

The media's responsibility — This is a very important time for the world's TV networks. Television will be the most effective means of communication in the New Age. There will be a great demand for the skills and art of communication. Cities and villages in every corner of the world will be reached and become informed. It is through communication that the world will be truly integrated. It is important, therefore, that television is properly organized to meet its new responsibilities.

THE NEW POLITICS: THE WILL OF THE PEOPLE

Dissolving old patterns — The dissolution of ancient patterns of thought and behaviour has begun. Polarities will dissolve. Extreme differences between rich and poor will begin to disappear. The rich will fulfil their duties and keep what they need within reason, sharing the excess. Once someone knows 'the Lord is with him' he can give up greed.

Even gurus and prophets are now beginning to realize that salvation is not achieved through the acquisition of phenomenal powers, but only in being humble to the Lord, seated in the heart.

Political and religious rigidities will dissolve. New forms of government will arise across the globe.

"By the will of the Lord, the seed of awareness is cracking open now." People everywhere are becoming aware, and will be unwilling to be dominated by others when their destiny is to be free. Governments everywhere will have to listen to the people. "Government will be by the people, for the people."

No one will be able to explain or comprehend fully this new sense of awareness, but we will witness it and experience it.

Maitreya has already prepared His platform. Everything is being made ready. When Maitreya speaks about creation, existence and purpose, they will be easily understood by the masses. (Aug 1988)

Future forms of government — Right across the world present political systems are being diluted and will eventually give birth to new systems of government which will be much more representational. Ordinary people, intellectuals, educationalists and others from a variety of walks of life will find they have a genuine voice in government. This will replace control of the masses through ideology. Evolution means evolution towards freedom. (Jun 1988)

New political era — There is a purpose in life for everyone. "It is divine to be a road-sweeper, or to sit on a throne. Everything is divine as long as whatever you do you do with detachment."

Faced with such awareness, all divisive politics can only crumble. Everyone will experience themselves as unique. They will reject the old political system. This is the end of an old road — a new road begins.

Everything is moving so fast now that events are beyond the control of the politicians. All political systems that divide the world, that create rich and poor, will come to an end.

A new political era has begun in which awareness informs everyone of their basic human rights, their liberties and their responsibilities to themselves and each other. There will be resistance to this new political approach — particularly in China, Russia, Japan and South Africa — but it will not succeed. The divisions are increasing now, but in the end these politicians will have to give in to the new energies that are sweeping the world. (Feb 1990)

Moral and spiritual dimension in politics — Many church leaders are coming out in defence of the people. They are challenging the politicians to address the moral and spiritual dimension, which cannot be circumvented by anyone holding power. If this dimension is avoided, a crisis necessarily follows.

There are some political leaders who are beginning to realize that commercialization by itself is a shallow creed. A clear rethink of principles would yield other priorities, such as meeting basic needs first, which would re-order economic and political policy.

As an example, it is clear that one basic need is adequate shelter. If this becomes a priority, it is obvious that within a relatively short space of time no one in Great Britain will be sleeping rough. The only reason this is not the case at present here (and in the USA and in other relatively wealthy European countries) is that this need is not considered a priority. (Jun 1988)

The UK: Socialism and Conservatism — The mellowing process is visibly under way in the UK. The present government is undergoing changes. It cannot stick to the current ideology of conservatism, "which is nothing but the seed of attachment". Socialism at least emphasizes sharing. But to be detached takes a long time. It requires awareness. It is not an easy process.

Socialists, on the other hand, have to learn the art of self-preservation. Conditions must be created around the individual so that he can realize that he, as an individual, is important.

The process of inculcation, of imposition, by forcing ideologies into the minds of people, is beginning to dissolve round the world, both in religious and in political fields. Consensus will replace it. (Oct 1988)

Spiritual leaders — Politicians have not been able to solve the strife in Sri Lanka, the Punjab, and other areas. A process of awakening the people has begun under the inspiration of several spiritual leaders who are coming to the fore now. They are using the media as their medium of communication, although the substance of their message is different from that of American preachers who also employ media facilities. (Oct 1988)

Church leaders — The Pope will speak out now about the necessity for sharing the world's food and resources. The Archbishop of Canterbury will also speak out publicly about discrepancies between people and government. (Oct 1988)

Third World debt — The debt will be written off. There is no possibility of doing anything else. There is no way in which this debt can be recovered.

It is not through an increased burden on taxpayers in creditor nations that the solution will be found to this dilemma. Instead, money which has hitherto been spent on defence will be found to meet this situation. Defence will no longer be the first priority as tensions begin to decrease around the world.

Further, the new technology of light will make present weapons obsolete. With the technology of light it is possible to pinpoint a needle on planet Earth.

Light is not an energy that we 'make'. We simply harness it.

In addition, cheap sources of energy will be found. This will ease the plight of many nations. (Apr 1989)

The environment will become the number one issue — In China, Russia and America people are openly asking politicians for justification of defence spending. In some Latin American countries politicians are beginning to work in harmony with the people. Similarly, no one can ignore environmental issues now. The environment will become the 'number one' issue throughout the world.

There is a link between the inner and the outer environment. The moment you become aware of yourself, the environment within your mind, spirit and body is under your control. Then this development spreads to the family, then nationwide.

Politicians will no longer be able to control the people through the rule of Parliament without adequate representation of the people's will. The will of the people will prevail. (Apr 1989)

New politics: the opposition will form a coalition — The main opposition parties will come together in a coalition which does not stand for socialism, capitalism or any other ism. A new trend in "human politics" will take place which will not be based on the philosophy of divide and rule. Politics will be transformed into the art of making people more aware of themselves and their potential. Politicians and people will find a common harmony in the search for peace and happiness. (Apr 1989)

Harmony — Eventually the old names and labels will disappear. China, Russia, the Middle East, Catholics, Protestants — they will all lose their intensity to divide although they will still be respected.

In future there will be harmony between all these groups and nations. There will be no sense of superiority, of good or bad. All will be in balance. (Apr 1989)

Awareness — Awareness is growing everywhere, among nations, people and even animals and plants. Problems are beginning to be solved automatically as this awareness brings people into closer harmony with nature.

Life, nature, energy, consciousness, all are becoming harmonious.

The young are demanding that they play their part and that their voice be heard. Before, everything was decided by the elders but all that is changing. It will be the 'end of the road' for politicians unless they willingly get into step with the New Age. This is beginning to happen in South Africa, for instance.

Mrs Thatcher is wrong when she claims that East Germany is following democracy. "No one is following anything other than their own path." (Oct 1989)

New energy is creating awareness — The new energy is creating awareness in the people of Eastern Europe and we are seeing the old regimes dissolving before our eyes. But they will not follow the West and adopt their style of democracy. They will create their own models of government.

This new energy is already beginning to affect the West. As it creates awareness of the Self in individuals, so they become aware of their environment and their sense of duty and responsibility. This will make people take to the streets in America and Britain and demand that the voice of the people be heard in their parliaments.

The wealth of the nations should remain that of the nations and not be used to create chaos and confusion in the name of peace, by manufacturing more arms and weapons.

Politicians must realize that the only way they can stay in power is by representing and voicing the wishes of the people. "Politicians whose creed is 'market forces' will find that their time is over."

Capitalism, in its pure form, is at an end in Europe. In future, countries will model their governments on a form of democratic socialism. Gradually this will become the model for all nations as the most effective way to ensure that the voice and will of the people is properly represented. (Nov 1989)

The media — The future will be modelled on the concept of balancing between the environment and energy and so will politics. All those who indulge in creating divisions in life and politics are finished. "I have pulled the plug out. There is no energy left there," says Maitreya.

The days of the media who cover up political corruption and scandals, and hide the truth, are numbered. Soon, the media will be open and reflect the corruption and chaos of politics and the judiciary. The judiciary cannot be independent of the constitution. It must be part of it and properly accountable.

"If you want to be happy make sure that your neighbour is happy. If you are rich and he is poor then share with him." (Oct 1989)

Politics, an art of harmony — Present-day politicians are baffled by their inability to achieve any of their policies. No longer is the rule of force an effective instrument of control in the world. Those politicians who try to govern by divide and rule, and by creating chaos and confusion, are finished. In the New Age, politicians will respond readily to public opinion and they will develop the art of harmony. Intellectuals, scientists and doctors will be drawn into politics as ideologies disappear.

The people's voice — "How is it that the people's voice is becoming the foundation of political systems throughout the world?" It will become the foundation of society, of political and of educational systems.

New politics — The old forms of polarized politics will disappear. The concepts of democracy and capitalism will change. There is no room for communism for it meant loss of freedom.

Democracy allowed limited freedom, while capitalism meant freedom only for the haves and the rich.

Nothing can remain stagnant — Every second, changes are taking place, so fast that there is no point in holding on to old modes of political and religious control. Nothing can remain stagnant and no one knows which direction changes will take. That is why it is vital that we should not cling to old ideas, but be detached.

Federal governments — In future all countries and nations will be ruled by Federal Governments. For example, there will be the Federal States of Europe under which 70 per cent of all decision making will lie at the centre. Major policy areas such as environment, education, welfare and scientific research will be controlled by the Federal government.

Interdependence — The time has come for the leaders to recall their armies and satisfy the needs and demands of their people. Basically, these are for peace, happiness and security. The voice of the people will assert itself and become the basis of future policies, even in Northern Ireland, despite the present and tragic appearances to the contrary.

Every nation is interdependent, every individual like brother and sister. The old politics of divide and rule are finished. (Oct 1990)

World political changes — The political spectrum of the world has changed for the better, despite all appearances. The will and voice of the people will become the guiding light of all countries and nations.

Even in the Soviet Union you will see such changes coming very quickly. This is also true for South Africa.

The people have awakened and they will join hands in delight and happiness.

Military rule in Africa is coming to an end. In future, all newly independent states will be supervised through a probationary period by the United Nations to ensure that they do not succumb to totalitarianism or military dictatorship.

The role of the United Nations — "The purpose, goal and aim of the United Nations is and must be to serve the cause of humanity and not to become a political force controlled by the strong. Neither America nor the Soviet Union can ever rule the entire world.

"It is becoming a powerful institution that will be able to watch over the welfare of the world.

"Be strong: defend the true welfare of your nation and country with honesty, sincerity and detachment. You will witness miraculous happenings. Nations will then be at peace. Those who want war will fade away."

Nations are awakened — Much good will come out of the events in the Gulf. A new concept of politics will emerge, in which the nations' destinies will be in the hands of intellectuals, philosophers and religious thinkers. Many countries will unite to finance one another's needs, especially the needs of the poor in the Third World.

The nations of the world are awakened now. The wealth is there but the will to share and work together is still required. The leaders of the world are being guided by Maitreya. "Once I guide you, you will follow Me."

The good of mankind — Despite the turmoil, what is happening around the world is for the good of mankind. Politicians will look for guidance, and the will of the people will become the constitution of nations and countries.

Who is the superpower? — The US and the USSR are no longer superpowers. Humanity is the superpower. The will of the nation and country will be based on the will of the people. The people will make sure politicians do not make mischief. In Africa, India, Pakistan, Japan and many other countries, people have been awakened. They are now demanding their rights.

New Age politics — Politics the world over are undergoing rapid change. The politics of the New Age will be by the people, for the people. The United Nations will become a powerful instrument, and will provide the defence of weaker nations. The US and the USSR, too, will work for the welfare of weaker nations.

The educational systems are also changing. Parents are being brought in. The local authority will not decide everything. (Nov 1991)

The New Age dawns — Gradual political transformations have taken and are taking place around the world. Politicians are realizing that the dawn of a New Age is breaking. The sacredness of nationhood will be better understood.

Fundamentalism wanes rapidly — All fundamentalisms will wane rapidly. Fundamentalism is like a big tumour; it will burst. There is no place for fundamentalism in the New Age.

In the New Age there will be an aura of consciousness, an awareness, an inner openness which enables people to look within for peace, grace and happiness.

Isms lead to self-destruction. All types of temptation can be found in isms; corruption, duplicities and dishonesty in life all come from isms. People who indulge in fundamentalisms, whether these be economic, religious or political, either run away, or, if they remain stuck, destroy themselves.

Shift of power — The budgeting system of central government will be changed now. When national policies fail to generate happiness and prosperity at home, the political process leads automatically to pockets of war so that attention is focused on problems elsewhere. The focus shifts from home to other parts of the world and the masses forget the problems at home for the time being.

When the people remember their problems at home they go against the politicians in power. When the Russians brought the army home from Afghanistan there was nothing left in the kitty. They turned to the West for help. The house is shattered but there is little help.

The role of central government is to defend the nation and country. The local authorities and the people are sandwiched between the failures of central government. The local authorities are for the local people and together they have to take charge of their local affairs.

With local freedom, crime will retreat, and the local environment (ie with people working together and taking charge of their own affairs) will generate a national environment of happiness and friendliness.

When home affairs are not in order, look after these first. The time is now. (Jul 1992)

Consensus building — Although we may not realize it fully, the political spectrum is now changing. The old models cannot provide the answers. There will be a more pragmatic 'mix' at local levels to try to solve the problems of people in the area.

Socialism and capitalism will converge — Power politics will give way to the politics of food, shelter and protection. This will spread the world over. Socialism and capitalism will converge. They are the two wheels which are essential. Politics cannot function with only one wheel.

Commercialization — Commercialization and its destructive competitiveness are fast coming to an end. All projects with only profit in mind are doomed now.

The technology of light will fulfil all our needs instantly. So where is the need for commercialization and competitiveness?

Our future on this planet is destined to be one of happiness where everyone can enjoy life to the full. Corruption and chaos have been created by politicians and the Masters have come to end all of that and to make the politicians realize that they are not the masters but the servants of the people.

CHANGES SWEEPING THROUGH THE WORLD

The laws of evolution — The Lord guides one and all in every station of life. No one is 'immune' in creation. We are all interdependent. Once you realize what the laws of evolution are, you manipulate them, but you do not break them.

In the USSR, the one who will replace Mr Gorbachev will be a more effective leader in the sense that he will channel and protect the energy which has been unleashed. People will not be 'let loose' (that is, to carry out mindless and destructive acts).

"History will not be repeated." The changes which are taking place around the globe are due to this new energy which makes people aware of 'energies' and 'environment'. This is not a matter of individual countries. Policies are being forged globally.

Did this come about through 'scientists' or 'politicians'? The energy is there, bringing nations closer to a realization of their interdependence. (Jan 1990)

Afghanistan — All the factions will get together and will rule together "in the name of Islam". (Nov 1988)

Power vacuum — We think of creation coming out of a 'big bang'. But before the big bang there was a vacuum. In Afghanistan at present there is a vacuum. There are two forces, and neither can prevail. So-called stalemates are stepping stones on the way to this power vacuum. When this vacuum is reached, isms dissolve in it, and all shades of opinion get together and develop a consensus.

Similarly in China, there are very strong streams of opinion. When the government cannot rule, when there is a stalemate, a vacuum will prevail. The vacuum is a healing process. Isms will dissolve, there will be a consensus, and the evolutionary forces which have been arrested temporarily will again come into play. (Jun 1989)

Central America — The situation in Nicaragua will improve. The trend will be for the US to withdraw from military involvement in the area as a whole. (Apr 1988)

Nicaragua — A lull in the fighting will lead to "government by the people". The people's voice will be "enshrined and respected". (Nov 1988)

Governments and guerrillas — Conflict between governments and guerrilla forces the world over will begin to decrease. People will come to the negotiating table. In particular, examine this process in the Sudan, Ethiopia and Nicaragua.

This is partly due to the fact that both the USA and the USSR are looking at the constructive side of global existence and are taking up their responsibilities. They will decrease the supply of weapons to developing countries, and, instead, will supply food and the means for better health and education. (Oct 1988)

Aura of democracy — In Latin America as a whole the 'aura' of democracy will begin to flourish. Even the seemingly intractable situation in Peru will improve. (Oct 1988)

China: New energy — The process which has swept through the Soviet Union is already starting to work changes in China. The new energy has reached the cities and villages, and people are crying out for freedom. The politicians have accepted that change has to happen but they want to manage it by opening the doors gradually and so avoid the chaos and confusion that threatens to overwhelm Mr Gorbachev. Nothing has appeared in the media as yet, but it will create great interest when big events start to happen. (Jan 1990)

China: Religion — There are signs in China that people are beginning to frequent churches and temples more, and this same process is also occurring in the USSR. (May 1988)

China: The people's voice will be respected — China cannot survive more than a few months in its present form. The existing style of government will come to an end and the people's voice will be respected. Politicians are beginning to invite the people to speak. The army is essentially on the side of the people. This attitude is true even of people in key positions. "Babies must be looked after by their mothers. The armed forces are being inspired to play the role of 'mother' to look after the nation and the country." The generals are saying: "You cannot ask us to kill the people." Some politicians are frightened; they have no control over the armed forces.

One experience of Maitreya is enough to transform the life of a person. (Mar 1990)

China: The doors are being opened — The doors are being opened quietly in China, encouraging the people to express their desire for greater freedom and democracy. Politicians, industrialists and diplomats are being invited from other countries to talk to the Chinese leaders. All this is taking place without publicity. The politicians there are playing their cards very cleverly in order not to upset the stability of the nation. But events and developments taking place in China will shake the Western world when they hear about them.

Eventually, China will replace Russia as a dominant influence in the world. They have maintained their cultural and social discipline, unlike Japan, where the mixing of their own cultural values with Western ones has resulted in a serious confusion of identity. (May 1990)

China: The dominant force — China will become the dominant force in the East. It has discipline, tradition, philosophy and science. In China people are shedding ideologies at a rapid rate. This process of awareness is spreading so rapidly that the media generally cannot keep pace. But when this reality is brought to the fore, China will occupy a leading place in Asia.

Meanwhile, the Soviet Union is becoming concerned and is trying to make China appear as a threatening dark horse. But this tactic will not work. (Jun 1990)

China: Changes within the government — The rulers have become aware that the will of the people cannot be trampled on any more. Vast changes are taking place in China, and many changes are taking place within the government. (Aug 1990)

China: Maitreya — Maitreya has appeared to some Chinese politicians. They have been made to realize that their time is over. Changes are not yet being reported in the media, but they are occurring very fast. (Aug 1991)

China: Radical changes — The radical changes towards greater freedom and democracy that have already swept Eastern Europe are quietly under way in China.

The government has become conscious of the growing demands and awareness of the Chinese people. The leaders are responding very positively and they do not need European politicians telling them what to do. The past has gone. The government has begun to open the doors to its own people first. It is already encouraging the establishment of a private sector of business and ownership. In the second stage, the rest of the world will be invited to take part in the construction of Chinese industry. This will be followed by the gradual development of religious freedom. China will become the most powerful nation in the East, particularly now that the Soviet Union has been dismantled. It will be the centre of a rich culture of humanitarian philosophies. (Sep 1991)

China: Parliamentary representation — Watch for developments, for the people are asking for parliamentary representation and the authorities are beginning to consider it. They are aware that they cannot resist the winds of change that have swept through the Eastern bloc. There will be no violent upheavals. There will be a smooth transition and an intermingling of the people with the institutions.

It will be the same on the African continent and in the Middle East. The days of the dictators, the sultans and sheikhs are ending. Now is the time for government by the people, for the people. (Jan 1992)

China: "Match the dollars" — China is on the way to being a very powerful country. For the present it will have capitalism as an aspect but it will still retain values of life pertinent to its civilization, unlike Russia where the values of life have been destroyed. Capitalism on its own cannot survive in the world. Socialism on its own cannot survive either. China's economy will become very strong: it will "match the dollars". (Aug 1993)

India: Religion and ideology — The use of religion and ideology in a violent way has given rise to trouble in the Punjab and the demand for a separate Sikh state. It has resulted in confrontation between Sikhs and Hindus and also between Sikhs and Indian government troops. This will give way to a more conciliatory mood. Ultimately there will be talks between the various representative groups in the conflict and major problems will be solved.

In this regard, Maitreya has already begun to act. (Apr 1988)

India: Harmony — Increasingly, the turmoil in the Punjab will give way to greater harmony. Violence will be seen for what it is, and ways will be found to effect a satisfactory process of conciliation. (Jun 1988)

India: Greater participation — "These ideologies must come to an end. This issue [Kashmir] cannot be resolved by fighting."

"There will be no war between India and Pakistan." India is now experiencing great changes in her political and economic life. People are beginning to participate to a greater degree. (Mar 1990)

India: Self-realization — The politics of dynasty are coming to an end. Now the politics of ideology are setting in. But the true colours of the political ideologists are coming to light. They are clutching at the last straw in their desperate attempts for power, by the dangerous tactics of stirring up religious fears and prejudices. But a new flower is beginning to grow among the political chaos and corruption. A new political party will emerge based on the principle of Self-realization. Through the experience of the teachings of Maitreya — of honesty of mind, sincerity of heart and detachment — people will realize that there is no difference between Rama, Krishna and Allah. So if a temple is built next to a mosque, that is not un-divine. (Nov 1990)

India: The duty of the politicians — Maitreya says to Indian politicians: "Be what you are. Do not bring isms into politics. The duty of the politicians is to uphold the spectrum of diverse opinions.

"As a result of 'dynasty', of the strong versus the weak, chaos will prevail in the short term. The tumour has burst open. In the longer term, a cleansing process is under way." (Jun 1991)

India: Unity in diversity — Gradually, all opinions, religions and divisions will be united. "I want My garden to be restored. It will be full of diversity, yet united. It will be beautiful and flourishing."

That unification is already beginning. The Western style of politics and democracy is coming to an end in India, for it has not created unity. (Jun 1991)

India: Change — That same positive energy will also sweep through India and Pakistan. The domination by rich land-owners and their families over the lives of so many millions will end. The people will soon have the means and ability to grow enough food to feed themselves. (Sep 1991)

India: Nepotism is over — The radical changes that we have seen in Eastern Europe will occur in India. The rule of nepotism is over. We shall see the same demands for state autonomy based on government by the people and for the people. Foreign policy and defence will remain centrally controlled. (Oct 1991)

India: Political vacuum — Maitreya has made it clear that God is not interested in having this or that particular temple; it is people who want this. God does not want a temple to Ram.

The politicians want to rule the masses through religious tensions. But there is no real religion in these fundamentalisms. In India, there is a political vacuum at present. (Oct 1991)

Israel-Arab problem — An Arab editor who lives in London recently made contact with Maitreya and will give out a message to all Arabs and Israelis.

People in Israel have a deep desire to be near the Lord. The Israelis are disillusioned with the politicians. The people are telling them openly "We want to live at peace with the Arabs." Each country will have its own respective homeland. Lebanon will be restored to the Lebanese. The Palestinians will have their own country. The Israelis will be back in their own country. The Israeli army will put down their arms.

Maitreya can appear to people in any form. When a politician has a direct experience of Him, that politician changes. This is happening now. Maitreya has appeared before a number of politicians around the world. Great changes are taking place, and will continue to take place. He has also appeared before a number of religious leaders. "You are free from this moment. When you see Me no one will be able to force you to fight against each other." (Apr 1988)

[Note: An interesting movement was recently founded by Israelis called The 21st Year, which advocates non-support of and non-violent resistance to military action in the Occupied Territories.]

Israel: Messiah — Maitreya appeared to four elderly Israelis in a remote village. They recognized Him immediately as the Messiah. He told them that the politicians would begin to respect the will of the people. The Israeli people will give up the occupation in the West Bank, in Gaza and in Lebanon. (Jul 1988)

Israel and Palestine — Maitreya has appeared to thousands of people in Israel, in a form in which He would be recognized by them, including a number of Rabbis. These Rabbis will develop a role not dissimilar to that of the House of Lords in the UK. They will keep an eye on the politicians "so that they do not destroy the fabric of society", and they will be able "to defend the voice of the people".

Among all the peoples, those who are really looking fervently for the Lord are the Jews. Whether the Israeli politicians like it or not, Maitreya has intervened, to restore equilibrium. Whatever these politicians do, the Palestinians will have their own homeland. The process can be somewhat speeded up or delayed, but nothing can prevent the ultimate outcome. (Nov 1988)

Israelis and Palestinians — Awareness is embracing ordinary Israelis and Palestinians. Palestinians need a place to live. They will have their own homeland, peacefully. This issue will not be settled by the leaders, but by the people. The leaders will be forced to accept the will of the Israeli and the Palestinian people. The leaders will then work as servants of the people.

Israelis and Palestinians will live alongside each other in greater harmony despite all the difficulties they have faced, and a greater sharing of wealth in the region will take place.

"When your mind, spirit and body are in confusion, you need to purify them. What is the purifying force? Awareness. Awareness is growing now and bringing Israelis and Palestinians together." (Jun 1991)

Saudi Arabia: Changes — The Royal House of Saudi Arabia has kept its people in ignorance and controlled them through old modes and traditions. It has maintained a firm grip on Islam through its control of Mecca. The people have not developed the art of communication, but have remained in a conditioned state of mind, spirit, and body.

But changes will take place very fast, as the people begin looking for liberties and freedom.

Throughout the Middle East, people are saying: "I am a human individual and I have rights." They are questioning the conditions of politics and religion imposed on them. The doors are opening slowly. (Jan 1990)

The rigid control of thought and behaviour that was imposed on the masses in the name of the Koran is coming to an end. These rigidities have destroyed the people's independence. Now the voice of the people will be heard. The same process is taking place in Iran and Iraq. (Feb 1990)

Democracy in the Middle East — A process has started that will see democracy established throughout the Middle East. In the name of Allah, the Islamic Constitution has been awakened and we shall see the Arab nations working together and sharing together.

At one time, no one dreamt of democracy in the Middle East, but now everyone is talking about it. For the first time this concept is being discussed, which means that the nations will be run by the people, for the people. (Feb 1991)

The Middle East: A new dawn — The process of government by the people, for the people has gathered a momentum such that you will find a new dawn arising in the relations between the Israelis and Arab countries, in which there will be a peaceful settlement.

What is breaking open cannot be stopped now. The hardline and orthodox approaches will dissolve. (Dec 1991)

Iran and Iraq — Despite outward appearances, fast changes are taking place at ground level in both countries. In Iran the religious leaders will not be able to rule the masses as they have done until now. They are trying to bring in 'younger blood' so that they can continue to hold on to power, but the old political faces will go.

Governments everywhere will evolve towards a variety of forms which reflect "government for the people, by the people". (Aug 1993)

The African continent — Maitreya's words here are: "Purity is in darkness." Africa will generate a very positive force in life. This is because the African people as a whole are not confused mentally or spiritually. Mentally and spiritually they are not bankrupt, despite their poverty. (Apr 1988)

Africa and the food issue — The African continent must be looked after by those who are strong.

It will become a global duty to provide the first thing in life: food. This will become the basic duty of the United Nations, which will play the most important role. "Food will pour out." Certain disciples at the United Nations have been trained by Maitreya and will have an unwavering dedication to this cause. There will be no shortage of food. This policy has already begun.

This message will become so forceful from Maitreya's Day of Declaration onwards that governments will begin to take heed. Politicians are also looking for solutions. It will harness much basic goodwill in an appropriate direction.

The Great Powers will continue along the path of co-operation and the African continent will become the key place to grow food. In this venture, major powers and African countries will co-operate.

Smaller African countries will get together. Increased co-operation will be of mutual benefit and will be seen to work. Both Ethiopia and the Sudan are in a critical situation. At the present time there are difficulties with various aid agencies in Ethiopia. The government has removed aid workers from war zones. Nevertheless, we will witness a speedy recovery from famine.

In Angola, the process of mediation between opposing foreign powers involved there (in particular, Cuba, the USSR, South Africa and the USA) will ultimately result in the withdrawal of foreign troops. (May 1988)

Africa will grow more food — African countries are now undergoing fast changes. Africa will grow more food, and more food will be supplied by the United Nations. Although many who are in a position to look after their nations and countries are fighting, all is not 'doom and gloom'.

In Ethiopia changes in government are imminent. Politicians will begin to look after their people.

In the Sudan, political isms are coming to an end. Senior politicians are saying: "Let us call this 'social democracy'; let's supply the basic needs of life for the people." (Mar 1990)

Africa: Political changes — Great political changes are taking place in Africa. Ideologically based governments, such as Marxist regimes, will disintegrate. There will be government for the people, by the people. For the first time, the United Nations will become a watchdog to prevent major powers from supplying arms to fight ideological wars on the African continent.

As public and political awareness continues to grow in this area, the resources of the world will be harnessed to make living standards simpler, cleaner and healthier for everyone. (Jun 1990)

Creating war — "The Zulu chiefs know their days are numbered, so they create war. The younger generation does not believe in war." (Jun 1991)

British Imperialism — Maitreya asks African leaders: "Have you been fit enough to run your own countries?" The idea of 'freedom' in Africa has been nothing other than the expression of the politics of the US and the USSR. They did not like the slow but sure evolution of Africa, which they called 'British imperialism'. Yet, wherever British imperialism went it established a high standard of administration and justice; it established a system. But because of the animosities of the US and the USSR, they coined the words 'freedom' and 'independence'. Britain was the giver of justice, of assured standards of administration. Wherever Britain went, it ruled justly, without undue force.

Now Africa is ruled by the military, who are supplied by the Americans and the Russians. They have really ruled Africa by force of arms. African wars are the seeds of confusion and chaos. (Jun 1991)

Africa: UN as the watchdog — The growing power of the United Nations means that no African politician can get away with starving his people for his own political ends.

Day by day, the UN is becoming the watchdog for the welfare of starving people the world over. Its powers are increasing all the time as it receives growing backing from the major powers: America, the Soviet Union, China and the European countries. The dictatorships that made their own people suffer will not be able to resist the power of the UN.

Maitreya has released positive power into the African continent and soon we shall see that its people will be able to grow more food for themselves. Western nations will also be sending teams of agricultural experts to help African countries develop their farming industries. (Sep 1991)

South Africa: Consensus — Confrontation will eventually give way to consensus. Although it may be difficult to believe now, the day will come when President Botha and Desmond Tutu will sit down together and work out a solution. According to Maitreya, politics is the art of bringing harmony into life. (Apr 1998)

A process has begun — Maitreya is trying to cleanse the mind, spirit and body of this country [South Africa] through individuals, white and black alike, who are in a position to influence their country's destiny. Although outwardly clashes and divergent views hold sway, inwardly a process has begun which will lead white and black leaders to the negotiating table. It is possible that we may witness the initiation of this process within months. (Jun 1988)

The release of Nelson Mandela — Winnie Mandela, the wife of the black South African leader Nelson Mandela who has been in prison for 25 years, gave a press conference on the occasion of his 70th birthday on 18 July 1988 and said that she did not think her husband's release was 'on the cards' for years to come. According to Maitreya, Nelson Mandela will be released before the end of the year* — it will be "a Christmas bonus"! Subsequently, the hostages in Beirut will be released. (Nov 1988)

[*Nelson Mandela was officially released from prison on 11 February 1990. However, on 9 December 1988 he had been moved to an isolated cottage with pool, chef and gardens in a minimum security prison, and was also allowed to receive visitors.]

No turning back — There is no turning back. History cannot be repeated. The old cycles have come to an end in which 'I ruled you' or 'you ruled me'. (Feb 1990)

South Africa: The barriers — The barriers between white and black are beginning to be erected again. The government thought that when they freed Nelson Mandela he would have a magnetic effect on the black people and distract them from their demands for electoral freedom. But though he is a powerful symbol he is not a man of power.

The black tribal chiefs have been cultivated by the white authorities and persuaded that they should develop only their individual tribal powers. This is creating problem after problem as the black people turn against each other.

The whites will stay in power so long as the tribal chiefs stay in power and the black people are divided among themselves. (Apr 1990)

South Africa: Dawn — As the dawn of togetherness comes closer, evil forces will try to ensure that this dawn does not arise; again, through fear. (Sep 1990)

The US and the USSR — The process of glasnost in Russia may equally be understood as the necessity of letting go of 'old ways' to make way for the new. This process, and this necessity, applies not only to Russia but to many other countries East and West, North and South. Viewed in this global way, we may begin to understand the inevitable upheavals which are going on around the world. It is a prelude to much-needed change towards a more equitable society where freedom is not achieved at the expense of justice, nor justice at the expense of freedom.

Both Russia and the US would prefer to hide their weak points, and the tendency to control other countries is still strong. However, increasingly they will begin to interfere less, and this process will continue, contributing to an improved climate in world affairs and growing confidence in the future. Maitreya's influence will play its part to ensure that this new climate prevails.

Maitreya has appeared to a military leader in a very senior position in the USSR. This man has had a profound realization as a consequence of this encounter which will lead to a reorientation of aims. It is important to realize that Maitreya can appear in a variety of guises, but always in a form that the person concerned can recognize in a meaningful way. In this case, for example, the Russian military leader recognized Him as the Christ. (May 1988)

The USSR: Crystallized form has cracked open — The moment people in Russia realized they couldn't make any progress, the crystallized form of communism 'cracked open'. "Every force is important. It is not right to say communism, *per se*, is against freedom. Because it has cracked open, new forces are pouring in and producing a mixture of communism, socialism, democracy, etc. No one can stop this process. It will continue and will ultimately create an equilibrium." (Aug 1988)

Communism is not evil — If America had its way the Soviet Union would disintegrate. Maitreya has awakened the communist leaders and told them that communism is not evil. It has certain qualities that democracy does not have. Democracy has certain destructive elements which create rich and poor, the haves and have-nots.

Freedom does not mean breaking essential habits of life. After the Second World War the Soviet people came together to work and co-operate to rebuild their shattered lands. They should not throw all of this away.

Now they need freedom of movement within the Union, but not to undo everything they have achieved. They need freedom at home, and to allow freedom to spread its wings in speech and thought.

But it is essential that the economy and defence should remain centrally organized. It would be destructive if every state decided to break away. The Soviet leaders have now been awakened to the dangers of what is happening. (Jan 1991)

The old guard has taken charge — The old guard has taken charge in order to prevent the collapse of the Soviet Union.

America thought she had a free hand in the Middle East and elsewhere because the Soviet Union had too many problems of its own. This is at an end as the Soviets begin to make their presence felt in world politics once again. (Feb 1991)

Autonomy in the Soviet Union — Individual states will soon have autonomy over everything except defence and the economy. There will be no chaos or civil war, for it is the hand of Maitreya Himself which is guiding events through awareness. In awareness, there is no division, no yes or no. There is only unity which contains all diversity.

Some aspects of central government cannot be done away with entirely. The defence and economy will continue to be administered by central government. The republics will probably make contributions for defence on a pro rata basis. (Aug 1991)

Inspiring the Russians — Maitreya has also awakened politicians in the Soviet Union. He has told them: "Do not destroy all your own habits. These must be preserved until people learn the meaning of freedom." He has also asked them to 'play their cards' in the Middle East (ie to engage in constructive diplomacy). "Do not allow this war to continue." "No one will be a loser, no one a victor." (Feb 1991)

The USA — America was adamant about capitalism. Now it realizes capitalism on its own cannot bring harmony. Americans are becoming open to the flow of different forces.

In the political sphere, all these different elements will gradually converge, creating equilibrium. "Equilibrium creates harmony."

"Do not say: 'I am right, you are wrong.'"

For all politicians, educationalists, doctors, etc, the message is: "Everyone is important. Life itself cannot be dissected." For politicians the particular message is: "You are here to work for the masses, the people, to create harmony instead of divisions." (Aug 1988)

Independence — The movement towards independence has already begun in America. Individual states want to govern themselves and do not see why their money should go to Washington.

Only a few states are prosperous, while there are many millions of poor people in America. Meanwhile the drug problem has reached huge proportions. The American states want to tackle the problems of controlling poverty, drug abuse and ignorance.

"The heart of a person is My parliament where I give experiences. It is My temple. When I speak there, changes take place in the individual's mind, spirit and body and no one can stop them." (Jan 1990)

USA: Power shift to individual states — Just as the individual is becoming aware, so awareness is governing nations and countries. No politician can impose ideologies on nations. What has happened in the USSR is about to happen, in a somewhat different form, in the US. Individual states are going to seek their own powers, destiny and guidance, free from excessive control at the centre. California, for example, will point out that it has a certain degree of wealth, and at the same time a range of social problems it must solve. Defence will be centrally governed. Central government cannot be done away with completely, but increasingly it will be a case of 'looking after your own house first' — that is, looking after the unemployed, dealing with the drug problem, education and general health issues, violence in the cities, etc, on a local, regional basis.

In America, political corruption is such that even senators and some members of the judiciary are on the payroll of drug dealers. (Aug 1991)

Fundamentalism in the US — Fundamentalism in the name of Christ is also counter-productive. Christ is Oneness. "Do not take donations from the poor while you, the leaders, live in luxury." President G.H. Bush has opened the door to the fundamentalists so that he can win the presidential elections. (Nov 1991)

There will be changes — It is difficult to govern a people who have lost faith. American society has reached danger point: the tempo of life is too fast, lacking in compassion; it suffocates people who cannot keep up. There is too much suffering. Here, too, there will be changes; America cannot be left as it is. (Dec 1991)

Freedom and independence — America will be next to undergo change. Individual states will demand freedom from Washington to run their own economies and evolve their own legislation. The people are demanding independence, as are the Croatians. A number of demonstrations in New York and in California have been violently put down by the police. (Dec 1991)

Disintegration in America — The disintegration that is taking place in the former Soviet Union is now happening in America. The Los Angeles riots are not an isolated outburst. Every state is crumbling and it is worsening day by day.

The states are desperately turning to the Federal government for aid, but it is not forthcoming. America is suffering in retribution for that country's indiscriminate bombing of Iraq. (May 1992)

Greater autonomy — Just as the 80 regions of the Russian Federation are seeking greater autonomy, the same process is occurring in the United States. Each state wants a greater say in managing its own affairs (education, health, housing, police forces, etc.) Each state is willing to pay its due share of taxes to central government, but at present the feeling is that too great a share goes to the centre, leaving insufficient funds for local management of local affairs. There will be a change of policy. Central government will concern itself with defence and national priorities. (Sep 1993)

German reunification — The two Germanys will be reunited. Symbolically this will have a powerful effect on Western Europe, for they represent between them the ending of communism and the ending of capitalism. What will emerge is social democracy, which will become the political model for Europe and the rest of the world. No one can stop this process. (Feb 1990)

Britain: Consensus politics — At the moment the political scene here is in disarray with all parties lacking strength and engaged in bickering and blaming one another for the country's ills. While they argue, the nation waits and judges their suitability to lead.

The people have been awakened to the hypocrisies of politicians. One day, a new system will emerge in which Britain's problems will be resolved by consensus politics served by politicians who listen to what the people are saying. The rich man and the poor man will be able to share the platform of influence under this new system. The atmosphere is already developing. (Jun 1991)

UK: Disintegration — This country faces the same disintegration as America. Are the people happy? No, there is no happiness here, there is so much friction and confusion.
There is going to be a massive revolt as people take to the streets and demand action to bring back harmony and justice. Not even the police or the military will be able to control it. (May 1992)

Government for the people, by the people — From 1982 onwards, problems in an embryonic stage were highlighted in the media which today are growing fast in Britain. It becomes the duty of one and all to make fellow citizens aware of the happenings and to work for the general security and happiness of all, and to do away with the coined myth of non-interference: a 'mind your own business' attitude so cultivated in human behaviour and relationships that sectarian politics are able to withstand people power.

The role of central government is to defend the affairs of nation and country but not to interfere with local authorities. Local authorities enjoy spending on behalf of the people. Government is for the people, by the people. (Jul 1992)

Northern Ireland: Positive changes — Despite all appearances to the contrary, there will be changes. Current processes leading to positive changes are not reported in the media. There will be greater autonomy and communities will take greater control of local affairs in a more satisfactory way. Although the UK will be responsible for overall defence, its influence in other areas will lessen. At the local level, the people will be represented in a type of regional parliament in which both Protestants and Catholics will be represented. Better links between them will develop. Regional representation in a parliament will also develop in Wales and Scotland. (Aug 1993)

Independent — Scotland and Wales will become independent. (Aug 1991)

Europe — Identity

Europeanization — Mrs Thatcher is right to be concerned about the process of Europeanization. The aim should not be to create a giant, a monolith which then imposes its will on the European nations concerned. Nations should not merge into 'one' and thereby lose their identity. "Even if you merge with Me, your individual identity remains." The individual identity of a nation must likewise be enshrined. At the same time, nations can and will experience brotherhood, common goals and common aspirations. But it is "un-divine" for a giant to devour your identity, both in the case of individuals and of nations. (Oct 1988)

Commercial greed — Just as an individual's identity is sacred, so the identity of nations is sacred. The moment mind, spirit and body lose their centre of gravity, breakdown ensues. The same thing goes for nations. When the centre of gravity shifts from individual nations to a European centre, havoc ensues.

A major motive for Europeanization is commercial greed. But no one will want to hand over power; trade will continue, but national boundaries will be preserved. Those who threaten national sovereignty will not succeed. (May 1989)

The European Community — The ideals of the EC must not become too lofty and threaten the cultural and national identities of the individual countries. These are sacred and must not be interfered with. But the EC does have a role in terms of nourishing the nations of the world. (Nov 1989)

Different nationalities — The concept of Europeanization was and is to create wider market opportunities and not to sacrifice national identity. Be what you are. Identity is sacred. Even when the individual Self merges in the Supreme Being, individuality remains sacred.

This political effort to merge the nationalities into one will fail. It cannot and will not work. The destiny of everyone is to be what they are and not what others are.

Mrs Thatcher, having realized the truth that it is wrong to sacrifice the nation to create wider market forces, has now begun to understand the realities of life. It is still not too late. If the British people were asked to ballot the idea of Europeanization they would reject it. Mrs Thatcher was right to raise the alarm about this issue. (Nov 1990)

Individual identity is sacred — The drive towards a common European culture is a political blunder and cannot survive. It is not an ideology or a political philosophy. It is a means of creating freedom to sell goods here and there.

We must ask who is making money and who is making sacrifices. Individual identity is sacred for countries and for people. Even in a family everyone has a separate identity and cannot get on well all the time. All want privacy. We need the privacy of our identity to survive and maintain our purpose for existence. Politicians are sacrificing this in the name of economic forces.

Europeanization will not happen and it will not work. National identities will be preserved along with their individual parliaments and sovereignties. The only outlets for market forces will be to influence trade and commerce. (Dec 1990)

Federal ideas — As people become aware of their destiny, nations come closer, but they will retain their identity. If you lose your identity, you are as if blind. Without identity you lead a life of confusion and chaos. (Nov 1991)

No federal Europe — There will be no common European nation. If the politicians think they can play with the lives of people to try and balance the books, or to kill off nations in the name of pounds and pence, they are mistaken. It will never happen. The whole concept is already dead. It is only a matter of time before everyone can see this for themselves; the process has already started.

The people of Europe do not want it. If a referendum were held tomorrow the people would say No to Federalism.

It is only the politicians who are disassociated from the realities of life. They tell everyone that everything is fine when everything is far from fine. The idea of removing national borders would be disastrous and as such will not happen.

Look at the two Germanys, which until recently existed as separate nations. Already we are seeing the rebirth of Nazism and savage attacks on foreign workers. Remove national boundaries and people lose their sense of identity; they feel vulnerable and lash out in fear. No, France will remain France and Britain, Britain. (Dec 1991)

Europe: Common defence — The dawn of a New Age is now beginning to break in the Western world.

"The sacredness of a nation cannot be played with. Any effort to do so will lead to confusion." Many politicians are realizing the strength, the power, the essence of nationhood. In short, the European nations will unite for the purposes of common defence and common economic issues, while preserving the sacredness of their own nationhood. (Dec 1991)

The sacredness of nations — The current European experiment (ie ever-closer political and economic union) has not worked. There can be a convergence along certain lines, but the identity of a nation remains sacred. Humans (ideologues) cannot destroy it. (Aug 1993)

The Maastricht Treaty — This treaty cannot work. The French will remain French; the British will remain British, and so on. The nations will retain their sacred individuality. Food, shelter and protection must be given priority so that the seeds of destructive nationalism and racism cannot grow.

Free trade is not the same as the abolishing of all border controls. To abolish these is to allow the drug business to flourish. If we allow this, the national identities will suffer. This suffering itself gives rise to nationalism and racism, which are the seeds of destruction.

Once the identity is destroyed there is darkness. Identity is the space between the Self and the Lord. Without identity there is no life. (Sep 1993)

NATO — NATO and all military strategic organizations are crumbling now. The armies are moving back to their own countries. They are important — but only within their own boundaries.

NATO will assume a new form under the auspices of the United Nations. Its function will be to look after nations and countries the world over, and protect them against war. The

Russians, the Chinese and the Japanese will also be involved in this protective 'policing' role. (Dec 1991)

CHAPTER SEVEN

THE SCIENCE OF LIGHT

Cells, light and matter — All living cells are interconnected, with Light between them. Every atom is interconnected with the Light. The time will come when we can transform that Light. What happens? The body dematerializes. Adepts and Masters can do this. One day you will be able to do it. Matter can be transported from one place to another through Light. Thus the astral body of one who has departed can materialize. This is the power of Light. In time, scientists will be able to understand these processes, these laws of nature. When you become aware, conscious and detached, you will not manipulate these laws for selfish ends. Your mind will become stable. You will not struggle. Awareness creates a different kind of knowledge and wisdom.

Light — One should not be attached to Light; it is like beauty, to be appreciated. The universe, created by the Creator, is in that Light.

A Swami asked Maitreya: "How can we give the bounties of nature to people when they come to us in need?" Maitreya answered: "Look within." The Swami looked within. He found that out of the golden light whatever he wished for materialized. Some swamis are materializing, and giving, food.

Magic — Scientists wonder how some Masters, such as Sai Baba, are able to materialize things. This is not magic. Magic does not last.

"Miracles in themselves are not important. What is important is You (the Self) and Me (the Self)."

Scientists are learning to master the Technology of Light, sometimes called by Him [Maitreya] "the bright light". When you look at the bright light through the third eye, it energizes you the moment you touch it.

In the physical body, the seat of this light is the pineal gland and it is from here that all the functions of the body are controlled. When this light leaves, you are no longer there. When you bring the bright light back to the body, it is resurrected.

Until now, only yogis and gurus have mastered the art of directing this bright light, at the mental and spiritual levels. Yet these are not 'godly powers'.

Maitreya inspires some scientists who are working with the Technology of Light. Eventually, fewer hospitals will be needed; computers will be adapted to this new technology; medicines we now use will become defunct; a new mode of transport will develop, using the magnetic field and the energy of the Seven Rays.

Mind is like a computer; it needs someone to use it. How do you use the mind? Through the agency of consciousness. Consciousness is governed by light. The moment the relationship is articulated between mind-consciousness-light, you will see big changes. The rays, the colours, will trigger mind and spirit. Then, even a child of five or six will be able to interpret at a deeper level the structure of the atom.

This type of civilization already exists on other planets, where this 'science of light' is developed. The aeroplanes and ships we know now will be things of the past. There will be no need of oil or petrol.

The age of light — We are now entering the age of light. The Hierarchy is training scientists through experiences of phenomenal powers by demonstrating the use of the science of light to achieve transfiguration, transportation and communication.

When light is at your command you do not need guns and bullets. The time is fast coming when there will be no need for prisons, as individuals can be controlled from space. Terrorism will disappear because there will be no place for terrorists to hide. He who masters space can control the entire planet. The ambition of the politicians is now moving into space from where all movement on Earth can be controlled. But Maitreya warns that if the politicians play with this science of light and abuse it, it will destroy them.

He has a clear message to the world's political leaders: no wars can now be won, and spending vast amounts of money on international arms programmes is a complete waste.

Consider what happened to the £14 million Trident missile that exploded recently. Maitreya warns that there will be more such demonstrations if the politicians do not understand.

Humanity has naively believed that they are the only ones in space. But there are others there, far advanced, who have always watched over us, teaching us not to kill, to respect others, and to learn to be happy and free. They have always protected humanity and they will not allow it to destroy itself by the exploitation of science in space.

Our prime task now is to look after the environment. This will become the responsibility of every individual, politician, guru, saint and scientist. Our energies will be spent in making it healthy again. When that happens there will be less suffering, disease and poverty.

Colour: new technology of light — The new technology of colour and vibration will provide all the energy we shall need. It will be the "inner technology of evolution". Already, scientists in Russia have experimented with colour technology (the technology of light) and have incubated a human brain. The research has been carried out and the knowledge of this technology is waiting to be used. (Apr 1989)

The technology of light — "It is your destiny to know the technology of light, but be detached from it." Science is evolving very fast. The USA and the USSR will be able to colonize space. From space, our activities on the ground can be controlled. A nation which masters this technology could, in principle, control other nations. This is why at this stage, "the Lord intervenes, to maintain equilibrium."

It is the duty of religious people, gurus, etc, rather than just singing hymns and mantrams, to explain these processes, their dangers and consequently the necessity for detachment.

Call for disarmament — Why are the Russians and the Americans moving so quickly on the talks for disarmament? There is good reason behind their confident calls for major disarmament. It is because they have been told by their scientists that all the weapons they are making will be rendered useless by the coming technology of light.

They now have the technology to monitor every movement on Earth — of armies, tanks, planes and even submarines beneath the sea. Their scientists have been trained by their 'big brothers', who in the past have been described as the 'Space Brothers', those evolved beings who have always been with us, watching and guiding humanity.

Not only does this technology (a sophisticated extension of the US Star Wars concept) make pin-point surveillance possible, it can also be used to control men and machines. For instance, if a terrorist was located on a plane thousands of feet in the air, holding a gun or a bomb, he could be "frozen" in the act of terrorism. Likewise a submarine beneath the waves could be drained of energy and rendered powerless.

Obviously, this technology could be dangerous if misused and Maitreya warns that if any politician attempts this he will bring destruction on himself.

Only a few top Russian and American politicians know of this technology, President George H. Bush among them. Others, like Mrs Thatcher, as was apparent at the recent NATO conference, do not, which is why they feel it necessary to cling to their tanks and guns for defence. When she and the other leaders are told, there will be confusion and chaos. But it means the end of NATO.

The 'Brothers' have used this technology in other ways in recent years. For example, how was it that the Iran-Iraq war suddenly came to an end? No one had seriously done anything about it — certainly the superpowers were quite happy to watch these two nations smash each other to pieces while they themselves prepared to step into the Middle East vacuum that this confrontation was creating.

The change began on the battlefield where soldiers suddenly experienced a 'mirror-image' of themselves superimposed upon the face of the enemy they were about to kill. These soldiers, who had been misled by their politicians and spiritual leaders, began to ask: why am I killing? Then it was the turn of the generals to have these experiences and soon they were insisting that all this killing and fighting was not worth it. (Jun 1989)

Defence — No one will be able to maintain defence as a top priority now. This is neither ideology nor opinion. The technology of light renders present defence requirements obsolete. One can understand how to use and control this technology. But do not become attached even to Light or you will be carried away. No one can claim this Light.

Defence budgets — "If you play with the technology of light with a view to destroying one another, the electrical energies can become defunct and planes will be destroyed as a result."

About three months ago in the UK two military planes equipped with highly sophisticated Star Wars-type technology were experimenting during low-level flight with laser beams to penetrate radar systems.

The planes crashed. This is all the public knew. Yet each plane was worth not less than £20 million. This could have been a matter for investigation by Parliament, yet no such investigation took place. "The defence budget of nations will become the last priority." (Mar 1990)

The technology of light in healing — Drugs and surgery will no longer be needed as doctors are trained in the use of the technology of light in healing. Scientists in Russia and America are already experimenting with genetic engineering and this will develop until the time will come when they can transmit genetic information into a sick organ to rejuvenate it without the use of surgery. Eventually the need for so many hospitals will diminish, as people will be able to undergo treatment within hours for even the most serious conditions. (Jun 1989)

Surgery will vanish — The art of dying will be taught. The technology of the future will be nothing other than Light. Through the knowledge and use of the seven colours the technology will evolve. Mind, spirit and body will be healed. Surgery will vanish.

Solar energy — This is the energy of the new age — there will be no need for nuclear energy. The power of the sun will be used for heating, transportation and driving industry. The 'Brothers' are teaching the engineers how to store solar energy right now.

Space probes — The scientists could create havoc in the universe with nuclear-powered space probes. There are certain points in the universe which control the energies of creation. If they are disturbed, it is like setting free the atoms from their nuclear bonds. This can create disasters such as earthquakes and floods on Earth.

The distant planets have their own gravitational force which holds them in place and maintains their pattern of evolution. Nuclear-powered probes can upset the balance and lead to disastrous consequences.

Scientists will be given experiences by Maitreya to make them aware of the danger of their research. "The moment you come near the powers of creation you will be tempted to use them. If you do not know how to handle them they will destroy you. Certain yogis can approach these powers but with detachment. Therefore they do not harm them. The scientists, however, do not possess this detachment."

Scientists are also playing dangerous games in other ways. They are searching to find the secrets of consciousness. They are now experimenting with animals, playing with genes to discover where this conscious energy comes from, where it goes to after death.

So many experiments are being carried out behind closed doors that if the public knew about them there would be an outcry and a demand to end them. "The scientists are playing with the forces of life." (Sep 1989)

US space probe — The latest American space probe which carries plutonium on board could disturb the energies of space in unforeseen ways. "It could trigger nuclear explosions. There are different patterns of energy in space than those on Earth and the chemical reactions cannot be predicted." The scientists should not play with the forces of nature so blindly. The Space Brothers, however, are watching and will, when necessary, take the appropriate steps to prevent disaster. (Oct 1989)

Maitreya had neutralized the plutonium load on board the recently launched US space probe. The scientists will not be allowed to go beyond the boundaries of their knowledge. If the Master [Maitreya] had not intervened the probe could have triggered nuclear explosions on Earth that would have been beyond human understanding." (Oct 1989)

Star Wars — American scientists have not given up the "game of Star Wars". They have realized that the Russians have gone well beyond the technology used in the Star Wars programme and are desperately trying to catch up. They are attempting to create the technology to control not only the planet but space itself. But the Space Brothers are watching. "Scientists will not be allowed to use technology to interfere with the laws of creation. Their technology might have to be destroyed because it could even interfere with the evolution of the [Space] Brothers themselves." (Oct 1989)

Mini technology — American scientists will succeed in developing Star Wars weaponry, "a mini technology of light". They need it as an umbrella in case it rains. (Jul 1991)

The technology of light, and sound rays — The Star Wars technology is being carried out, not in space, but behind the secrecy of closed doors. It is being used in prisons, hospitals and by the armed forces of Russia, America and Britain.

Scientists are developing light and sound rays of the most dangerous kind which, if they escaped, could kill living tissue and cause instantaneous cancer. These laser weapons have been fitted to aircraft and submarines. The same technology has also been adapted for civil use in prisons where operations are being carried out on certain categories of prisoner to wipe out particular memory areas.

If these operations were known about there would be a huge outcry by those concerned with the infringement of the civil rights and liberties of prisoners.

A certain professor at a well-known London hospital is also experimenting too much with human genes. He has been using techniques with genes to heal people, but without telling his patients. A few weeks ago he got the shock of his life when Maitreya gave him an experience and made his memory disappear. The professor was worried that somehow the genes had entered his blood. What he is doing is a dangerous practice which can alter people's personalities and make them schizophrenic. (Jan 1990)

The science of the 21st century — Scientists are being taught by the Space Brothers the art of producing energy through light. The effects of the ozone problem will disappear but the climatic changes that are under way are still bound to take place. The days and nights will be warmer across the globe. We shall see changes in human behaviour as people spend more time resting and less time working. They will enjoy more recreational activities. The plant and animal kingdoms will also be affected, with a number of species disappearing. We shall find that society will think in global terms and policies will be developed globally. People will draw closer together, learning to share and live together in harmony.

The scientists are being taught how to materialize through the technology of light, so that objects can be transmitted from one part of the world to another. This technology — using colour, sound and vibration — is the science of the 21st century. It will make society more prosperous and happy. People will enjoy life more, many diseases will be healed instantaneously.

As the scientists learn to develop the rays of light, they will be able to penetrate not only the physical brain but the mind itself. Experiments are already being successfully carried out in healing the mind, particularly with people who have become addicted to drugs. Basically, the rays dissolve the conditioning factors of the mind which trap the personality.

Many experiments with the technology of light are being undertaken in Russia. This is because the Space Brothers set up a community in that country 15 years ago. Russia was chosen because it was such a closed society, where commercial pressures did not affect scientific research. Today, the Russians are well ahead of the rest of the world in this field. That is why Russia leads the way in calling for arms reductions. (Nov 1989)

Energy source — The technology of light is the technology that will meet all our energy needs in the 21st century. It will need no huge budgets to maintain because it will be devised and controlled by intellectuals who do not look for billions of pounds of profits to satisfy them. Once built, the technology will last for 2,500 years, until the next cycle of evolution. Environment and energy will be the top priorities of the new era. Last will be defence "because there will be nothing to defend."

The benefits — As the technology of light evolves we shall soon see the benefits. It will remove the possibility of any country threatening another, as the security of the planet can be maintained from space. We shall find less and less need for hospitals as the technology will make it possible for patients to be treated in local clinics.

The planet will become very vibrant with plenty of food for all and a clear atmosphere. Living conditions will improve for everyone and people will experience a meaning in life. Crime will begin to recede and people will be able to enjoy life. They will find that it is not all just work, work, work.

Regulate life on Earth — Scientists have been inspired by Maitreya to develop the technology of light to be able to regulate life on Earth. If, in future, any politician attempts to press the nuclear button, he can be frozen by the use of this space technology.

Biological weapons — Even biological weapons can be nullified. It only takes a split second for Light to transform them. They then become defunct. This is also true of other types of weapons.

Science fiction — Science fiction writers are not mad to depict the things they do. They are able to go into the subtler regions of the mind and transform what they see into stories. They are able to see the blueprint of the future.

World awareness — Keep an eye on the skies over Britain, Europe, the whole world. There will be much activity. People will report that they have seen big flashes in the sky, that they saw something land, that people came out, that people returned.

This is a time when highly evolved beings are moving into the world, in every nation and country, giving experiences to people, showing them a higher life, a higher wisdom. Now for the first time people across the world are feeling that they have a mind, spirit and body; that these must be catered for, that there must be equilibrium, which creates awareness, which leads to salvation. (Feb 1990)

UFOs and the Space Brothers — There are always signs when the Space Brothers are due to arrive anywhere on Earth. If you look into the night sky and you see that it is much brighter than it would normally be, that is a sure sign that the Brothers are due. Whenever their lightships enter the Earth's atmosphere they cause atmospheric reactions which result in the sky becoming brighter, a phenomenon that can be seen at night.

Space landings — In Canada, Space Brothers landed in the far north and fishermen there witnessed the event. Governments are now being pressured to open up about what they know. People will also be talking [about it] more openly. (May 1990)

Nowhere have there been more space landings than in North America. The Space People are here to help, and sometimes give experiences to ordinary people who subsequently present a puzzle for scientists. (Dec 1991)

Extra-planetary help — Already, there are beings from more evolved planets in our solar system living on Earth. In the United Nations there are records of the fact that they are acting in some instances as advisers in government circles in various countries. Much inspiration is being given in the medical field also, particularly with reference to the technology of light.

Enlightened beings can control this technology of light but they do not misuse it. In important instances, they have prevented its misuse. Their role is protective and inspirational.
.

CHAPTER EIGHT

THE EMERGENCE OF MAITREYA

Self-awareness — Maitreya is continuing to give experiences to people in all walks of life. His purpose is to free people. "If you can keep your mind and spirit free, then you can understand reality."

A graphic illustration of how He works is the method He has used to enable even thieves to gain self-awareness. On one occasion when a burglar was about to force open a safe, Maitreya enabled this man to witness the opening of the safe seemingly of its own accord, before the burglar could 'have a go' at it. The man was startled, and asked himself: "Who is doing this? I am not doing this!" He ran away. But in that split second, he experienced a moment of self-awareness. This type of experience has apparently occurred on a number of occasions.

The signs of Maitreya's presence in the world will continue to increase. He is going to flood the world with such happenings that the mind can never comprehend it.

The signs are there for those who need them, to strengthen our faith and to give us the necessary courage and conviction to emerge from a state of complacency in order to take on, together, the myriad necessary tasks of salvage in the world.

Self reliance — The USSR and the USA could have given much more help to the poorer countries up until now. At present, Maitreya is enabling many people to experience Him in a variety of ways. These people belong to the top and middle ranks in many poorer countries. One of the results will be that responsibilities will shift to each country individually. The theme of self-reliance is close to Maitreya's heart, but this goal for all is not to be confused with indifference on the part of those in a position to render assistance. Many people, and many countries, are in need of help now. As the reality of global interdependence becomes an established fact in our awareness, so the fact that 'all men are brothers' will be increasingly translated into structures and practical programmes of action that reflect this reality. (Jun 1988)

Do not run after me — Maitreya says to the people: "Never run after me. I am always with you. If you run after the 'powers' of saints, etc, you will get lost. To run is to run away from your Self. I am in your heart. Be honest, sincere, detached, and you will experience Me within. The ultimate can never be achieved by running away from the Self."

Direct experience — "I do not want you to believe in me. I want you to experience me. Doubts make a person weak." Maitreya has given experiences to soldiers in the desert. They wake up and see or experience something which puzzles them at first. Later, they become aware of the folly of war, regardless of which side they are on.

Signs — "When the baby cries too much, the mother comes to him and comforts him. To those who cry, I give glimpses or signs. Happiness is momentary only, if derived from this. The happiest moment is when you see Me in your heart."

Jehovah's Witnesses — Maitreya has appeared at meetings of Jehovah's Witnesses. The intransigent view of the Lord's transcendence, the unwillingness to accept anything other than the Bible in a certain fashion, leads to contradiction.

Maitreya has posed this question at those meetings: "You say God cannot come in human form." (According to their doctrine, Jesus is the perfect man, not God, and is God's agent in establishing the Rule of God.) "Since everything is God, He can appear anywhere or everywhere. How is it that God created individual forms? These too, are God. He can appear in absolute or relative form. How can you say the Almighty cannot come in human flesh?"

In thinking about this, the 'closed' mind becomes puzzled. There is conflict. Some Jehovah's Witnesses have had certain experiences as a result of Maitreya's presence among them which have led them to abandon an entrenched, ideological position.

Maitreya at the UN — Maitreya has appeared to several UN representatives and politicians, in a variety of guises. He sat next to [then Secretary General] Javier Perez de Cuellar, who thought he was a colleague. Maitreya suggested that the United Nations is not "the football ground of the politicians" and that Perez de Cuellar could travel to various trouble spots on his own and ascertain matters for himself.

Maitreya also appeared to President George H. Bush. Initially Mr Bush did not recognize the man who addressed him, and subsequently thought he was a bodyguard. In the ensuing conversation, Mr Bush was somewhat taken aback, wondering how a bodyguard could know so much.

Maitreya also appeared to Mr Gorbachev, in the guise of a colleague. He suggested to Gorbachev that since he spoke so much about democracy it was necessary to initiate that process at home in the USSR.

"Those who doubt Me will find I will come before them and talk to them." After a few days they may realize something has taken place. (Sep 1990)

The African famine — Maitreya is already intervening directly to help the starving people of Ethiopia. "I do not have to wait for people or governments." Miracles are taking place as food suddenly appears from nowhere. The soldiers who at the moment are stopping the relief supplies from reaching the people will discover that they are fighting their own brothers and sisters. They will stop fighting and help to feed the hungry children. The Ethiopian leaders are beginning to panic and look for a way of fleeing the country.

Many strange events are taking place. Once, Maitreya showed His group of Swamis a small baby crying from hunger inside a hut in the desert. The mother had two other hungry children to feed. She prayed desperately to God to give her food for her family. Maitreya told a Swami to materialize food for the mother. He did so, but the mother had no memory of it suddenly appearing in front of her. She thought that God had answered her prayers and ran to tell the villagers.

But Maitreya does not want the media to come in and give publicity to these miracles. He only wants to feed His people.

Sai Baba has also moved about the world feeding the hungry and materializing medical supplies where they were needed.

Experiencing Maitreya — "If you take two steps, I take four steps ahead of you. You cannot destroy the Lord's creation."

Messengers — Governments are asking for advice, and He has sent His messengers. In the East, Maitreya has been accepted as the World Teacher and He is now moving into Africa. In the West the Swamis will soon be speaking out openly about Maitreya and spreading His word. (Dec 1990)

Maitreya's meetings — Maitreya is meeting different groups of people two or three times a month. These meetings can include 40 or 50 people, who attend by invitation. Two weeks ago such a meeting took place. Five or six journalists from the Middle East, India and Canada attended. After Christmas, a gradual process of more open meetings with Maitreya will unfold. These will take place in different parts of the UK. (Dec 1990)

Communicating Maitreya's teaching — The associate explained that under Maitreya's guidance he had engaged in correspondence with local authorities, including those in the borough he lives in. He communicated much of Maitreya's teaching.

"The first letter I got was like that of a governor* writing to a prison inmate, rather as if I had been 'a bad boy'. That was the tone. The second reply was governmental; quoting rules and regulations. When the third reply came, 'the governor was awakened' because the teaching in the letters he was receiving was not from an ordinary person.

"The fourth reply offered help. But 'the prisoner' wrote back to say this was not important. What is important is to serve as a servant of the people, not as a master of the people."

To the question of how 'the governor' (the local authority official) was awakened, the associate quoted Maitreya as saying:

"The moment they read it, I stir their hearts. This creates vibrations in mind, spirit and body. These are automatic processes. It is the innate, natural desire of every human individual to find the Lord." (Jul 1992)

[* Head prison official]

Journalists — A growing number of journalists are meeting Maitreya, both in Britain and abroad. Right motive and a willingness to serve the cause of truth are necessary qualities. In growing numbers, journalists are also beginning to meet close associates of Maitreya. (Jun 1988)

Journalists visit Maitreya's Ashram — Many journalists, in particular from Holland and Canada, are now returning to Europe after visiting Maitreya's Ashram in Mysore, South India. (Jan 1991)

Praise and blame — "I am involved with everyone. The day you experience My presence you will realize the truth. Detachment will grow. The Self does not involve itself with praise and blame. Do not praise Me. You do not have to please Me. Please yourself by respecting your Self."

At the eleventh hour — The difference between the 11th and 12th hour is such that it can transform the course of evolution. He who comes with the powers of the Lord comes at the 11th hour to reveal and redeem. We are all waiting. The 11th hour is not far off.

Maitreya's press conference and Day of Declaration — Maitreya has trained and will continue to train a number of journalists.

The plan to have a press conference that will lead to His Day of Declaration still holds. Certain events must take place in the world first, but once they have taken place both the press conference and the Day of Declaration could follow in weeks or months.

On the Day of Declaration, Maitreya is going to 'embrace' every individual. They will feel His 'touch', even physically. Then "the food will pour out".

Many people have had a direct experience of Maitreya, and people are beginning to talk to each other, realizing they are not alone or unique in the experiences they have had.

Maitreya's gift to the world — Nations will be free to express their will and the voice of the people will be enshrined in national constitutions across the world — that is Maitreya's gift to the world.

Politicians who think they are clever and powerful will be helpless as the energy of this gift sweeps across the nations.

An even greater gift will be that Maitreya will be among the poor and needy. He will be among them, guiding them, and giving them spiritual warmth. He will be with the people in the streets who are sleeping rough and suffering injustice.

Maitreya will come "like a thief in the night" — He will come "like a thief in the night", startling the world, which will ask: "Who is he?" When He tells them Who He is then the onus will be upon Him to fulfil the hopes and aspirations of the people, to help them seek freedom, for nobody wants a life of slavery.

Maitreya says: "The last time I came, as Jesus, it was written in the Bible that when I appeared again the very elements of nature would be disturbed."

All this energy has been released because man has upset nature. This energy transforms everything and everyone, making them aware.

The World Teacher — These are electrifying times, and soon they will reach a crescendo which will flash around the world. Maitreya will appear and call Himself the World Teacher. He will say that He is not a prophet, an idealist nor a messiah, but a World Teacher, and here are My teachings. He will tell us all: I am with you and you are with Me. I experience you and you experience Me. That awareness will transform each and every one.

Day of Declaration — Preparations are well in hand for Maitreya to speak to the world via satellite television. Every nation and country will be linked by satellite to experience the presence and teachings of Maitreya. Those who watch, listen and respond will find themselves gradually undergoing transfor-mation.

On the Day of Declaration "people will enter churches, temples and mosques, and church bells will ring". It will be a day of rejoicing.

I will choose My moment — It is difficult for people to understand that although Maitreya is among us no one can 'deliver' Maitreya.

Maitreya Himself says: "Without disturbing anyone, I will choose My moment."

Maitreya mysteriously appeared 'out of the blue' to 6,000 people at a prayer meeting on Saturday, 11 June, 1988 in Nairobi, Kenya. The crowd immediately recognized Him as Jesus Christ and knelt down. (He appeared in their image of Jesus). He spoke to them in Swahili for 15 minutes, then disappeared, leaving dozens miraculously cured of their ailments. Photographs of the event were carried by media around the world.

Job Mutungi, editor of the *Kenya Times*, witnessed Maitreya's miraculous appearance in Nairobi: "The tall figure of a bare-footed, white-robed and bearded man appeared from nowhere and stood in the middle of the crowd... Everyone was murmuring something. People were flat on the ground, weeping uncontrollably in praise and worship, in total submission to the occasion... In clear Swahili, which had no trace of accent, the strange man announced that the people of Kenya were blessed..."

The Prayer for the New Age

I am the creator of the universe.
I am the father and mother of the universe.
Everything came from me.
Everything shall return to me.
Mind, spirit and body are my temples,
For the Self to realize in them
My supreme Being and Becoming.

The Prayer for the New Age, given by Maitreya, the World Teacher, is a great mantram or affirmation with an invocative effect. It will be a powerful tool in the recognition by us that man and God are One, that there is no separation. The 'I' is the Divine Principle behind all creation. The Self emanates from, and is identical to, the Divine Principle.

The most effective way to use this mantram is to say or think the words with focused will, while holding the attention at the ajna centre between the eyebrows. When the mind grasps the meaning of the concepts, and simultaneously the will is brought to bear, those concepts will be activated and the mantram will work. If it is said seriously every day, there will grow inside you a realization of your true Self.

Share International

Begun in 1982, this unique magazine features each month: up-to-date information about Maitreya, the World Teacher; an article from a Master of Wisdom; expansions of the esoteric teachings; articles by and interviews with people on the leading edge in every field of endeavour; news from UN agencies and reports of positive developments in the transformation of our world; Benjamin Creme's answers to a variety of topical questions submitted by subscribers and the public.

Share International brings together the two major directions of New Age thinking — the political and the spiritual. It shows the synthesis underlying the political, social, economic, and spiritual changes now occurring on a global scale, and seeks to stimulate practical action to rebuild our world along more just and compassionate lines.

Share International covers news, events, and comments bearing on Maitreya's priorities: an adequate supply of the right food, adequate housing and shelter for all, healthcare and education as universal rights, and the maintenance of ecological balance in the world.

Excerpts from the magazine are published on the internet at: *www.share-international.org*

Versions of *Share International* are available in Dutch, French, German, Japanese, and Spanish. For subscription information, contact the appropriate office below. *ISSN 0169-1341*

For North, Central and South America,
Australia, New Zealand and the Philippines
Share International
PO Box 971, North Hollywood, CA 91603 USA

For the UK
Share International
PO Box 3677, London NW5 1RU, UK

For the rest of the world
Share International
PO Box 41877, 1009 DB Amsterdam, Holland

Further Reading

The Reappearance of the Christ and the Masters of Wisdom
by Benjamin Creme

In his first book, Benjamin Creme gives the background and pertinent information concerning the emergence of Maitreya (the Christ), as World Teacher for the New Age now dawning. Expected under different names by all religious groups, Maitreya comes to help us create co-operation among the many ideological factions, galvanize world goodwill and sharing, and inspire sweeping political, social, economic and environmental reforms. Benjamin Creme puts the most profound event of the last 2,000 years into its correct historical and esoteric context and describes what effect the World Teacher's presence will have on both the world's institutions and the average person. Through his telepathic contact with a Master of Wisdom, Creme offers insights on such subjects as the soul and reincarnation; fear of death; telepathy; meditation; nuclear energy; ancient civilizations; UFOs; problems of the developing world; a new economic order; the Antichrist; and the 'last judgement'.

1st edition 1979, ISBN 0-936604-00-X, 254pp.

Messages from Maitreya the Christ

During the years of preparation for His emergence, Maitreya gave 140 Messages through Benjamin Creme during public lectures in London from 1977 to 1982. The method used was mental overshadowing and a telepathic rapport thus set up.

Maitreya's Messages of sharing, co-operation and unity inspire readers to spread the news of His reappearance and to work urgently for the rescue of millions suffering from poverty and starvation in a world of plenty. In Message No. 11 Maitreya says: "My Plan is to show you that the way out of your problems is to listen again to the true voice of God within your hearts, to share the produce of this most bountiful of worlds among your brothers and sisters everywhere...." (5 January 1978)

Maitreya's words are a unique source of wisdom, hope and succour at this critical time of world change, and when read aloud these profound yet simple Messages invoke His energy and blessing.

1st edition Vol. I 1981, Vol. II 1986. 2nd, combined, edition 1992, reprinted 2001. ISBN 90-71484-22-X, 286pp.

Transmission: A Meditation for the New Age
by Benjamin Creme

Transmission Meditation is a form of group meditation for the purpose of 'stepping down' (transforming) spiritual energies which thus become accessible and useful to the general public. It is the creation, in co-operation with the Hierarchy of Masters, of a vortex or pool of higher energy for the benefit of humanity.

Introduced in 1974 by Benjamin Creme, under the direction of his Master, this is a form of service which is simple to do and is at the same time a powerful means of personal growth. The meditation is a combination of two yogas: Karma Yoga (yoga of service) and Laya Yoga (yoga of energy or chakras). It is a service in which we can be involved for the rest of our lives knowing that we are helping the evolution of humanity into, and beyond, the New Age. There are hundreds of Transmission Meditation groups active in many countries around the world.

In this practical and inspiring book Benjamin Creme describes the aims, technique and results of Transmission Meditation, as well as the underlying purpose of the meditation for the development of disciples.

1st edition 1983. 4th edition 1998. ISBN 90-71484-17-3, 204pp.

A Master Speaks

Humanity is guided from behind the scenes by a highly evolved and illumined group of men Who have preceded us along the path of evolution. These Masters of Wisdom, as They are called, seldom appear openly, but usually work through Their disciples – men and women who influence society through their work in science, education, art, religion, politics, and in every department of life.

British artist Benjamin Creme is a disciple of a Master with Whom he is in close telepathic contact. Since the launching of Share International, the magazine of which Benjamin Creme is editor, his Master has contributed to every issue an inspiring article on a wide range of subjects: reason and intuition; the new civilization; health and healing; the art of living; the need for synthesis; justice is divine; the Son of Man; human rights; the law of rebirth; the end of hunger; sharing for peace; the rise of people power; the brightest future; co-operation – and many more.

The major purpose of these articles is to draw attention to the needs of the present and the immediate future time, and to give information about the teachings of Maitreya, the Master of all the

Masters. This third edition contains all 223 articles from the first 22 volumes of Share International.
1st edition 1985. 3rd expanded edition 2004. ISBN 90-71484-29-7 452pp.

Maitreya's Mission, Volume One by Benjamin Creme

The first of a trilogy of books which describe the emergence and teachings of Maitreya, the World Teacher. As human consciousness steadily matures, many of the ancient 'mysteries' are now being revealed. This volume can be seen as a guidebook for humanity as it travels on the evolutionary journey. The book's canvas is vast: from the new teachings of the Christ to meditation and karma; from life after death, and reincarnation, to healing and social transformation; from initiation and the role of service to the Seven Rays; from Leonardo da Vinci and Mozart to Sathya Sai Baba. It sets the scene and prepares the way for the work of Maitreya, as World Teacher, and the creation of a new and better life for all. It is a powerful message of hope.
1st edition 1986. 3rd edition 1993, reprinted 2003.
ISBN 90-71484-08-4, 419pp.

Maitreya's Mission, Volume Two by Benjamin Creme

This inspiring and heart-warming book offers new hope and guidance to a suffering world on the threshold of a Golden Age. It presents the teachings of Maitreya, the World Teacher, on both the outer, practical, and inner, spiritual levels; His uniquely accurate forecasts of world events, which have astonished international media; and His miraculous appearances which have brought hope and inspiration to many thousands. It also contains a series of unique interviews with Benjamin Creme's Master which throw new and revealing light on some of the greatest problems facing humanity.

This book covers an enormous range: Maitreya's teachings; the growth of consciousness; new forms of government; commercialization and market forces; the principal of sharing; life in the New Age; schools without walls; the Technology of Light; crop circles; the Self; telepathy; disease and death; energy and thought; Transmission Meditation; the soul's purpose. Also includes transcripts of Benjamin Creme's inspiring talks on 'The Overcoming of Fear' and 'The Call to Service'.
1st edition 1993, reprinted 2004. ISBN 90-71484-11-4, 753pp.

Maitreya's Mission, Volume Three by *Benjamin Creme*

Benjamin Creme presents a compelling vision of the future. With Maitreya, the World Teacher, and His disciples the Masters of Wisdom openly offering Their guidance, humanity will create a civilization worthy of its divine potential. Peace will be established; sharing the world's resources the norm; maintaining our environment a top priority. The new education will teach the fact of the soul and the evolution of consciousness. The cities of the world will be transformed into centres of great beauty.

This book offers invaluable wisdom on a vast range of topics. It includes Maitreya's priorities for the future and interviews with a Master of Wisdom on 'The Challenge of the 21st Century'. It explores karma and reincarnation, the origin of humanity, meditation and service, the Plan of evolution, and other fundamental concepts of the Ageless Wisdom Teachings. It includes a fascinating look from an esoteric, spiritual perspective at ten famous artists – among them da Vinci, Michelangelo and Rembrandt – by Benjamin Creme, himself an artist.

Like the first two volumes of *Maitreya's Mission*, this work combines profound spiritual truths with practical solutions to today's most vexing problems. It is indeed a message of hope for a humanity ready to "begin the creation of a civilization such as this world has never yet seen". *1st edition 1997. ISBN 90-71484-15-7, 704pp.*

The Great Approach: New Light and Life for Humanity *by Benjamin Creme*

This prophetic book addresses the problems of our chaotic world and its gradual change under the influence of a group of perfected men, the Masters of Wisdom, Who, with Their leader Maitreya, the World Teacher, are returning openly to the world for the first time in 98,000 years.

The book covers such topics as: sharing; the USA in a quandary; ethnic conflicts; crime and violence; environment and pollution; genetic engineering; science and religion; the nature of light; health and healing; education; miracles; the soul and incarnation. An extraordinary synthesis of knowledge, it throws a searchlight on the future and predicts our highest achievements of thought to reveal the amazing scientific discoveries which lie ahead. It shows us a world in which war is a thing of the past, and the needs of all are met.

1st edition 2001. ISBN 90-71484-23-8, 320pp.

The Art of Co-operation by Benjamin Creme

The *Art of Co-operation* deals with the most pressing problems of our time, and their solution, from the point of view of the Ageless Wisdom Teachings that, for millennia, have revealed the forces underlying the outer world. Benjamin Creme brings these teachings up to date, preparing the way for the imminent emergence of Maitreya, the World Teacher, and His group of Masters of Wisdom.

This volume looks at a world locked in ancient competition, trying to solve its problems by old and out-worn methods, while the answer – co-operation – lies in our own hands. It shows the way to a world of justice, freedom and peace through a growing appreciation of the unity underlying all life. Maitreya will inspire in us this growing realization.

Topics include: the necessity of co-operation; the USA and competition; organism versus organization; opportunity for service; fear of loss; karma; love; courage and detachment; overcoming of glamour; how the Masters teach; unity in diversity; consensus; trust.

1st edition 2002. ISBN 90-71484-26-2, 235pp.

The Ageless Wisdom Teaching by Benjamin Creme

An overview of humanity's spiritual legacy, this booklet serves as a concise and easy-to-understand introduction to the Ageless Wisdom Teaching. It explains the basic tenets of esotericism, including: source of the Teaching; the emergence of the World Teacher; rebirth and reincarnation; the Law of Cause and Effect; the Plan of evolution; origin of man; meditation and service; future changes. Also included is an esoteric glossary and a recommended reading list.

1st edition 1996, reprinted 2006. ISBN 90-71484-13-0, 76pp

~ ~ ~

These books have been translated and published in Dutch, French, German, Japanese and Spanish by groups responding to this message. Some have also been published in Chinese, Croatian, Finnish, Greek, Hebrew, Italian, Latvian, Portuguese, Romanian, Russian, Slovenian and Swedish. Further translations are planned. Books, as well as audio and video cassettes, are available from local booksellers.